Early praise
from John Grisham

Back in the 1980s, I had the privilege of serving two terms in the Mississippi House of Representatives. I was inspired to seek office because I was embarrassed that my state still had no kindergarten system. My state was in dire need of many progressive reforms. I took the oath, swore to uphold the seriously outdated constitution, and started filing bills to shake up things. None of them passed.

In those days, and for decades before, the state of North Carolina was the unquestioned leader of modern reforms in the South. It was viewed by us and by legislators from other states as the model of a sensible, workable, state government that got things done and tried to take care of its more vulnerable citizens.

Many times, in the middle of a debate, someone said, "This is what they're doing in North Carolina, and it's working." Or, "North Carolina passed this law twenty years ago." These were powerful statements because the state's legislature was serious about education and equality.

Those days are gone. In 2013, hardcore conservative Republicans won big and put together supermajorities in both the House and Senate. With a like-minded leader in the governor's office, they immediately waged war against teachers and schools, the poor, women, elections, the courts, the environment, and those with darker skin.

The changes in North Carolina are shocking and depressing. Gene Nichol was either in the ring or agitating from a front-row seat. He knows this sad story because he was there.

The war is still raging. And he's still fighting.

John Grisham
Chapel Hill, N.C.
August 19, 2019

Early praise
for Indecent Assembly

"The radical right chose the once-moderate state of North Carolina as a test site for its project of remaking the nation by rigging the rules of governance and misinforming the people. What will it mean for your life and our country if they succeed nationally? To read this searing survey from the front lines by democracy champion Gene Nichol is to be forearmed."

—Nancy MacLean, author of *Democracy in Chains: The Deep History of the Radical Right's Stealth Plan for America*

"Gene Nichol, the Tar Heel State's progressive conscience, provides a searing indictment of North Carolina's lurch to the political right. Nichol pulls no punches, but provides plenty of documentation, as he tracks the legislature's effort to repeal the twentieth century. If you care about North Carolina, read this book."

—Rob Christensen, longtime North Carolina political reporter, columnist, and author

"Gene Nichol has long been a clarion voice on issues of race and poverty in North Carolina. Unbeloved by the powerful and beloved by the disadvantaged, in his latest book he unsparingly sets forth the politics of what he calls the state legislature's "Blueprint for the War on Democracy and Equality." Without fear or favor, Nichol tells the story of a state once known for moderation on issues of race, but that has become ground zero in partisan extremism and the resurgence of racial recidivism in America."

—Ted Shaw, Julius Chambers Distinguished Professor, University of North Carolina, and former director-counsel and president of the NAACP Legal Defense and Education Fund

"Gene Nichol has long won admiration for his courage and eloquence in forthrightly championing the interests of the oppressed and the neglected. In this electrifying new book, he demonstrates that the assault of the Republican-dominated North Carolina legislature on the poor is more than ultraconservative; it represents nothing less than a war of annihilation against our most revered, most fundamental constitutional rights. This is a must-read book—not only for Tar Heels, but for all who abhor injustice and who cherish our republic."

—William E. Leuchtenburg, William Rand Kenan Jr. professor emeritus of history, University of North Carolina, and past president of the American Historical Association

INDECENT ASSEMBLY

INDECENT ASSEMBLY

The North Carolina Legislature's Blueprint for the War on Democracy and Equality

GENE NICHOL

—Blair—

Printed in the United States of America
Cover design by Laura Williams
Interior design by April Leidig

Blair is an imprint of Carolina Wren Press.

The mission of Blair/Carolina Wren Press is to seek out, nurture, and promote literary work by new and underrepresented writers.

We gratefully acknowledge the ongoing support of general operations by the Durham Arts Council's United Arts Fund.

ISBN: 978-1-949467-27-7

Library of Congress Control Number: 2020930206

For my girls:

Glenn, Jesse, Jenny,

Soren, and Belle

CONTENTS

By Rev. Dr. William J. Barber, II
Dr. Timothy B. Tyson

If you read this eloquent and deeply informed book, you will see that Gene Nichol's insights into the mercenary politics of our time resonate far beyond the North Carolina state line. Readers across America will find themes, schemes, and real human beings wedged in struggles that rage in many corners of this nation. If these strike a familiar chord, likely it is because North Carolina has provided a laboratory for the cruel and corrupt policies far-right extremists sooner or later pursue in many other places. The author's observations illuminate the far-flung, corporate-bankrolled assault on moral values that most Americans have experienced, not just North Carolinians. In fact, Gene is "not from around here," a phrase southerners have long used to dismiss someone damn fool enough to tell the truth in public. He is from Texas, which is different, though not different enough these days.

Like many of humanity's sublime truth-tellers, Nichol sees with the love and intimacy of an insider, partly because he has lived and worked in this state for almost two decades in jobs that offer deep knowledge of politics and poverty. Though Gene Nichol's intimate sense of place brings one kind of clarity, his years of public advocacy and academic prominence in similar bellwether states like Colorado and Virginia grant him a complementary vantage point. That is, he also comes with the clarity of the outsider who often notices things so commonplace to homegrown folks that they may be harder for us to see.

By the time he came to us, first as the dean of the UNC School of Law, then as the director of the UNC Center on Poverty, Work, and Opportunity, Nichol's reputation for courage and candor already stood tall—notably his celebrated insistence on defending the First Amendment at some starchy liberal arts institution in Williamsburg. When we heard rumblings that the political appointees on the University of North Carolina Board of Governors intended to get him fired if he did not stop telling the truth about the damage inflicted on our state by Gov. Pat McCrory and his Republican supermajority, we just laughed. What on earth, we wondered, made them think they might stampede Gene Nichol? An old journalist's adage, "R.F.P.," which translates, roughly, "Read the doggone paper," sprang to mind.

We knew our man, and not just from reading the paper, though his editorials in the *Raleigh News & Observer* shined facts and faces through the fog of far-right ideology. Gene was hard to miss, given his constant presence in the Forward Together Moral Movement, better known to the nation as "Moral Monday." The movement's nickname came from the wildly successful campaign of weekly demonstrations we held on Monday afternoons in the spring of 2013. Governor McCrory had campaigned as a "business moderate," promised not to sign any new laws to restrict abortion rights, and won by a whopping twelve-point margin. He also rode a Tea Party wave in 2012, which washed in a Republican supermajority with the votes to pass anything they wanted. Since 2010, local libertarian potentate Art Pope had poured millions into North Carolina politics, with help from a vast web of far-right funders from far away, put together by billionaires Charles and David Koch. Widely known as the "Kochtopus," their daisy chain of dollars has woven a fortune into American politics, truckloads in North Carolina, through dozens of money-pumps such as Americans for Prosperity, the American Legislative Exchange Council (ALEC), and the State Policy Network. The GOP supermajority immediately began passing a raft of mean-spirited attacks on poor people, public schools, hard-pressed teachers, voting rights, environmental protection, and LGBTQ+ equality, among other poisonous policies.

Not only brave but conceivably a mite cantankerous, Gene Nichol refused to cede the public square to icy ideologues like Art Pope. He insisted that North Carolina confront the ruthless indifference to humanity that marked "this unforgiveable war on poor people," as he put it. "It is a rank violation of our history, our scriptures, and our constitutions." His urgency resonated from the heart of the statewide grassroots "Moral Monday" movement. We saw firsthand and no doubt fed his passion after he helped lead Moral Monday's Poverty Tour, in which we loaded journalists, activists, and community leaders onto a bus and went directly to the places where people directly suffered from these hard-hearted policies. Legislative hacks and panicky administrators attempted to shut him up, but his eloquence, often amplified by Republican threats and reprisals, became the state's pillar of fire by night. Moral Monday activists and many other admirers began to tout his bravery at every opportunity. Gene made light of these claims. "I'm a tenured law professor," he often said. "Nothing takes less courage than being a tenured law professor."

When the confrontation came to a head, though, the authoritarians in the General Assembly threatened to fire Nichol from UNC if he refused to shut up, generally, and if he dared speak at an upcoming Moral Monday rally in Charlotte, specifically. Charlotte is the GOP former governor Pat McCrory's hometown, and we suspected McCrory feared that if Nichol took to the stump down there, his mama might read the *Charlotte Observer* and find out what her son had been doing in Raleigh. Nichol walked tall into the Charlotte rally, seemingly unphased. Invited to speak, he rattled off the most shameful array of the state's abysmal poverty statistics and then declared, "Our governor and our General Assembly looked at these strong inequalities and decided to make them deeper."

The far-right Civitas Institute responded to Nichol by filing a

Freedom of Information Act request for all of his emails over two months. Threatened by budget cuts, the University asked him to comply, an exercise that turned up nothing improper, or even interesting, with the possible exception of a comedic tirade sent to Gene by one of us who shall go unnamed but apparently is not a preacher. Always touchy, these lockstep Republicans, led by Art Pope, Governor McCrory's budget director and by far the largest donor to their party, did manage to close down the UNC Poverty Center to punish Nichol for his speeches and newspaper columns. "For a crowd that talks so much about liberty," he responded, "they sure do love to shut people up."

The far-right extremists, fueled by rivers of far-right money, have "waged the stoutest war against people of color and low-income citizens seen in the United States in a half-century," Nichol declared. "All-white Republican caucuses, dominating both houses, have behaved essentially like a White People's party—attacking the participatory rights, antidiscrimination guarantees, educational opportunities, and equal dignity of African Americans." His scalpel-like pen traced with precision the way that southern white conservatives, funded by the ultrawealthy whose interests they represent, battered the poor while they brayed about Jesus, prayed about family values while preying upon actual families. This book unmasks that meanness and madness, and Nichol tells the story far better than we can.

It is worth noting, however, what some *other conservative voices* saw happening in Raleigh. Only six months after Gov. Pat McCrory and the far-right supermajority took the oath of office, *American Conservative*—a right-wing magazine founded by Patrick Buchanan, perhaps the most rightward presidential candidate in modern American history (George Wallace is his only competition)—published an article on the right-wing revolution that Nichol writes about in this book. "How Raleigh's Republicans Forgot the Working Class," a telling title, excoriated the hardcore, Koch-fueled libertarians for making "policy choices that hurt working-class families combined with an inability to defend their reforms without relying on stale conservative rhetoric."

The problem, said *American Conservative*, is that Republican leadership ruled the General Assembly with a veto-proof supermajority but had lost touch with North Carolina. "Given the state's bipartisan tradition of striking a balance between economic growth and maintaining a social safety net," the editors continued, "North Carolina is simply not well suited for libertarian governance. Education is a prime example: the right to a K–12 education is enshrined in the state constitution, and public education is broadly seen as a public good." *American Conservative* also noted that the state continued to have the fifth highest unemployment rate in the nation and that "North Carolina's unemployment is largely structural, not cyclical; there were simply no jobs to be found." And yet the Republicans stripped 70,000 citizens of their federal unemployment benefits, while another 100,000 would lose their benefits at the end of the year.

That made the deep cuts to community colleges, where workers might have retooled for new jobs, seem cruelly indifferent to the state's poor and working class. Slashing teacher pay and per-pupil expenditures for children, charged the editors, had hurt working families and dampened North Carolina's economic prospects. Intoxicated by power and infatuated with rigid ideology, Raleigh Republicans forgot the best interests of their constituents. Strengthening public schools, alternately, "would affirm the role that education plays in social mobility for working-class families. Instead, public schoolteachers felt disrespected, and Republicans, in thrall to far-right libertarian dogma, were tagged as the anti-education party."

In a socially conservative state like North Carolina, abortion ought to be a winning issue for Republicans, *American Conservative* claimed, but even here the GOP leadership had managed to alienate *80 percent* of all voters when the House attached antiabortion measures to a law banning sharia and passed the bill at 2:00 in the morning. The Senate then attached their version to a motorcycle safety bill, ridiculed by women's rights advocates as the "Motorcycle Vagina Act." The magazine's editors swung their heaviest hammer, however, at the Raleigh Republicans' repeal of the Earned Income Tax Credit. If this "conservative anti-poverty measure," rather than been cut adrift, instead had been made permanent, they charged, that might have offset the "increased burden on the working-class families in the bottom 40 percent of taxpayers under the new tax regime—and deprive protestors of their most effective rhetorical weapon."

Needless to say, the Republicans in Raleigh paid this critique no mind, and it became their undoing. But that is another story.

Over the course of a decade, Gene Nichol convened his congregation at the militarized wailing wall going up not between America and Mexico, but between "street people" and "loft people" in our downtowns, between our country and its heart. He stood with Moral Monday's pilgrims amid the blue-tarp encampments of impoverished men, women, and children, often huddled in the cold woods a stone's throw from our most affluent gated communities. He stood at dawn on downtown sidewalks with families hoping for food or shelter or a doctor for a sick child. He stood in rural trailer parks and on city street corners, listening to the stories of the invisible poor. He stood in the pulpits of small-town churches in counties where more than half of the children frequently do not get enough to eat.

In roadside motels and on long drives home, Nichol penned eloquent, profound, and irrefutable newspaper columns that compelled North Carolina to face the far-right assault against our most vulnerable neighbors and against our most deeply held moral values—and the denigration of democracy necessary to pull it off. Nichol also offers a moral compass and a shining lighthouse for America's journey, much as he has for many years in North Carolina. It was not just what Gene Nichol stood for, but where and how he stood for it. In a landscape luminous from the Appalachians to the Outer Banks, here stood a man to match the mountains and the sea. His transformative labors evoke James Baldwin's dictum: "Not everything that is confronted can be changed; but nothing can be changed until it is confronted."

CHAPTER ONE

North Carolina

A "Laboratory for Extremism"[1]

The broad and generalized frame of the story has been told well, pervasively, and sometimes even passionately. North Carolina, "once considered a beacon of far sightedness in the South"[2] and a "paragon of Southern moderation"[3] has, since 2011, but especially since 2013, undergone a "powerful Republican revolution." A state long dominated by "business-minded moderate Democrats" has been, at least politically, turned upside down.[4]

A complex stew resulting from the rise of an assertive Tea Party, the weakening and then near collapse of a corruption-plagued and seemingly disengaged North Carolina Democratic Party, the massive investments of right-wing political donors, and an ascendant backlash to the election of Barack Obama led to a Republican takeover of both houses of the General Assembly in the 2010 election.[5] For two years, Democratic governor Bev Purdue acted as something of a counterweight to the boldest Republican ambitions. But Republican Pat McCrory won the governor's race in 2012, giving his party firm and uncontestable control over all three branches of state government for the first time since 1870.[6] The grip included veto-proof Republican majorities in both houses. McCrory quickly proved he was no match for the legislative leaders—even if he wanted to be.[7] And the lawmakers were not about to sit on their hands.

So a cascade of changes rapidly came. Strict voter regulations aimed at curtailing turnout; repeal of racial justice guarantees;

new and generous school voucher programs for private and religious schools; potent and demeaning abortion restrictions; expansive new firearm possession and carry rights; attacks on teacher tenure and representation; dramatic cuts to K–12 and higher education budgets; eased, "business-friendly" environmental regulations; internationally derided anti-LGBTQ+ measures; brutal cuts to an array of social programs designed to assist the poor; a formal and consistent opposition to Obamacare and Medicaid expansion; the largest cut to a state unemployment compensation program in American history; massive tax breaks for the wealthiest Tar Heels and out-of-state corporations accompanied by, astonishingly, tax increases for low-income workers—operating under the odd premise that giving money to the wealthy makes them virtuous and giving money to poor people makes them venal.

And the whole package was safeguarded by among the most aggressive racial and political gerrymandering crusades ever witnessed in the United States; direct and relentless attacks on the independence of the North Carolina courts; rarely before seen intrusions on traditional local government prerogatives; retaliatory violations of long-established boundaries of separation of powers; and, to top it off, fulsome attacks on democracy itself.

Powerful Senate leader Ralph Hise could accurately brag that the North Carolina Republican General Assembly had, by 2016, amassed "the most conservative record of any state legislature in the nation." The dean of North Carolina political columnists, Rob Christensen, wrote that "there has been a bigger and quicker shift to the right here than in any other state in the country."[8] The *New York Times* decried "North Carolina's pioneering work in bigotry."[9] The *Washington Post* opined that the state's General Assembly had "turned back 50 years of progress on civil rights and gutted the social safety net." Other states began to follow what was overtly deemed the "North Carolina playbook." And the *New York Times Magazine* frantically asked, in a now Trump-based era, "Is North Carolina the future of American politics?"[10]

So that is my starting point. In a very brief period of time (really four or five years), North Carolina moved from being a "beacon of southern progress" to what national newspapers readily call "a laboratory" for extremism—a "poster child for regressive, conservative policies."[11]

Second, as a reminder, the citizens of North Carolina did not sit idly by as their state government was brutally recast. A massive "Moral Monday" protest movement was launched and remarkably executed in response. Following the creation of a potent and active coalition by Rev. William J. Barber and the North Carolina NAACP in 2007 (the HK on J [Historic Thousands on James Street] coalition), Moral Monday leaders started weekly protests at the statehouse in Raleigh on April 29, 2013. That day, Rev. Barber and sixteen others were arrested for peacefully challenging the unfolding Republican legislative crusade, defying what Barber called "regressivism on steroids."[12]

Soon thousands of supporters joined the ranks—week after week—gathering in huge, nonviolent throngs both in Raleigh and across North Carolina. In February 2014, the Moral Monday march drew more than one hundred thousand people to the steps of the legislative building, making it the largest racial justice rally in the South since the Selma-to-Montgomery march of 1965.[13] The governor and Republican General Assembly leaders called the multiracial protesters outside agitators, old hippies, loony liberals, and morons—echoing the responses of 1960s southern segregationists.[14] By the end of 2014, more than a thousand people had been arrested at statehouse protests.[15] Rev. Barber told demonstrators, "We can no longer allow the ultraconservatives to have the moral megaphone." As the protests increasingly drew the attention of the world, Barber noted, "If you are going to change the nation, you have to change the South, and if you are going to change the South, you have to focus on these legislatures."[16]

The Moral Monday movement didn't drive Republicans from control of the General Assembly. But it has had potent impact in

North Carolina and, increasingly, beyond. (In full disclosure, I have been much involved in the Moral Monday movement and in the protests and poverty tours that preceded it, and I've worked with Rev. Barber long enough to believe, as Cornel West put it, Barber is "the closest person we have to Martin Luther King Jr. in our midst."[17]) First, the Moral Monday protests worked to thwart and slow the unimpeded reign of the legislature. Republican leaders sought to enact dramatic economic, legal, and social change without significant pushback, delay, or debate. Democratic lawmakers were often both leaderless and demonstrably powerless to contest the cascade.

If Republicans aimed to remake North Carolina without troubling controversy, Rev. Barber and his colleagues made that impossible. The movement also, in a sense, revitalized the state Democratic Party. Barber made sure the protests remained a moral, rather than a partisan, crusade. But as Democratic pollster Tom Jensen put it, "Barber really stepped in to fill the void of progressive leadership for Democrats when they'd been put out completely in the wilderness."[18]

Thanks largely to the burgeoning demonstrations, Governor Pat McCrory's approval ratings began to drop notably. He'd won by twelve points in the election of 2012, but by the end of the summer of 2013, McCrory's approval rating was decidedly underwater. Democrat Roy Cooper narrowly beat McCrory in 2016. He likely would not have done so without the emotionally charged and pervasively visible protests. Democrats regained enough seats in 2018 to, finally, at least, eliminate the Republican supermajorities dominating both legislative houses.[19] The same could likely be said of those campaigns. Cranky Republican leaders would complain, "Barber and the Moral Monday crowd gave Democratic base voters a reason to be excited, to be active and to vote."[20] But maybe most important, the Moral Monday protests helped convince North Carolinians and, later, the country at large that an invigorated engagement in the democratic process provides the surest basis for securing the sort of society they hope to achieve.

All that said, North Carolina Republicans still held significant majorities in both houses of the General Assembly after the 2018 elections. At the time of this writing, Republicans retain a 66–55 edge in the House and a 29–21 lead in the Senate.[21] The laws of North Carolina are still launched from the Republican caucuses in each chamber, and Republican lawmakers retain the distorted security of grotesquely gerrymandered electoral districts, though litigation will likely persist until a new federal census demands a complete restart. On occasion now, thankfully, the products of Republican lawmakers may be constrained by a bolstered gubernatorial veto power. But the North Carolina General Assembly remains, first to last, a Republican outfit—following the same singular and destructive agenda it has pursued the last eight years. That agenda has inflicted damage on the people of North Carolina and directly threatens both their well-being and their children's futures. It is that agenda, writ large, that will be the focus of this book.

I concentrate on the legislative record of the Republican General Assembly rather than the political strategies that have led to its ascendancy or, more congenial to me, the impetus of the Moral Monday and Democratic Party forces that have risen to oppose it, for two reasons. The first is simple and direct. Though much has been written of particular legislative programs and areas of repeated and pointed focus for North Carolina's Republican lawmakers, relatively little study seeks to examine the agenda, and now at least partial legacy, of the General Assembly more broadly. It is one thing to read of day-by-day accretions and extensions. And, no doubt, they alone, individually, without more, can justifiably spark outrage. But it's another matter to see what is now nearly a decade's accumulation laid out in a package. When I began studying the General Assembly's record of both attempt and accomplishment, I was, it's fair to say, a member of the determined, perhaps even angered, opposition. Studying the Republican lawmakers' work as a whole, though, can readily move one past that comparatively less-alarmed state. As my friend, historian Dan Carter, wrote a few years ago, in explaining how he answers when folks ask if what's happening in North Carolina is as bad as it looks, Carter always responds, "It's worse. It's a lot worse than you think it is."[22]

My second reason is more important. It has to do with the nature of the General Assembly's crusade—the categories and themes and beachheads of their assault. What they're doing, what they repeatedly show they are after. Characterizations of the work product of the North Carolina legislature typically run, understandably, along traditional headings of punditry: liberal-conservative, left-right, moderate-radical, extremist-mainstream, reformist-revolutionary, and the like. And there is accuracy in these labels, or at least meaningful suggestion. But they can miss the basics, the defining, undergirding essentials, as well.

In the chapters that follow I will argue and, I hope, demonstrate, without pulling punches, that since 2011 the North Carolina Republican General Assembly has waged the stoutest war against people of color and low-income citizens seen in the United States in a half century. All-white Republican caucuses, dominating both houses, have behaved essentially like a white people's party—attacking the participatory rights, antidiscrimination guarantees, educational opportunities, and equal dignity of African Americans. Poor Tar Heels have been targeted, demonized, shamed, and economically penalized—essentially treated as outcasts to the commonwealth—deserving disdain rather than brotherhood.

Women, I'll show, have repeatedly been denied equal dignity in reproductive decisions in ways that effectively deny their full and functioning humanity in favor of a patronizing and authoritarian state decision-maker insistent upon enforcing its own vision of a meaningful life on diminished subjects. And the North Carolina General Assembly has also, I'll argue, repeatedly moved to officially disparage, debilitate, and demean LGBTQ+ Tar Heels to, in effect, brand them as strangers, denying their membership and endangering their prospects. The General Assembly's treatment of public education and the environment has reflected similar demarcations of insiders and outsiders—favoring the powerful at the continued, and augmented, expense of the marginalized and already burdened.

These bold and often singular steps can be accurately characterized as ultraconservative and extreme. But, foundationally, they represent a broad and animating war on equality—seeking to undo much of the broad mandate of the modern equal protection clause. They constitute an overarching attack on the Fourteenth Amendment itself—the most consequential provision of the U.S. Constitution. They should be seen as such. The Civil War amendment's principal author sought to assure "equal justice for any person, no matter whence he comes, or how poor, how weak, how simple, how friendless."[23] The North Carolina General Assembly's actions have been in direct opposition to this noted and defining ideal.

And Republican lawmakers have not stopped there. They have not been satisfied with bold and sustained alterations to our substantive legal regime—the rights and duties of Tar Heels. They have also attacked the foundations of American constitutional government as well: independent judicial review, separation of powers, the rule of law, and the defining operational values of democracy itself. As I will explain, the General Assembly has interfered with the judicial election process, it has limited judicial review of legislative acts, manipulated the size of the Court of Appeals for partisan purposes, aided Republican candidates in supreme court races, interfered with gubernatorial appointment powers, threatened disobedient judges with shortened terms, cancelled judicial primaries, gerrymandered the districts of disfavored judges, and more. The entire state judiciary is under potent assault.

Republican lawmakers have also used legislative powers more ruthlessly than any other state assembly to tilt the democratic process in their direction. They passed the most aggressive voter suppression and political gerrymandering plans in a half century. They have specialized in "sore loser" laws—effectively overturning the results of municipal and other local elections when unhappy with the choices of the voters. Republican lawmakers have even been willing to cast aside the American democracy's most foundational rule: if you lose an election, you respect the will of the voters and move on. The General Assembly has, instead, chosen to dramatically diminish the authorities of the governor and attorney general's offices when their favored candidates didn't prevail. No need to turn the keys to the governor's mansion over to one's successor, the theory goes—just burn it down. Democratic norms are, apparently, for losers. All that matters is power.

Attacking the Fundaments

It is possible, of course, to characterize these assaults on equality, democracy, and judicial review as radical, or extreme, or, I guess, even as ultraconservative, which North Carolina Republicans seem to think they are. But the General Assembly's war on equality and its war on democratic and constitutional norms is actually a rejection of, an assault on, the structures and foundational premises of the American democracy itself, on the developed assurances of the American promise. The power-grabbing moves do not reflect the normal give-and-take of traditional politics. Instead they challenge, and move to overthrow, the foundations, the fundaments of our premises of governance. I've long been taken with that word, *fundaments*. It means, broadly, the "basic principle, the underlying foundation or theory" of a system.[24] But it can also suggest "a base or foundation, especially of a building"—the fundaments upon which we have built. Chris Hedges has written that "every democracy needs a liberal fundament, a Bill of Rights enshrined in law and spirit, for this alone gives democracy the chance for self-correction and reform."[25] Yale historian Timothy Snyder more recently noted, in fretting over Donald Trump, that "history can remind us of the fragile fundaments of our own democracy."[26]

Foundations of governance—like judicial independence, the rule of law, and separation of powers—have taken us centuries to develop and secure. Casting them out in a temporary craving for power mocks our history and the bold legacy of our forebears. It sells our meaning and sacrifice for an ill-intentioned mess of pottage. Preferring tribe to the defining constitutional norm of equality irrefutably breaks the most important promises we have made to one another as a people. It ought to be deemed beyond the pay grade of an even overambitious state legislature. A rejection of our fundaments, of course, is a more serious business than merely being careless, or mistaken, or hyperzealous, or simply wrong. It is more scornful of our story, our meaning. More contrary to the red, white, and blue. It sets aside our binding ideals. It assumes all that matters is the temporary authority of a favored partisan grouping, not the norms that define us as a state and as a nation. It is, not to put too fine a point on it, unpatriotic.

This means, then, that the political battle presently being waged in North Carolina is not only brutal; it is defining. The stakes are larger than ideological ascendancies. They touch, directly, perhaps even permanently, the character we seek as a people. The leaders of the Republican North Carolina General Assembly never profess to campaign as crusaders for an altered vision of American constitutional government—but that platform is what they increasingly carry out, regardless of what they might say. So the political war in North Carolina is about more than politics, at least politics in the typical sense. It is about the promises that constitute us as a commonwealth. It is about our constitutive assurances to one another. It is about our hard-secured traditions of governance. It is about our character as a people. At its core, it is about a struggle for our own decency.

This is a book about the politics of North Carolina, but it is also a warning beacon for other states as well. The *New York Times* has claimed, "North Carolina experienced its political cataclysm a few years ahead of the rest of the country."[27] The *Atlantic* writes that "nowhere is the battle between liberal and conservative visions of government fiercer than in North Carolina."[28] *Vox* adds that

"North Carolina has become a playbook for Republicans across the country."[29] My own congressman, David Price, also a thoughtful political scientist, now concludes, "We've become Exhibit A of our country's political trends."[30] Perhaps more precisely, Rick Hasen, the noted election law scholar from the University of California, Irvine, has written: "North Carolina set a precedent in playing a kind of hardball that we haven't seen in other places. Does it spiral out of control? This has been more asymmetric with Republicans, but I don't think it would always stay that way."[31] In other words, what happens in Raleigh may not stay in Raleigh.

CHAPTER TWO

Governing as a White People's Party

It's obvious. It's planned. They want to think, here, that the world belongs to a certain race of people and they don't want the rest of us to be equal. —Rosanell Eaton, ninety-four-year-old civil rights and voting activist, Warrenton, North Carolina, 2017[32]

There is no moral issue. It is wrong—deadly wrong—to deny any of your fellow Americans the right to vote in this country. —President Lyndon Johnson, calling for passage of the 1965 Voting Rights Act[33]

I am loath to write first of race. The reason is simple. When a lot of folks in North Carolina read claims about race, they stop paying attention. Especially white ones.

Still, the last decade's assault on the interests, rights, dignity, and opportunities for full participation of African Americans constitutes the plainest rejection of our history and aspirations of constitutive promise yet seen in modern North Carolina. The repeatedly demonstrated willingness to overtly exclude and marginalize black citizens has presented, I think, the strongest surprise and perhaps the greatest heartbreak, for Tar Heels of long-standing. One of the state's most common refrains, as the third decade of the twenty-first century approaches, is "I never thought we would go through this again." Who would have guessed that a state, particularly North Carolina, would reopen foundational questions about racial equality and inclusion? That we would seek to dislodge and dismember this well-settled aspirational core?

Too much energy, courage, sweat, spirit, faith, and blood has been spent over too many generations, even centuries, to revisit the very heart of the matter: the notion that we all count, that we are all empowered members of the polity. The "arc of the moral universe is long," as Dr. King repeatedly said, "but it bends toward justice."[34] The contemplated and interjecting arc doesn't carve out new and ambitious fronts aimed at a studied reversal and reconsideration of America's foundational tenets. It most pointedly does not call into question anew the essential underpinnings, the idea that we're all in this together, that we are all fully authorized participants. We have, in recent years, though, learned to expect to be surprised. The givens are no longer that.

The rejection of racial equity as an accepted and defining social goal is particularly tough medicine in a state with North Carolina's sometimes inspiring but often brutal racial history. The discard and depletion of the beckoning norm of constitutional equality is appalling in a commonwealth already desperately riven with racial disparity—in virtually every component of its social ordering. In income, in wealth, in power, in health, in education, in housing, in employment, in safety, in status, in proffered life prospect. In a state constantly declaring its pledged commitment to "liberty and justice for all," whose state charter deems it "self-evident that all persons are created equal," that "all political power is vested in and derived from the people," and "is instituted solely for the good of the whole," where "no person shall be denied the equal protection of the laws, nor be subjected to discrimination by the State because of race, color, religion or national origin."[35]

Removing the hard work of effective racial integration and inclusion from the shared political agenda defeats the meaning of the claimed commonwealth. And that these steps should be undertaken pointedly, repeatedly, aggressively, and (seemingly) relentlessly by a governing political party that operates in all meaningful ways as a white people's party moves beyond the tolerable limits of American constitutional democracy. The North Carolina General Assembly's war on African Americans, I will argue, standing alone, fatally undermines its legitimacy as a governing institution. It also patently violates North Carolina's defining purpose as a civic polity.

A Word in Perspective

North Carolinians typically believe that their state's racial history was, broadly speaking, comparatively less horrifying than that of an array of our southern neighbors. And there is at least some evidence to back up the "less terrorizing" verdict. Rob Christensen, for example, writes that after the demise of North Carolina's harshest white supremacist campaigns, it "adopted a milder form of racial segregation than most of the South, as business leaders sought to avoid the violence and disruption that could harm efforts to recruit northern corporations."[36] More pointedly, as my colleagues Robert Korstad and James Leloudis have noted, at almost the same moment that George Wallace launched his governorship on the steps of the Alabama statehouse, committing the entirety of his energy to defending "Segregation now! Segregation tomorrow! Segregation forever!" Terry Sanford was preparing to launch his noted North Carolina Fund, arguing that the state could not join the American economic mainstream until it invested in the full potential of all its people and ensured equal rights for all. Three months later, at North Carolina A & T State University, Sanford declared, "We must move forward as one people or we will not move forward at all. We cannot move forward as whites or Negroes. We can only move forward as North Carolinians."[37]

But, as Christensen also suggests, "the state's reputation for racial moderation has typically been overstated." North Carolina's history is often "presented as a soothing narrative—a politically moderate state, run by reasonable business-oriented leaders that have worked together to help a poor state pull itself up by the bootstraps."[38] Thus Tar Heels "avoided the demagogues of other southern states, such as South Carolina's Cole Blease, Mississippi's Theodore Bilbo, and Georgia's Eugene Talmadge." Still, the truth,

Christensen notes, is decidedly "more complicated." North Carolina is the state of Frank Porter Graham, Terry Sanford, Bill Friday, Pauli Murray, and, later, Jim Hunt, Henry Frye, Ella Baker, Floyd McKissick, the Greensboro Four, Ann Atwater, and Julius Chambers. But it has also produced, perhaps more readily and regularly, committed white supremacists like Furnifold Simmons, Charles Aycock, Alfred Moore Waddell, Cameron Morrison, Thomas Dixon, Josephus Daniels, Willis Smith, I. Beverly Lake, Jim Gardner, and Jesse Helms. If North Carolina has experienced stretches of racial moderation, it has also produced the nation's only murderous municipal coup in Wilmington in 1898,[39] inflicted more than one hundred documented racial lynchings from 1877 to 1955,[40] seen expansive periods with the nation's highest state Ku Klux Klan membership,[41] and suffered the injustices of the Wilmington Ten and the violent rampage of the Greensboro Massacre in the 1970s.[42] North Carolina's racial history has not always tracked the very worst of the American South, but it has been, without doubt, brutal, bloody, and reprehensible.

And the impact of history persists.

In 2019 twice as many African-American Tar Heels live in poverty as whites, and more than twice as many blacks are unemployed.[43] The gulf is worse for kids. Almost three times as many black children are poor compared with white ones. The disparity is greater for kids younger than five years old. Much higher rates of hunger and a lack of health insurance appear in the black community. About three times as many African Americans have mortgages that are underwater. Amazingly, black North Carolina households have only about one-sixteenth of the family wealth—the accumulation of income and assets over time and, often, over generations—on average compared with white households. Three times as many black families report a negative net worth. Most of the state's counties experiencing beyond-daunting child poverty rates (approaching 50 percent)—Northampton, Chowan, Scotland, Vance, and Edgecombe—have high percentages of African-

American residents. The same is true of North Carolina's ten federally designated persistent-poverty counties.[44] Poverty and race, in the Tar Heel State, are constant and pervasive companions. Ever has it been so. From our first day until this one.

Black kids also attend, very disproportionately, North Carolina's highest poverty public schools.[45] Under our state's odd A–F grading system, almost all high-poverty schools receive exceedingly poor grades, while almost all high-wealth schools excel. A recent university study found that black students make up 26 percent of the state's public school enrollees but receive more than half of all suspensions. In Chapel Hill–Carrboro, where I live, black students make up 13 percent of the enrollment but receive 53 percent of the suspensions. Twice as many white Tar Heels have a college degree compared with African Americans. And, most stunning, 57 percent of North Carolina Department of Correction prisoners are black, though 22 percent of the state's population is African American. A little more than a third of the prison cohort is white, though whites constitute more than 70 percent of the population overall. North Carolina incarcerates 203 whites and 915 blacks per 100,000 in population. And an unending cascade of irrefutable empirical studies demonstrate massive and unexplainable racial disparities in policing, employment, housing, and health care. North Carolina reflects, and notably amplifies, national trends recently documented by the Pew Research Center: "America remains two societies—one white and one black as measured by key demographic indicators of social and economic well-being. Blacks, on average, are at least twice as likely to be poor or unemployed; they earn, by household, little more than half of what white households claim, and they possess only about 8% of the net wealth enjoyed by white peers."[46]

In other words, unless the term is to be drained of all meaning, there can be no doubt that, at this moment, still, North Carolina experiences an intense, pervasive, and systematic (meaning, "of, or relating to, the entire body of an organism") regime of racial subordination. Yet the brutal, widespread, and racialized disparity triggers no correspondingly ambitious policy programs or proposals. It is not derided in the statehouse or in notable committee hearings. State leaders raise no chorus of exigency. Perennial, debilitating systemic racial subordination is assumed to be as natural and untroubling as the sun's easterly morning rise. One could add, I think noncontroversially, that if the respective racial roles were somehow to be reversed, with white Tar Heels experiencing subordination on every front, the state would surely deem the crisis one of unspeakable urgency. Legislatures would be summoned into emergency session. Unresponsive leaders would be politically dispatched. As my colleague Dr. Jarvis Hall puts it, "The only acceptable response would be revolt."[47]

The New Republican Racial Legislative Agenda

Upon assuming control of both houses of the legislature in 2011, Republican supermajorities went to work securing their favorable control of the electoral process. Maps were passed, as demanded by a new census, redrawing both federal and state electoral districts. Each set was eventually ruled unconstitutional by the federal courts for markedly diluting the voting rights of African Americans. The challenged districts created for the U.S. House of Representatives had been constructed to dilute the effective participation of black Tar Heels, not to comply, as the legislature had asserted, with the demands of the federal Voting Rights Act, the court ruled. Black voters were packed into contorted districts that limited their electoral effectiveness. The U.S. Supreme Court, after a six-year saga, agreed.[48]

The Republican legislative plan for their own (state) districts was more ambitious and notably more flagrant. Another federal court ruled that here the General Assembly had "unjustifiably and unconstitutionally relied on race in drawing district lines" in 2011. The "overriding priority of the redistricting plan was to draw a predetermined, race-based number of districts." Judge James Wynn was frank to say the scheme to discriminate was a "widespread, serious, and longstanding constitutional violation." It was, Wynn added, "among the largest racial gerrymanders ever confronted by a federal court." In effect, it deprived an ample percentage of North Carolinians "a constitutionally adequate voice in the state legislature," defeating foundational ties of "popular sovereignty." Tough words. Unusual ones from a federal judge.[49]

Still, Republican leaders dragged their feet, stuck to their positions, and appealed every move, often delaying the implementation of a meaningful remedy and pressing their (judicially declared) impermissible advantage. Eventually, on the congressional side, a three-judge federal tribunal, in exasperation, declared:

> We continue to lament that North Carolina voters have now been deprived of a constitutional congressional districting plan—and, therefore, constitutional representation in Congress—for six years and three election cycles.[50]

The massive state-based gerrymander, federal courts concluded, had

> [so] unjustifiably relied on race to distort dozens of legislative district lines, and thereby potentially distort the outcome of elections and the composition and responsiveness of the legislature, the districting plans [under which the General Assembly had been elected] interfered with the very mechanism by which people confer their sovereignty on the General Assembly and hold the General Assembly accountable.[51]

By seeking so potently to disenfranchise black Tar Heels, in other words, the North Carolina Republican General Assembly had undermined its own legitimacy. It had broken the bonds necessitated for the essential consent of the governed. It had also, in the process, cast aside the foundational American premise of representative government.

So pronounced was the persistent violation that in 2019 a Wake County state judge, Brian Collins, ruled that two electorally adopted amendments to the North Carolina constitution were invalid because the legislature had forfeited the authority, under Article XIII of the state charter, to place proposed amendments on the ballot for adoption by the citizenry. The state constitution, the court reasoned, requires a 3/5 vote of the General Assembly for electoral consideration. However,

> the unconstitutional racial gerrymander tainted the 3/5 majority required by the state constitution before an amendment proposed can be submitted for a vote, breaking the appropriate chain of popular sovereignty between North Carolina citizens and their representatives. An illegally constituted General Assembly does not represent the people of North Carolina and therefore is not empowered to pass legislation that would amend the state constitution.[52]

Judge Collins's decision actually echoed an earlier conclusion by Judge James Wynn and the three-judge federal court exploring the ramifications of the General Assembly's foundational 2011 statehouse racial gerrymander: "As James Madison warned, a legislature that is itself insulated by virtue of an invidious gerrymander can enact additional legislation to restrict voting rights and thereby firmly cement its unjustified control of the organs of both state and federal government."[53]

Nor did the Republican General Assembly limit its anti–African American, racialized tampering to state and federal electoral districts. In July 2015 the Republican-controlled General Assembly, using a "truncated process" without "soliciting input from the affected parties or the local delegations," unilaterally recast the Greensboro city council districts. The surprise plan was sponsored by Republican senator Trudy Wade, though, oddly, when the alteration was challenged in the federal courts, she claimed legislative immunity and refused to explain why she had sponsored it.

Apparently Senator Wade was annoyed that Greensboro elections had produced a comfortable majority of Democratic councilors on the eight-member panel—including four African-American incumbents. Accordingly, she moved to restructure the local election process and redraw the new districts to double-bunk incumbents in ways that would ensure at least some of them knocked others from the council.

Federal Judge Catherine Eagles invalidated the measure, concluding it was designed in major part to suppress the effectiveness of black voters and candidates through yet another Republican-inspired racial gerrymander.[54] Once again, the federal courts were less enthusiastic about disenfranchising black people than the leadership of the General Assembly had been. In the 2019 legislative session, Republican legislators introduced a similar hit on city government elections in Winston-Salem. There, the unsolicited districting changes would have double-bunked an array of African-American incumbents—effectively overturning previous electoral and likely future candidate prospects. Hostility to the proposed statute in Winston-Salem was so intense, however, that the Republican sponsors eventually dropped it.[55] Even in North Carolina you can't always get what you want.

The Republican General Assembly also has not limited its race-based electoral interference to district gerrymandering. In 2013 it passed an array of voting restrictions, including a biased voter identification requirement aimed at tightening access to the ballot.[56] The provision ended same-day voter registration, notably shortened the early voting period, ended out-of-precinct voting, and restricted various early registration practices. As the voter access bill was being considered, the U.S. Supreme Court handed down its controversial ruling in *Shelby County v. Holder*, invalidating the preclearance requirements of the federal Voting Rights Act.[57] Chief Justice John Roberts famously wrote that "things have changed dramatically" in the American South—"discriminatory evasions of federal decrees are rare." Sen. Thomas Apodaca, one of the North Carolina voting statute's principal sponsors, announced giddily to WRAL news, "Now we can go on with the full bill."[58] Hot dog.

Unsurprisingly, the "monster" voter ID bill passed by the N.C. General Assembly in 2013—described by election law scholars as, in total, the most restrictive electoral measure passed by a state government in the last half century[59]—was immediately challenged in the federal courts. The federal court extensively explored the motivation and methods behind the statute's enactment. It concluded and demonstrably proved that Republicans had studied every voting provision or mechanism that elevated black turnout and then eliminated or restricted each practice "with almost surgical precision." The law reflected targeted racial suppression; its impacts could not sensibly be regarded as accidental or based on permissible justifications. Thus the central requirements of the act were invalidated. The claimed interest in ballot integrity was held to be a mere ruse. No evidence of in-person voter fraud could be provided. The judges noted that the speed of the Republicans' post–Shelby County gyrations revealed the lawmakers' actual intentions. "Neither this legislature, nor, as far as we can tell, any other legislature in the country," the three-judge panel wrote, "has ever done so much, so fast, to restrict access to the franchise."[60] First place. Yet again. (Another voter ID bill was passed in 2018 after the adoption of a state constitutional amendment. It, too, was invalidated, at least temporarily, by the federal courts.)[61]

The "surgical precision" the federal courts decried reappeared in the lead-up to the 2016 elections. Dallas Woodhouse, then executive director of the state Republican Party, wrote to Republican-majority local electoral boards (which Woodhouse played a role in appointing), urging them to double down on racial suppression. In an email to GOP appointees, he warned them "to make party line changes to early voting" by limiting hours and keeping polling sites closed on Sundays—taking aim at the "souls to the polls" efforts of many black churches in North Carolina. Woodhouse warned any recalcitrant Republicans of being deemed "traitors to the party." A number of counties quickly complied. Woodhouse described himself as an "unabashed partisan," proclaiming, "Our folks are angry and opposed to Sunday voting." By overtly pressing a Republican policy to eliminate "souls to the polls" programs, Woodhouse stepped beyond the traditional pretense embraced by his party colleagues. We're targeting black folks, he effectively explained, because they are our adversaries. Our opposition is "unabashed." Sen. Bob Rucho and Rep. David Lewis, whom the federal judges had already found to have engaged in systemic race discrimination, wrote to the state elections board in enthusiastic support, backing Woodhouse's play.[62]

The General Assembly also moved dramatically to diminish the rights of African Americans in the criminal justice system. In 2009 North Carolina (then under Democratic control) enacted the groundbreaking Racial Justice Act, which required courts to vacate a death sentence where it was proven to be "sought or obtained on the basis of race." The goal of the statute was to ensure that if North Carolina was to continue to have a death penalty, every effort would be made to ensure that racial bias played no role in its implementation. The statute was aimed particularly at racially discriminatory practices in death cases, including bias in jury selection. In April 2012 Cumberland County Superior Court Judge Greg Weeks overturned Marcus Robinson's death sentence after concluding that highly reliable evidence proved that North Carolina prosecutors intentionally discriminated against black defendants in selecting juries in capital cases. A few months later, three other previously convicted death penalty defendants proved that prosecutors had blocked African Americans from jury service, and their death sentences (not the underlying conviction) were vacated.

In June 2013 the Republican General Assembly decided it had seen enough and repealed the Racial Justice Act. Rather than moving to cure the injustices revealed in the early racial justice act cases, the legislature decided to kill the messenger. Gov. Pat McCrory signed the repeal bill, claiming it would merely remove needless "procedural roadblocks" to the death penalty in North Carolina. A freshman legislator who opposed the repeal said:

> Even though I'm new here, I understand that there was evidence of racial bias when the legislature adopted the Racial Justice Act. Subsequent court cases confirmed this bias. So why are we reversing the law now given all of this evidence?[63]

Democratic Sen. Martin Nesbitt asked even more pointedly, "If we have somebody on death row because they're black, wouldn't we want to find that out?"[64] Republican legislators and the Republican governor, apparently, thought not.

The racialized Republican agenda in education has produced an exuberant embrace of expanded, segregating charter schools and generous, unregulated, discriminatory private school voucher programs. The 1996 state law that opened the door to public charter schools contained a numerical cap (one hundred) and required that within a year of a charter's opening, the school must reflect the racial and ethnic composition of the district in which it is located. In 2013 the Republican General Assembly lifted the cap on charter schools and repealed the diversity requirement, demanding, instead, only that charter schools "make efforts" to achieve racial diversity.[65]

The result was predictable. A 2017 study by the *Raleigh News & Observer* concluded that "charter schools in North Carolina are more segregated than traditional public schools and have more affluent students."[66] Most charters, the study found, have "either a largely white population or a largely minority population." Charter schools are thus more white and less Latinx than schools run by local districts. In traditional public schools, more than half of the enrolled students come from low-income families, but in charters, the report determined, only about a third of kids were poor. A 2019 study by the North Carolina Justice Center traced the segregating impact of charters on the traditional school system. The proliferation of charter schools "exacerbates racial segregation," it concluded. In 72 percent of the counties containing at least one such school, charters increased the degree of racial segregation in the district. Charter schools "tend to skew whiter than other schools in the same county."[67] Eliminating the diversity requirement has had its impact.

In 2018 the Republican General Assembly took segregation efforts a groundbreaking step further. Lawmakers passed a measure permitting four suburban towns in Mecklenburg County, with mostly white populations, to create their own charter schools and limit enrollments to students from within their borders—effectively withdrawing from the broad and more racially and economically diverse Charlotte-Mecklenburg school district.[68] The law also would allow the municipalities—Cornelius, Huntersville, Matthews, and Mint Hill—to spend property tax dollars on the charters. Irv Joiner of the NC NAACP described the move as "an effort to go back to the 1900s with Jim Crow, setting up white enclaves." James Ford, a North Carolina teacher of the year, wrote in the *Charlotte Observer* that the bill was "a design for racial and economic segregation. . . . We've seen this before. Only this time it's not white flight, it's building a 'white fence.' "[69]

Looking more broadly, as the Black Lives Matter movement swept the nation in 2013 and 2014—fueled by revelations of police brutality caught on ever-pervasive cameras—the North Carolina General Assembly bucked the national trend by making it more difficult to obtain or publish police video camera footage. The new statute allows ready access only to those pictured in the footage or their relatives. Journalists and members of the public are now required to obtain a court order to view the footage. The law also barred willing police departments from releasing footage independently since all requests now had to be directed to the judicial system. And police departments were given the presumptive power to close off access to footage if necessary to protect an officer's reputation or an active criminal investigation.[70] The North Carolina ACLU protested vehemently, calling the law "extremely restrictive." Body-camera footage "should be a tool to make law enforcement more transparent and accountable to the communities they serve," Suzanna Birdsong explained, "but this shameful law will make it nearly impossible to achieve those goals."[71]

In the fall of 2016 Charlotte experienced massive protests in response to the police shooting of Keith Lamont Scott.[72] (It was during the internationally televised protests that North Carolina Republican congressman Robert Pittenger explained to the BBC that the black demonstrators on the streets of Charlotte "hate white people because white people are successful and they're not."[73]) Following the long-lived demonstrations revealing intense poverty, inequality, and racial tension, Republican state representatives Justin Burr and Chris Millis introduced H.B. 330. Rather than addressing the issues of police brutality and racial inequity that triggered the protests, the bill proposed civil and criminal immunity for drivers who hit protestors on the road without a permit, so long as the drivers exercised due care. Republican Rep. Michael Speciale offered his enthusiastic support, explaining: "These people . . . are nuts to run in front of cars like they do . . . and say me and my buddy here are going to stop this two and a half ton vehicle. If somebody does bump somebody, why should they be liable?"[74] H.B. 330 passed the House in April 2017 but stalled in the Senate after a murderous white nationalist ran over protesters, killing a heroic young woman in Charlottesville, Virginia, three months later.

Of course, H.B. 330 was hardly the Republican General Assembly's first interaction with large, unhappy demonstrations. The Moral Monday movement, led by Rev. William Barber—head of the NC NAACP and the state's leading civil rights activist—began in 2013 in response to the legislature's dramatically altered political agenda. Relations with the citizen protesters were hardly welcoming. Sen. Thom Goolsby, for example, referred to the demonstrators who regularly assembled by the tens of thousands as "Moral Morons." After more than nine hundred protesters were arrested, leaders convened the Legislative Services Commission in 2014 to revise the rules of conduct in the Legislative Building. Senate Minority Leader Democrat Josh Stein called it "deeply concerning that we are changing the rules in which the people can enter the people's house without any public comment or opportunity for the full chamber to consider those rules." NAACP lawyer Irv Joiner argued, "These rules do no more than give the General Assembly police officers and the legislative leadership unbridled discretion to indiscriminately violate the rights of North Carolinians with whom they do not agree."[75]

Rev. Barber was arrested, yet again, during a sit-in protest at the Legislative Building on May 30, 2017, and was banned from entering the building in the future. General Assembly Police Chief Martin Brock and Legislative Services Officer Paul Coble sent Barber a letter in which they gloated, "Your release orders clearly state that you are not to go back to the North Carolina Legislative Building unless authorized to do so. At this time, I have not authorized you to return and this prohibition will be enforced until the resolution of your case in court."[76] Coble later threatened two young African-American activists for attempting to deliver a letter to House Speaker Tim Moore's office.[77] The petition, ironically, demanded an immediate redistricting effort in light of the U.S. Supreme Court's recent ruling that North Carolina's legislative districts were unconstitutional. The scene presented an interesting encapsulation of North Carolina's plight—an angry white bureaucrat threatening idealistic young African Americans with arrest for requesting legislative districts that don't deny the equal rights of black people.

Perhaps as notably, in 2015 the Republican General Assembly passed NCGS sec. 100-2.1, requiring the approval of the North Carolina Historical Commission before any monument can be moved and placing strict limitations on the removal, even temporarily, of

Confederate war memorials. The statute was apparently designed to prevent the removal of the "Silent Sam" Confederate monument at the gateway of the UNC–Chapel Hill campus—which had been the focus of pointed demonstrations for decades.[78] Distinguished southern historian Professor Harry Watson of UNC explained the statue's genesis in white supremacy:

> Beginning in the 1890s and going into the 1900s, the South had gone through a political cataclysm stripping black men of their rights without provoking a northern reaction. As a result, the white South was taking a victory lap (with the statue). They were saying they had in effect won the Civil War. They were saying, "We've reclaimed our homeland, and we can dictate racial relations without interference."[79]

After the horrors of the Charlottesville killing, Democratic governor Roy Cooper asked that the usurping and ill-motivated monuments law be repealed: "We cannot continue to glorify a war against the United States of America fought in the defense of slavery." The Republican General Assembly, however, refused to budge. After all, as one of the bill's principal sponsors, Sen. Tommy Tucker, had explained, the Civil War was not about slavery after all: "It was caused by the North and their tariffs over Southern goods."[80] Time to tear down the Lincoln Memorial.

I could go on. The list is not endless, but it is continuing, pervasive, enthusiastic, and assuredly long. It betrays North Carolina's immensely challenging history. It violates its constitutional promise. It closes off the state's future. It seeks to withdraw from America's national mission. And it potently wounds millions of our sisters and brothers.

Governing as a White People's Party

Practically speaking, the North Carolina Republican Party's racialized agenda raises an additional question: How does it work?

How does a state legislative assembly—in a commonwealth that is 22 percent African American and more than 40 percent citizens of color—adopt and carry forward an agenda that includes, as a central tenet, the diminution of rights of participation, equality, fairness, opportunity, and dignity of black Tar Heels? The answer to that question is straightforward, if horrifying. The North Carolina Republican General Assembly now operates as a white people's caucus.

As I've indicated, the Republican Party has controlled both houses of the General Assembly since 2010. It has often done so through very large majorities in the two chambers. From 2010 until 2018, Republicans enjoyed veto-proof supermajorities. Those margins were, thankfully, pared in the 2018 elections, eliminating the veto-proof chasm. Still, they remain large—ten seats in the House and eight in the notably smaller Senate. More alarming, all the Republican legislators, in both chambers, are white. As the surprisingly candid Republican Rep. Holly Grange of Wilmington put it in 2019, "On my side, there's not a lot of diversity; it's a middle-age white man's club."[81]

In 2019 there are twenty-six African-American representatives in the North Carolina House. There are ten black senators.[82] One Native American and two Indian Americans serve in the General Assembly. No people of Latinx descent do. But the overall numbers, scant as they are, still mislead. In the House, the twenty-six African Americans and one Native American are all Democrats. The sixty-five Republicans are white. In the Senate, the ten African Americans and two Indian Americans are Democrats. Every Republican (twenty-nine) is white. (Similar Republican tallies appeared in the 2010, 2012, 2014, and 2016 sessions.)

So when the majority caucuses in each chamber retire to their private deliberations to craft the laws of North Carolina, only white people attend (at least as participants). When the Republicans consider whether to repeal the Racial Justice Act, to make electoral participation more difficult for black voters, to gerrymander and misalign black-dominated voting districts, to politically harass and unseat black city councilmen, to adopt biased ID requirements, to further racially segregate the public schools, to create racialized (charter) school districts, to punish (often) predominantly black demonstrators, to shield police camera footage from public view, and to lionize Confederate monuments, no black voice is raised in protest. There are none in the room. Almost 150 years after the passage of the Fourteenth and Fifteenth Amendments to the U.S. Constitution, the North Carolina General Assembly is controlled by a white people's party.

In what other areas of twenty-first-century life would we countenance such opportunity-demolishing arrangements? We wouldn't accept an all-white justice system or whites-only universities or major businesses or sports programs or entertainment industries or public utilities or rotary clubs. We particularly wouldn't accept them in government, where they repudiate essential democratic premises and violate expressed constitutional constraints. And we surely would not accept aggressive efforts by any such organization to increase and sustain its grip on exclusion. Why in the world would we join, or support, or accept a "White People's Party"? Given the ubiquitous subordination continuously experienced by African Americans in North Carolina, it is astonishing that any political party—much less a dominant one—would launch, effectuate, and readily defend what constitutes a multifaceted and unrelenting campaign against people of color. Ignoring the challenging plight of black Tar Heels apparently has proven insufficient. Republican legislators have felt compelled to move further—burdening black citizens as if they were dreaded adversaries—and doing so with energy and dispatch, as if their oppressive opportunities were limited by the demographics, and the clock.

Imagine that, under a strange, somehow enforceable, truth-in-labeling demand, the North Carolina Republican Party was forced to rename itself as the White People's Party. Would a young, tech-driven, libertarian explain, "I don't like capital gains taxes, so I joined the White People's Party?" Would an accomplished and respected investment banker declare, "I'm committed to the carried interest exception, so I vote for the White People's Party?" Would a devout, patriotic, evangelical Christian forthrightly proclaim, "We need prayer in our classrooms, so I'm with the White People's Party?"

Of course not. Such justifications and protestations would immediately and conclusively be dismissed, even despised. No set of allegiances or commonalities would work to validate association with an overtly race-based political party. Admitted exclusion trumps the bartering of normal politics. It defeats the foundation of our polity. But is the reach of moral responsibility so thin that it can be escaped by the transparent tool of branding? Is it acceptable to operate as a white person's party as long as one never admits it? Does the fact of exclusion fade before a disingenuously proffered assertion of inclusive brotherhood? Can one, without blame, aid and abet the repudiation of equality? Is the labeling all that matters?

Too much blood has been spent, too many life chances crushed, to settle for pretense. Our leaders may be unaware of our history, but they can't escape its shadow. It makes no difference if the proponents of exclusion wear, as they do here, genial smiles and speak, oddly, of American values and Christian tenets. It has happened before. We all lose—not just African Americans and other citizens of color—when we retreat to a white people's politics. And we lose badly, perhaps irreparably. The muscular agenda of racism now embraced by the North Carolina Republican General Assembly is not an acceptable component of the barter and trade of democratic governance. It's a deal breaker. The deal breaker. All North Carolinians are diminished by it. All North Carolina Republicans are responsible for it. Each and every one.

I've been told repeatedly that it is rude and damagingly inappropriate—especially for a professor and a state employee—to mention the racial makeup of the Republican caucuses that dominate our legislature. It is unacceptable, the claim goes, to mention a "white people's party." It is apparently not troubling to *be* a white person's party—just to name it. This, of course, is the crowning exercise in political correctness. Words cannot be uttered, even when irrefutably true. Especially when irrefutably true. The racialized agenda of the North Carolina Republican General Assembly rejects, wholesale, the very undergirding of the American promise. It alone, even without regard to all of the stunning transgressions discussed in the additional nine chapters that follow, fatally shames and abases the people and aspirations of the Tar Heel State.

CHAPTER THREE

A War on Poor People

What we have to do is find a way to divide and conquer the people who are on assistance. We have to show respect for that woman who has cerebral palsy and had no choice in her condition, that needs help and that we should help. And we need to get those folks to look down at these people who choose to get into a condition that makes them dependent on the government and say, "At some point, you're on your own! We may end up taking care of those babies, but we're not taking care of you." And we've got to start having that serious discussion. It won't happen next year. Wrong time. Because it's going to be politically charged. One of the reasons why I may never run for another elected office is 'cause some of these things may just get me railroaded out of town. But in 2013 I honestly believe that we have to do it. —Thom Tillis, North Carolina House Speaker, Mars Hill, North Carolina[83]

North Carolina faces many challenges. Its greatest is likely poverty—wrenching economic hardship amid relative plenty. Poverty, of course, is a broad problem in the United States, even if a surprising one. Though we are, by sensible measures, the wealthiest nation on earth, we countenance higher levels of poverty, and especially child poverty, than other advanced countries. In 2018 the United Nations rapporteur on extreme poverty and human rights, Phillip Alston, found that the United States has now become "the most unequal society in the world" in ways that are "shockingly at odds with [its] immense wealth and founding commitment to human rights."[84]

Even as the richest nation, in terms of its poverty rate, the U.S. ranks thirty-fifth out of the thirty-seven countries of the Organization for Economic Development (OECD). It is also, Alston concluded, "the clear and constant outlier in child poverty; shocking numbers of its children are poor." America has, by far, the highest child poverty rate—about a quarter of its kids are poor compared to 14 percent in the other thirty-six OECD nations. We have the highest GINI (economic inequality) index. Of the ten wealthiest countries, the U.S. does the least to alleviate poverty. It has the weakest social safety net and among the worst rates of economic mobility. Poor people get rougher treatment than in any comparable nation. Thomas Piketty, the world's leading economic polarization scholar, has written that inequality in the U.S. is "probably higher than in any other society, at any time, anywhere in the world."[85]

North Carolina is, on average, even worse. About 14 percent of Tar Heels live in poverty (with an annual income of less than $25,900 for a family of four).[86] Twenty-two percent of all kids statewide are poor, almost a half million, the twelfth worst rate in the nation. Forty-two percent of Hispanic children and almost 40 percent of African-American and Native-American children live below the poverty threshold. About 650,000 of us overall live in extreme poverty, on incomes less than half of the traditional federal poverty threshold. That figure includes 10 percent of all children in North Carolina. Almost 1.8 million Tar Heels are classified as hungry—one of the nation's very highest rates. Nearly 560,000 North Carolina children, about one in four, didn't get enough to eat last year. The state's median income is markedly less than national figures. A third of Tar Heel workers make poverty-level wages—the second highest rate in the country.[87] The federal government reports that ten eastern North Carolina counties demonstrate "persistent poverty": Bertie, Bladen, Columbus, Halifax, Martin, Northampton, Pitt, Robeson, Tyrell, and Washington. That means that at least 20 percent of county residents have lived in poverty for more than thirty years.[88] Income inequality has risen dramatically in North Carolina over the last four decades. Over that period, inequality mushroomed in ninety-seven of one hundred counties. From 2000 to 2014, sixty-five North Carolina counties markedly expanded the polarizing trend.[89]

In 2014 Dr. Raj Chetty and his colleagues at the Equality of Opportunity Project concluded that Charlotte had the worst economic mobility of any major city in the United States: fiftieth out of fifty.[90] The U.S. Census Bureau announced that over the last decade, North Carolina experienced a steeper rise in concentrated poverty (census tracts where 20 percent or more of residents are poor) than any other state. Greensboro was identified several times in the last ten years as the hungriest or most food insecure city in America.[91] A national study named Lumberton and Roanoke Rapids as two of the three poorest cities in America.[92] A Wall Street study separately listed Goldsboro as the fifth poorest city in the nation. A Pew Research Center report on the shrinking middle class found that the share of adults in Goldsboro who are middle income fell from 60 percent in 2000 to 48 percent in 2014, the greatest decrease experienced by any metropolitan area in the nation.[93] Alternately, Hickory's dramatic, decade-long rise in unemployment was one of the most pronounced in the country.[93] North Carolina increasingly presents a leading edge of American economic distress.

A General Assembly Targets the Poor

Poverty was dramatically reduced in North Carolina between 1960 and 1970. A combination of the federal War on Poverty and the earlier-initiated North Carolina Fund[94] reduced the state poverty rate from a breathtaking 40.6 percent to 20 percent. By 1980 it had fallen further, to about 15 percent.[95] In the almost four decades since, the poverty rate has hovered in the 14–18 percent range. It has almost always exceeded federal levels, often markedly so. And since the potent crusades of Terry Sanford and the North Carolina Fund, poverty has never again reached a central place in Tar Heel politics. Political leaders of both parties have done relatively little to ensure that the plight of low-income citizens receive sustained attention. The Democratic Party, which dominated North Carolina for most of the post-Sanford period, often ignored the state's wrenching poverty.

When Republicans took control of both the legislature and governorship in 2013, however, low-income Tar Heels learned there is something notably worse than being ignored by their government. They can actually be targeted by it. A historic alteration in governing philosophies appeared almost immediately. Those struggling economically felt the most direct and sustained impact of the change. In 2013 the *New York Times* editorialized on "the decline of North Carolina," denouncing the "grotesque damage that a new Republican majority [has done] to the least fortunate."[96] National commentators began referring to North Carolina's altered economic policies, in particular, as "a conservative lab experiment"[97] in social and economic policy. The track record is stunning.

First (and still worst). When Republican power hit full throttle in 2013, Governor Pat McCrory, then House Speaker Thom Tillis, Senate president Phil Berger, and the General Assembly quickly did what other, especially southern, Republican-controlled states did—they rejected the Medicaid expansion proffered by the federal government under the voluntary terms of the Affordable Care Act. The decision was incredibly costly. It meant that more than 460,000 low-income Tar Heels were denied health care coverage despite the federal government being willing to foot the bill almost entirely.[98] North Carolina would forego tens of billions of federal health care dollars. Tar Heel tax dollars would be sent, absurdly, to pay for the health care of poor citizens in other states—states experiencing less poverty, lower unemployment, and much lower rates of uninsured citizens.

The state turned its back on tens of thousands of jobs annually. Hundreds of millions of state and local tax revenues were forfeited. Massive federal payments to distressed North Carolina hospitals for uncompensated care were turned away. Rural hospitals closed;

urban ones suffered greatly (and still do). Tens of thousands lost coverage for opioid addiction treatment, though we have one of the highest addiction rates in the country. Worst of all, sophisticated national studies revealed that a thousand or more poor Tar Heels die annually as a result of the Medicaid decision. Literally die.[99]

The reasons given for nonexpansion were difficult to pin down. Mostly they seemed to signal a distrust of the federal government and disdain for President Obama and the Affordable Care Act. But little more was said, typically, than "expanding Medicaid is not right for North Carolina," or as Senate leader Phil Berger put it, "We can't afford our current Medicaid system, much less an expanded one."[100] Subsequent efforts to join the heavy majority of states welcoming expansion between 2013 and 2019—including states with Republican leadership—received similarly curt, nonresponsive refusals. Despite the traumatic numbers and the subsequent clarity that the federal program had become widely embraced and accepted, state leaders remained unmoved (without fully explaining their stance)—seemingly well satisfied with the calamitous decision. At present, thirty-seven states (including Washington, D.C.) have adopted the Medicaid expansion. North Carolina now seems proud to stand as a silent, belligerent holdout—while its poorest citizens needlessly suffer.

As a result, we have notably higher percentages of uninsured than our Medicaid-joining state counterparts. After five years, according to national studies, the established track record in the expanding states reveals that "actual costs to states from expanding Medicaid are negligible," the "economic and public health benefits" obtained are massive, and "states across the political spectrum do not regret their decisions to expand Medicaid."[101] North Carolina seems tacitly to reply, "We're prepared to hold out to the last because we are so deeply opposed to universal health care coverage. Even as our economy is potently wounded, millions suffer, and tens of thousands of us die, the brutal costs are apparently thought to be worth it." The message seems to be "No additional poor Tar Heels are going to get free health care on our watch, even if the federal government wants to pay for it."

The no-Medicaid expansion decision was cruel, but the North Carolina Republicans at least had some company from other states, mostly in the South, in closing the health care door to impoverished residents. Next, though, they chose to march alone. Despite what were, at the time, soaring unemployment rates—the fifth highest in the country—the General Assembly quickly passed one of the steepest cuts to a state unemployment compensation program in American history. North Carolina became the only state in the country to withdraw from central aspects of the national unemployment program—slashing more than 170,000 unemployed residents from previously qualifying benefits. Again, the state refused to allow the federal government to put money into the pockets of poor Tar Heels—this time, those who had been unemployed for significant periods.[102]

Those still able to receive benefits soon learned that their payments had been cut by about a third. The maximum weekly benefit was reduced from $535 to $350. The length of time one could receive compensation was reduced from twenty-six weeks to twelve. After the changes, only 11 percent of the state's unemployed residents were receiving benefits—the lowest percentage in the country. The average duration for collecting benefits also fell to the bottom of the national barrel. The cuts resulted in North Carolina's unemployment compensation program moving from the middle of the pack to the stingiest in America.[103] Legislators seemed delighted.[104] When Urban League experts pointed out North Carolina's ignominious ranking to a legislative hearing, Rep. Dana Bumgardner, a Gaston County Republican, replied, "I think where we are is a good thing. What is the point of your presentation?"[105]

In 2014 the North Carolina Republican General Assembly continued its efforts to go where no state legislature has gone before by repealing the state's Earned Income Tax Credit (EITC). Despite constantly advertising themselves as existential, mission-defining tax cutters, Republican legislators elected to become the only state ever to eliminate a state EITC—thereby raising the tax bill owed by nearly a million working Tar Heels making about $30,000 to $40,000.[106] The lawmakers seemed to believe that raising the taxes of low-income workers somehow doesn't actually constitute a tax increase. (Maybe only the pocketbooks of high-income Tar Heels register as worthy of protection and enhancement.) Almost one in four North Carolina workers had qualified for the credit.[107] Ronald Reagan had been a potent supporter of EITC programs. They had typically been lauded by members of both parties as among the most inspiring and effective antipoverty measures. After all, they're available only to folks who work and gain income from wages, salaries, or self-employment. They can counter the impact of regressive state sales and property tax regimes for those at the bottom of the income scale—thus eliminating some of the need for welfare programs to support poor families.[108]

Research by the Center on Budget and Policy Priorities found that state EITC programs are "easy to administer, with nearly every dollar spent on the state credits going directly to the working families they were created to help. . . . They also [work] to reduce poverty, especially among children." The North Carolina General Assembly, it concluded, had earned the "dubious distinction" of being the only American government body to ever move in this fashion to make it harder for low-income working families to support their children.[109]

Next came a more overt, multiyear effort—despite North Carolina's extraordinarily steep poverty rates and daunting economic inequality—to shift the state's existing tax burden away from the wealthy and lodge it more robustly on the poor.[110] Republican lawmakers initially scrapped North Carolina's progressive income tax and replaced it with a flat tax, markedly lowering the rate for wealthier taxpayers.[111] Next they did away with the estate tax—a standard that already applied only to estates of $5 million or more.[112] A generous tax cut for corporations and additional shielding for out-of-state business profits earned in North Carolina followed. Then the General Assembly extended the sales tax to an array of new services, hitting low-income Tar Heels to help pay for gifts to the richest ones.

Then, in 2015, Republicans doubled down—again cutting the income tax rate for personal and corporate taxpayers and expanding regressive sales taxes to new categories of goods and services, including car and appliance repairs that fall more squarely on low- and middle-income taxpayers.[113] The General Assembly acted forcefully in the apparent belief that the main thing wrong with North Carolina is that those at the bottom have too much and those at the top don't have enough.

The North Carolina Budget and Tax Center released a study exploring who had benefitted and who had been burdened by the flurry of tax changes from 2013 to 2015. It found that the richest 1 percent of taxpayers enjoyed a cut of $14,977 per year. The next 4 percent got a decrease of almost $2,000. The fourth (highest) quintile received $465. The middle quintile saved $75. The bottom 40 percent received tax increases, not reductions—with the largest increases, on a percentage basis, saved for the poorest 20 percent. Three-quarters of the total tax benefit went to the top 20 percent of earners.[114] In 2015 Tar Heels making less than $20,000 annually paid 9.2 percent in state and local taxes. Those making more than $376,000 paid 5.3 percent. The adoption of a 5.2 percent flat income tax gave North Carolina millionaires, on average, a cut of $23,600. The middle quintile of taxpayers, on the other hand, got less than a hundred bucks. Our corporate income tax rate was 6.9 percent in 2013. As of 2020, it's 2.5 percent. More than 80 percent of the reduction went to wealthy out-of-state folks.[115] So the "tax-cutter" label that the North Carolina General Assembly so covets is actually inaccurate. Republican lawmakers gave massive cuts to the very wealthy, local and out-of-state, but they raised the taxes of the bottom 40 percent.[116]

And, sadly, they didn't stop there. Republican legislators also moved decisively to cut or burden an array of programs upon which low-income Tar Heels had traditionally relied. Childcare subsidies, which often make it possible for parents living at the edge of poverty to afford to work, were powerfully reduced. Reductions in funding, reimbursement rates, and restrictions on eligibility resulted in 30,000 fewer children receiving assistance in 2014 than in 2010 (dropping from 151,363 in 2010 to 121,113 in 2014).[117] As a result of cuts enacted by the General Assembly, North Carolina's nationally recognized pre-K program, despite dramatically rising demand, served 6,476 fewer low-income children in 2016 than it had in 2009.[118] The state's Oral Health Department received a cascade of cuts that dropped the number of dental hygienists who provide examinations at elementary schools throughout the state and help secure coverage for kids whose families can't afford dental care from eighty-four in 2006 to thirty-six in 2015. The staff cuts now leave thirty-five (of one hundred) counties without dental services.[119]

Continuing the trend, in late 2015, the General Assembly passed a bill that cut off food assistance (SNAP benefits) to 105,000 impoverished Tar Heels in the 77 most economically strapped counties of the state. North Carolina, you will recall, is the nation's fifth hungriest state. The SNAP benefits targeted provided, on average, $30 per week and were completely funded by the federal government. Declining the assistance saved no money for the state treasury. Funding intended for poor Tar Heels already having substantial difficulty making ends meet was simply returned to Washington.[120] Perhaps the food stamp decision should have been seen as unsurprising. It followed on the McCrory administration's odd determination, when the federal government temporarily shut down during budget deadlocks in 2013, to become the only state to preventatively suspend its Temporary Aid to Needy Families (TANF) program. The state Department of Health and Human Services instructed local offices that "no new approved applications for Work First should be processed because of the [possible] unavailability of federal funds."[121] The federal government assured state officials that any state dollars expended would be fully reimbursed. U.S. congressmen David Price and G. K. Butterfield explained, in a letter to the governor, that the national assurances had been deemed sufficient "by forty-nine other states." DHHS spokesperson Julie Henry explained the commitment wasn't good enough for North Carolina.

In October 2015, in order to help fund a new set of tax cuts almost exclusively benefitting wealthy residents, the General Assembly eliminated the state's appropriation for legal services. About a third of the already heavily overburdened staff of Legal Aid of North Carolina had to be terminated, though they were able to meet only about 20 percent of the legal need of poor Tar Heels even before the massive cuts were initiated.[122] Also, in a special session in 2016, the General Assembly slipped into another awful bill a provision making it clear that it was illegal for any municipality to increase the minimum wage.[123] In case any city or county government in the state ever attempted such an astonishing undertaking, the legislature wanted to be sure to stomp it out early.

It is true, thankfully, that state unemployment rates have improved since the close of the recession—following, as they typically do, national economic trends. Even poverty rates have declined slightly since 2015, as they have in the rest of the country. Still, more than one in seven Tar Heels lives in poverty today, markedly worse than the national average and among the poorest state showings. And even as brighter economic times have arrived in North Carolina and the rest of the country, poor Tar Heels have been disproportionately wounded by policies reducing their access to health care, child care, unemployment compensation, housing, food stamps, and legal services—as they have lost earned income tax credits and faced notably higher and more regressive sales taxes. The plight of the bottom third in a state is hardly enhanced by increasing their tax burdens and slashing their already too modest benefits. Unsurprisingly, waging war on poor people increases, rather than diminishes, their affliction.[124]

Declaring the Animus

The bold, groundbreaking list of Republican enactments that purposefully make life more difficult for poor Tar Heels in the last eight years has many other entries as well.[125] It is as long as it is shameful. And it continues to grow even now.

These enactments also reflect sentiments that, on occasion, have become overt in claims made by legislative leaders. This chapter opened with an extensive quote from former Speaker of the House (now U.S. senator from North Carolina) Thom Tillis. The Speaker was recorded addressing a group of Republican activists in Mars Hill, outlining a central purpose of his economic "reform" agenda reflected in the changes above. Tillis explained that it is crucial "to divide and conquer" low-income North Carolinians seeking government support: While "showing respect for that woman who has cerebral palsy and had no choice in her condition . . . we need to get [her] to look down at those people who get into a condition that makes them dependent on the government." Ideally, he explained, we want the cerebral palsy sufferer to say to her unworthy fellow citizen: "You're on your own. We may end up taking care of those babies, but we're not taking care of you." Tillis's dreamed-for dichotomy is filled with both venom and presumption that he was apparently eager to export. The unworthy recipient is to be despised. She's dependent. She caused her own plight. She wallows in it. We're not taking care of you, he condescendingly declaims, and your "babies"—your (plural) "babies" are the product of your dissolute life. Senator Tillis may not know you, surely has never met you, but he knows what makes you tick. And as the laws he helped enact show, he's out to punish your behavior, to treat it with the derision it deserves. He probably can even tell what the unworthy applicant looks like. All is clear in his mind's eye. More than clear. And, for once, he let it slip out.[126]

Three years later, Speaker Tillis reported significant pride in the economic policy shifts he had helped state government to initiate. He told *Governing Magazine*, "It puts us on a stage and lets them know that North Carolina has made more progress than any other state in the last three years on economic policy."[127] Tillis's potent declaration that there are worthy and, explicitly, quite unworthy poor people in North Carolina echoes the crasser claim made on the floor of the United States Senate, by his (now) colleague Richard Burr in opposing a requested extension of health care benefits for impoverished children. Burr declared that parents seeking such support were mere "hogs at the trough."[128] Both Burr and Tillis remind one of Republican congressman Robert Pittenger's explanation that Charlotte protestors flooding the streets after the Keith Lamont Scott killing were enraged because they "hate white people who are successful." Pittenger had added, sagely, that the government had spent too much money on welfare programs (for the demonstrators) "that ultimately hold people back."[129]

Rep. Michael Speciale, a Republican member of the General Assembly from New Bern, explained his support for heightened work requirements for food assistance recipients by saying, "Short of telling them, 'You can sleep all week,' how much more reasonable can it get?"[130] Senator Norman Samuelson of Pamlico County explained that in 2015 it was necessary to deny food stamps, completely paid for by the federal government, in the seventy-seven most economically strapped North Carolina counties, despite our soaring hunger rates—even though the money would simply be returned to Washington—because jobless recipients needed a shove to go to work: "I think you're going to see a lot of them go out and get that twenty-hour-a-week job now," instead of sitting back, taking it easy.[131] Rep. George Cleveland, from Onslow County, more famously asserted in a House Committee hearing in 2012 that "there is no extreme poverty in North Carolina." The federal government merely pads "agency figures to justify a poverty level that they want . . . they keep redefining it to get the poverty class they want."[132] There's no "real" deprivation here, he claimed. Representative Cleveland somehow missed the fact that more than 10 percent of the children in his own house district live in extreme poverty and that nearly four hundred children in the Onslow County School District were reported to the federal government as homeless.[133]

Perhaps even more telling, in 2015, the Republican General Assembly enacted a drug-screening requirement for North Carolina's Work First recipients.[134] The legislative sponsor of the new program indicated it was rooted in the belief, held by the bulk of his lawmaking colleagues, "that a large segment of the population that receives welfare benefits either abuses the system or does not use the benefits for the purpose intended."[135] The Work First program offers short-term cash benefits, training, and support services to families in extreme exigency. In 62 percent of Work First cases, only children get benefits. The drug tests are costly, administratively burdensome, and humiliating to poor applicants. The legislature asked for a progress report on the new initiative in early 2016. Of the thousands tested, twenty-one came back positive—less than 0.3 percent of applicants screened. Of the twenty-one test failures, twelve were still approved for partial payments because children were the beneficiaries. The National Institute on Drug Abuse reports that illicit drug use among Americans twelve or older, generally, is 9.4 percent.[136] To his credit, Rep. Craig Horn, a driving force behind the testing requirement in the state house, admitted the results made him question whether he had made unfair assumptions about the behavior of poor people. "I was frankly surprised," he said. "I had expected different numbers. Hopefully it's a good indicator." Nonetheless, Horn and his legislative colleagues opted to keep the wasteful, counterproductive, shaming hurdle in place.[137] At least it could be counted on to humiliate.

Rendering to the Rich, Stepping on the Necks of the Poor

I'd be among the first to concede that the Republicans of the North Carolina General Assembly are ambitious folks. As I'll argue throughout this book, there is a lot they want to do. They want to make it harder for black people to participate in elections. They want to stop women from controlling their own bodies. They want to shame and stigmatize LGBTQ+ people. They want to disparage and marginalize Hispanic immigrants. They want to dismantle the public schools. They want to radically constrain environmental regulation. They want to foster purchased elections. They want to diminish the power of judges and lay low their political adversaries. The list is long. And brutal.

But their true sweet spot, their principal raison d'être, the crusade to which they return enthusiastically in each succeeding session, is taking money and benefits from the impoverished and nearly impoverished in order to give more money, assets, and resources to, and to demand less from, the wealthy. Apparently, this is the core, defining premise of North Carolina Republicanism. It applies with full vigor, even though today the rich claim a larger share of our income and wealth than at any time in our history. It applies, enthusiastically, even when our economic inequality—the sprawling gulf between rich and poor—is greater than at any other moment in our long story. It is an unquenchable thirst. The shiny beacon that summons, no matter the circumstance or consequence. It prevails, come what may.

The repeated pattern—harsh cuts and new burdens for the vulnerable, generous largesse for the possessors of wealth—produces endless cadres of advocates and justifications. It is perhaps odd that so many would embrace its defense as their life's work. Both history and economics reject it. After all, if being the toughest on poor people reduced poverty, the United States would have the lowest poverty levels among the advanced nations, not the highest. Still, as John Kenneth Galbraith put it decades ago, "The modern conservative is engaged in one of man's oldest exercises in moral philosophy, the search for a superior moral justification for selfishness."[138]

North Carolina is presently engaged in the theory's boldest implementing outburst. We're home to many firsts. The first state to end its Earned Income Tax Credit; the first to so thoroughly disembowel its unemployment compensation program. First to join such steps with wholesale tax shifts—estate taxes, income taxes, sales taxes—radically increasing the obligations of the poor to ease the "plight" of the rich. Certainly we are among the very few to enthusiastically return federal dollars to Washington rather than allow them to reach the pockets of poor Tar Heels, even though it saves not a penny for state coffers. We've also shown real creativity in aiming new taxes—like sales taxes on car and appliance repairs—precisely and purposefully at low-income taxpayers. (I'm still waiting for a special excise tax on ramen noodles. Where is Anatole France when we need him?)

This nation-leading crusade against low-income people says much about our predisposition. But it also says a great deal about our politics. James Madison would have thought it difficult to thoroughly remove the economic interests of so great a percentage of the populace from one's legislative agenda. After all, the poor and near poor in North Carolina readily constitute at least 40 percent of the citizenry. That's a lot of folks to be left outside the fence. But ideology, tribe, race, religion, polarization, and cash register politics can combine to be extraordinarily potent forces—as ever, perhaps, in the South. Especially in the South.

This crusade against poor people says something about our commitment to constitutionalism, to a defining national project, as well. A society committed, foundationally, to "justice for all," to bold and declared norms of Fourteenth Amendment equality, to all legitimate state government authority being "instituted solely for the good of the whole," faces something of a hurdle in treating those at the bottom as effectively invisible. If America itself is based on an idea, the North Carolina General Assembly seems markedly unwilling to buy in.

And, perhaps most pointedly, wealthy and powerful Tar Heels using the levers of government to wrench too scarce resources from the most marginalized and vulnerable presents stunning moral challenges as well. Purposefully burdening the poor to further feather the expansive nests of the rich is not a mistake. It is not a policy error or a miscalculation. It is an opportunity and dignity-crushing penalty, not a boon. And for many—especially when it means health care is rejected—it is a potential death warrant as well.

Donald Trump is not the United States' leading outrage—bad as he is. That indignity is reserved for how North Carolina treats poor people, especially poor children. It is villainous to be the advanced world's "clear and constant outlier" (as Philip Alston of the United Nations has put it) with "shocking" levels of child poverty amid the world's greatest plenty—a condition that we embrace. No real democracy would accept this. No decent religion would tolerate it. If being the cruelest gives us no pause, what will? Leading the nation's charge in disparaging our poorest members demeans and indicts North Carolina. It is the kind of agenda that becomes difficult to explain to one's children. As John Prine once put it: "Take the star out of the window; let [our] conscience take a rest."[139]

CHAPTER FOUR

Denying the Equal Dignity of Women

The decision whether or not to bear a child is central to a woman's life, to her wellbeing and dignity. It is a decision she must make for herself. When government controls that decision for her, she is being treated as less than a fully adult human responsible for her own choices. . . . [She is] being denied both her full autonomy and full equality with men.
—Ruth Bader Ginsburg, *Planned Parenthood v. Casey* decision, 1992[140]

The U.S. Supreme Court famously decided in 1973's *Roe v. Wade* that the federal Constitution protects the personal right of a woman to terminate a pregnancy. The justices concluded that the due process clause of the Fourteenth Amendment extends a right to privacy broad enough to allow a woman to choose whether or not to have an abortion, free of overarching intrusion by the state.[141] The high court explained the genesis of the constitutional liberty more robustly in *Planned Parenthood of Pennsylvania v. Casey* almost two decades later. There, Republican justice Sandra Day O'Connor wrote:

> Our law affords constitutional protection to personal decisions relating to marriage, procreation, contraception, family relationships, child rearing, and education. Our cases recognize "the right of the *individual*, married or single, to be free from unwarranted governmental intrusion into matters so fundamentally affecting a person as the decision whether to bear or beget a child." Our precedents "have respected the private realm of family life which the state cannot enter." These matters, involving the most intimate and personal choices a

person may make in a lifetime, choices central to personal dignity and autonomy, are central to the liberty protected by the Fourteenth Amendment. At the heart of [that] liberty is the right to define one's own concept of existence, of meaning, of the universe, and of the mystery of human life. Beliefs about these matters could not define the attributes of personhood were they formed under compulsion of the State.[142]

It took the North Carolina Republican General Assembly no time, even before assuming full control of all three branches of state government, to launch a full-fledged attack on women's reproductive freedoms.[143] In 2011 Republican legislators passed the ironically entitled "Woman's Right to Know Act." It was immediately vetoed by then governor Beverly Purdue (Democrat). The General Assembly, in turn, overrode the veto—enacting one of the most totalitarian-leaning statutory regimes in North Carolina history. The "virtually unprecedented" intrusion on individual liberty was ultimately invalidated by the seemingly shocked federal courts--including that of well-known and markedly conservative Republican chief judge of the Fourth Circuit Court of Appeals, J. Harvie Wilkinson.[144] Its history, though, demonstrates not only the continuing crucial necessity of independent judicial review, but reminds us anew that those sufficiently arrogant to believe they speak for God can be capable of recklessly casting aside the central cornerstones of American constitutional government.

The Real-Time Sonogram Requirement and Forced, Partisan, Scripted Injurious Speech

The Woman's Right to Know Act requires a doctor to perform an ultrasound at least four but not more than seventy-two hours before any woman receives an abortion.[145] The physician must display the sonogram in a way that the woman can see it in real time. The doctor must then describe the fetus in detail, "including the presence, location, and dimensions of the unborn child within the uterus and the number of unborn children depicted." Then "the presence of external members and internal organs" must be noted. Next, the doctor must offer to allow the woman to listen to the fetal heart tone.[146] The woman may be allowed to "avert her eyes from the displayed images." She may also "refuse to hear the simultaneous explanation and medical description" by covering her eyes and ears.[147] (Never let it be said that the North Carolina General Assembly isn't sensitive—they won't force the doctor to hold her patient's eyes open.) The physician must convey the descriptions mandated by the statute in her own voice. The whole compelled conversation occurs, of course, while the woman is partially disrobed on an examination table in an extraordinarily vulnerable circumstance—this is not a doctor talking to a patient from behind the desk in an office with each fully clothed. It doesn't matter that the woman doesn't want it to happen. It doesn't matter that the doctor doesn't want it to happen. It doesn't matter that the doctor thinks it might be harmful to the patient. The law allows no therapeutic exception.[148] All recedes before the state's demand. A woman's body, her pocketbook, her senses, and her doctor are commandeered by the government to scare her out of exercising her constitutionally protected rights.

A doctor who fails to comply with the coerced regimen is subject to a financial damages claim, an injunction from performing future abortions, and the loss of his or her medical license. The "real-time" display is on top of a separate informed consent provision elsewhere in the act, demanding that, at least twenty-four hours before the procedure, the doctor explain the risks of the operation and "any adverse psychological effects associated with abortion."[149] The probable "gestational age of the unborn child" must be conveyed. And the physician must explain that financial assistance for the pregnancy may be available, that the father is obligated to pay child support, that there are ready alternatives to abortion, and that there is a state-sponsored website describing the features of a fetus.[150] There is also, separate still, a distinct abortion informed consent announcing the existence of "counseling for the patient to ensure she [is] certain about her decision to have an abortion."[151] No step to intimidate is left unpursued. The only "right" reflected in the "Right to Know Act" is the right to have the state coerce you not to exercise your established rights.

In late 2014 the U.S. Court of Appeals for the Fourth Circuit held the "Woman's Right to Know Act" to be a "virtually unprecedented" denial of the constitutional liberties of both a woman seeking an abortion and those of her doctor. It demands "starkly compelled speech that impedes First Amendment rights":

> Having to choose between blindfolding and earmuffing herself or watching and listening to unwanted information may in some remote way influence a woman in favor of carrying the child to term, [but] forced speech to unwilling or incapacitated listeners does not bear a constitutionally necessary connection to the protection of fetal life. Moreover, far from promoting the psychological health of women, this requirement risks the infliction of psychological harm on the woman who chooses not to receive the information. She must endure the embarrassing spectacle of averting her eyes and covering her ears while her physician—a person to whom she should be encouraged to listen—recites information to her. We can perceive no benefit to state interests from walling off patients and physicians in a manner antithetical to the very communication that lies at the heart of the informed consent process.[152]

The Fourth Circuit Court was also alarmed by the biased nature of the compelled message. The statute was overtly "ideological" and "promotes the viewpoint the state wishes to encourage," the court found. It "compels the physician to deliver the state's preferred message . . . on a volatile subject . . . in his or her own voice." By requiring health care providers "to deliver this information to a woman who takes steps not to hear it or would be harmed by hearing it, the state has moved from encouraging to lecturing," using doctors as its mouthpiece—regardless of the "psychological or emotional well-being of the patient." The U.S. Constitution, the judges concluded, does not permit government "to coerce doctors into voicing [this] message on behalf of the state in the manner and setting attempted here."[153] You could almost imagine the judges explaining, "This is North Carolina, not North Korea."

Back at It

Unfortunately, the breathtaking 2011 forced, narrated sonogram requirement has hardly been the only Republican General Assembly effort to demean the constitutional dignity of North Carolina women.[154] The sonogram law itself had allowed persons other than the woman seeking an abortion to bring lawsuits against health care providers who, in their opinion, failed to comply with the "Woman's Right to Know Act."[155] Oddly, if a patient wanted her name to be shielded in such an action, she had no right to demand it. The court, not the woman undergoing the procedure, made the decision. This provided an additional pathway to intimidate women who seek to undergo an abortion. A subsequent law, passed in 2015, requires that doctors send ultrasounds to a state agency whenever a woman obtains an abortion after sixteen weeks of pregnancy.[156] The agency, the Department of Health and Human Services, claimed that the intimate information would not be made public and that patient and doctor privacy would be protected. But it would be no small surprise if North Carolina women worried that a government that would force them to avert their eyes and cover their ears is not to be trusted with their personal information.

Melissa Reed of Planned Parenthood South Atlantic accused the General Assembly of again trying to intimidate women by requiring that "the most intimate piece of a woman's medical record" be shared with the state.[157] Another activist called it an additional "creepy scheme—something out of George Orwell's *1984*."[158] Who would have thought that sonograms would become such viable tools in crushing the dignity of women?

With almost no notice to anyone, on the eve of the July 4th holiday in 2013, Republican legislative leaders introduced a gutted motorcycle safety bill[159] and replaced it with an array of measures that critics claimed were aimed at forcing the closure of many, or most, abortion clinics in North Carolina.[160] The derisively tagged "motorcycle vagina bill" ushered in regulations meant to hold abortion clinics to standards closer to or the same as ambulatory surgical centers. The brief and unanticipated legislative debate showed another surprising turn—Republican legislators who had spent entire careers in dogged opposition to women seeking abortions were now touchingly concerned with their well-being.

Sen. Phil Berger explained, with only modest embarrassment, "Everyone in here is interested in protecting patient safety and women's health care—that's our primary concern." Sen. Trudy Wade (R-Guilford) assured "this whole bill is about making (abortion) safer for women." Sen. Warren Daniel (R-Burke) confirmed the provision was "about safety," first to last: "If we require burdensome regulations on orthopedic offices, and they can compete in the marketplace, abortion providers can too." The recording was replayed in the House. Rep. Jacqueline Schaffer (R-Mecklenburg) explained, "The state has an important interest in promoting the health and safety of women who receive an abortion." Rep. Ruth Samuelson, a noted antiabortion advocate, upped the ante: "We're not going to wait until women die in abortion clinics before we raise standards." Rep. Sarah Stevens (R-Mt. Airy) dismissed the widely shared skepticism. "Don't tell me it's not about health and safety—that's exactly what it's about. . . . I'm sorry if you don't believe it, but that's the truth."[161]

Opponents understandably doubted the General Assembly's newly unearthed concern over the health prospects of abortion seekers. The federal courts had already held, one might recall, that Republican abortion interventions had worked to actually jeopardize the health prospects of women seeking to exercise their reproductive freedoms. And the unaltered pattern reflected in all Republican abortion legislation was the closed, or closing, door. The fact that the statute appeared through such a truncated, deceptive, and insufficiently noticed process likely amplified skepticism. Republican governor Pat McCrory broke repeated campaign promises that he would sign no new abortion laws when he put his pen to the controversial measure.[162]

The General Assembly also moved to ban state teacher and employee insurance plans, and some city and county employee plans, from providing abortion coverage (though allowing exceptions for rape, incest, and the life of the policyholder). The rules, of course, disproportionately constrain low-income women. The state also prohibited Affordable Care Act health insurance plans offered in the state from including (with limited exceptions) abortion coverage. Republicans then banned sex-selective abortions without any evidence indicating that North Carolinians had been engaging in the practice. The law, though, adds yet another medically unnecessary hurdle to obtaining an abortion.[163]

In 2015 the Republican legislature adopted another deceptively named statute—the "Women and Children Protection Act."[164] It tripled the required waiting period for women seeking abortions—moving from twenty-four to seventy-two hours, the longest in the nation. Sponsors argued that the extension was essential to protect women from making hasty decisions they will come to regret. Yet other life-changing procedures require no such waiting period. Opponents, unsurprisingly, were angered by yet another dose of patronizing and insulting regulation: "This is not about supporting women," said Rep. Tricia Cotham (D-Mecklenburg). "This is about creating barriers that unfairly harm especially women of very limited financial means." Abortion is a "deeply personal decision," Cotham argued. "My womb and my uterus are not up for your political grab."[165] Governor McCrory again broke his pledge and signed the bill.[166]

The next year the General Assembly struck again. For decades, North Carolina had prohibited abortions after the twentieth week of pregnancy, allowing an exception to the ban when there was a substantial risk that the continuance of the pregnancy would threaten the life or gravely impair the health of the woman.[167] In 2016 the Republican legislature decided the exemption was not sufficiently restrictive. A post-twenty-week procedure would now be allowed only if an "immediate abortion is necessary to avert [a woman's] death" or there is a "serious risk of substantial and irreversible physical impairment of a major bodily function, not including any psychological or emotional condition." Another provision clarifies that this is not to include a likely suicide by the patient.[168]

I readily concede that many constitutional abortion issues can be wrenchingly difficult. Still, the arrogance of state lawmakers pronouncing such edicts is astounding. The North Carolina General Assembly deems itself empowered to decide that a woman who will likely be irreversibly impaired by her inability to terminate a pregnancy shall be barred from receiving such medical services because the impairment may not meet the statutory threshold of wounding a truly major body function. Or, even if a major body function is to be traumatized, the legislature will intervene unless the handicap can be deemed demonstrably irreversible. If it's likely a woman could perhaps recover, we will decide for her, the theory goes. She may bounce back after all. So we'll intercede. Even if a woman's doctor thinks she will suffer dramatic and life-threatening emotional harm if a pregnancy proceeds, the Republican caucus will make the choice—not the woman in consultation with the medical professionals. If a patient has potent and threatening psychological problems, she should have thought about that before she had sex. Thus sayeth the sages of the North Carolina state house.

The 2016 change, like much of the abortion regulation of the North Carolina Republican General Assembly, was held flatly unconstitutional by the federal courts a couple of years later.[169] Justice

O'Conner had long written that even late-term abortion laws must include exceptions to protect the health of the woman. And the new, groundbreaking North Carolina law no doubt transgressed that requirement. As Justice O'Connor had explained, "A woman's suffering is too intimate and personal for the state to insist upon its own vision of the woman's role, however dominant that vision has been in the course of our history."[170] Still, I am beyond perplexed at the hubris and the vanity of those who would insist on the ability (and the certainty) to make such wrenching determinations for others. And, I will irrelevantly concede, that the idea of the North Carolina legislature believing itself empowered to remove such choices from my wife or my family enrages me.

Crisis Pregnancy Centers

Any group of legislators that would force a doctor to repeat a Stalinist script in the ear of an unwilling, distressed patient and, in pursuit of a preferred ideological agenda, take it upon itself to foreclose medical treatment essential to the vital health of an endangered woman, does not respect the full and equal dignity of women as autonomous, independent, adult decision-makers. *Not to worry, we will decide for you* is the obvious claim. *We know, actually, what is best for you. Your autonomy must be forfeited before our obvious superiority.* Justice Ruth Bader Ginsburg has argued that "the decision whether or not to bear a child is central to a woman's life, her wellbeing and dignity. . . . [I]t is a decision she must make for herself; otherwise she is being denied both her full autonomy and full equality."[171] The Republican caucus of the North Carolina General Assembly—what (again) Republican Rep. Holly Grange of Wilmington calls "a middle-age white man's club"[172]—aggressively disagrees. So they have not been content with these regulatory measures, as coercive and indefensible as they are.

Our Republican lawmakers apparently believe strongly that North Carolina women should be heavily "counselled" not to have an abortion. To that end, each year the General Assembly sends millions of public dollars to Crisis Pregnancy Centers across the state.[173] Such centers do not provide traditional health care counselling.[174] They are often staffed by unlicensed volunteers and are not subject to regulation. Often, no medical professionals are present. Their mission is to convince women not to undergo an abortion. Studies indicate they frequently offer inaccurate information about the perils and impact of abortion.[175] The mission, they typically indicate, is to dissuade.

A national report published by Dr. Amy Bryant and Dr. Jonas Swartz of the UNC School of Medicine, appearing in the *AMA Journal of Ethics*, described the centers as follows:

> Crisis pregnancy centers are organizations that seek to intercept women with unintended pregnancies who might be considering abortion. Their mission is to prevent abortions by persuading women that adoption or parenting is a better option. They strive to give the impression that they are clinical centers, offering legitimate medical services and advice, yet they are exempt from regulatory, licensure, and credentialing oversight that apply to health care facilities. Because the religious ideology of the center owners and employees takes priority over the health and well-being of the women seeking care at the centers, women do not receive comprehensive, accurate, evidence-based clinical information about all available options. Although crisis pregnancy centers enjoy First Amendment rights protections, their propagation of misinformation should be regarded as an ethical violation that undermines women's health.[176]

The *Asheville Citizen-Times* has reported extensively on a local legislatively funded crisis pregnancy center, Mountain Area Pregnancy Services.[177] Pregnant women at the center get information only about adoption and parenting; the availability of abortion (or apparently contraception) is never broached.

> When women facing one of the most critical decisions of their lives walk through the door, portraits of Jesus cradling a newborn baby welcome them inside. Crosses dangle from the necklaces of staff, who often speak of the importance of religion in their lives. Most everything about Mountain Area Pregnancy Services reminds visitors that it is a Christian organization. "We respect life and we want to protect life," says Debbie Hrncir, a MAPS board member. "We want to show women who come here why life matters and why that organism inside them is living and is a human being."[178]

Counselling is offered "from a biblical perspective." This is "our ministry," Hrncir explains.

Dr. Amy Bryant responds:

> Until taxpayers can be assured that these centers conform to ethical standards of licensed medical facilities, offer sound medical advice and do not lead to harm, states should refrain from directly or indirectly funding these centers. The information they give women on their websites is grossly inaccurate and unfair. It's meant to scare women and pressure them into doing something that is ideologically driven, which is not to have an abortion.[179]

Republican senator Ralph Hise, who directed a $250,000 appropriation to Mountain Area Pregnancy Services last year, explained it is an "incredible" investment; "North Carolina has a long history of working with nonprofits."[180] Sen. Terry Van Duyn (D-Buncombe) countered that state funding for the religious center's operation "is simply a violation of the First Amendment." In the 2019 legislative session, Sen. Natasha Marcus, a Mecklenburg County Democrat, sought to remove state budget funding for crisis pregnancy centers. She argued "the state should not use taxpayer money to push a conservative religious set of beliefs," supporting "fake clinics" that are a threat to reproductive freedom.[181] The Republican Senate majority quickly dispatched the challenge.

An Equality-Defying Agenda

I have little doubt that the Republican caucus of the North Carolina General Assembly would like to outlaw, or largely outlaw, abortion in this state. At present, given *Roe v. Wade*, that is not possible. So, instead, Republicans leaders have sought to limit the availability of abortion in every way they could conceive. They limit the time frame for legal abortions, they restrict the acceptable motives for abortion, and they make abortion as expensive as possible—assuming that if they can't make abortion impossible for all women, they can at least make sure that poor and low-income women will be denied the right to choose to terminate a pregnancy. They effectively restrict abortion's geographic availability, they require complex record and reporting procedures, they demand long and singular waiting periods and informed consent determinations. They claim a right to try to aggressively "persuade" women not to abort. They lie and deceive in pursuit of an antichoice crusade, explaining a sudden, newfound commitment to the health and well-being of women seeking abortions. They force women into excruciating dilemmas, weighing their own physical health, even life-diminishing physical health, against legislators' preferred political or religious ideology. They trump individual and family determinations on intensely intimate decisions with government-compelled ideologies. They treat women and health care providers as if they were dissembling criminals. They demand disclosures and documentations meant to frighten those considering abortion.

Decisions they can't directly regulate, they seek to dominate through fear, shame, and intimidation. They force women's bodies—and pocketbooks and doctors—into the campaign, requiring unnecessary and sometimes harmful medical procedures in order to coerce Tar Heels from exercising their constitutionally assured rights. They make health care professionals behave like Soviet-era apparatchiks. They effectively urge rights-holders to undergo "counselling" that is essentially state-imposed propaganda. And then they hire religious organizations to spread the state-supported word—violating both the Fourteenth and First Amendments in a joyous two-for-one operation.

This is not the work of freedom.

This is not the work of equality.

CHAPTER FIVE

State-Proclaimed Disdain for LGBTQ+ Tar Heels

Not only is this new law a national embarrassment, it will set North Carolina's economy back. We're talking about discrimination here.
—North Carolina Attorney General Roy Cooper, announcing he would not defend H.B. 2, March 2016[182]

McCrory joins a dark list of Southern governors. This week, as then, North Carolina needed a leader who understood the damage this law might do—most importantly to its vulnerable citizens, but also to the face we present to businesses and workers considering our state. Instead, we got a late-night bill signing Wednesday and some campaign tweets. We got a state newly stained, and a governor joining a sorrowful list of those who decided not to lead us forward, but to bow to the worst in us.
—*Charlotte Observer*, March 24, 2016[183]

If the North Carolina General Assembly's crusades against African-American and impoverished Tar Heels have been their most sustained and agenda-defining legacies, and if the campaign against women's equal dignity the most covert, by far their most famous push—both nationally and internationally—has been a creative and multifaceted effort to use the power of the state to express derision for LGBTQ+ citizens. Republican legislators have sought readily, enthusiastically, and repeatedly to push frontiers in the denial of equal human dignity to the LGBTQ+ community—leading the *New York Times* editorial page to denounce the state's leadership, in 2016, as "pioneers in bigotry."[184] Through animus-driven constitutional amendments, expensive and sham litigation strategies, licenses to discriminate in government services, and universally denounced bathroom regulations meant to humiliate and even endanger the vulnerable, we have declared many thousands of our fellow North Carolinians officially diminished. We have proven steadfast and unapologetic in our siege. We've chosen to brag about it. As most of the nation celebrated notable expansions of gay and transgender liberties, we sought, consistently, to turn back the clock, seeking, apparently, to build a longed-for bridge to the 1950s. Republican officials expressed an unyielding and sanctimonious outrage as much of the world boycotted our despised efforts. The General Assembly's bold strategies have produced a dark, demeaning chapter in North Carolina history, and it's not over.

Amendment One

Almost a decade before state legislators launched their marginalizing LGBTQ+ campaign with the introduction of Amendment One in 2011, the U.S. Supreme Court had outlined a dramatically different vision of constitutional liberty in *Lawrence v. Texas*—a ruling invalidating state sodomy laws:

> Liberty protects the person from unwarranted government intrusions into a dwelling or other private spaces. In our tradition, the State is not omnipresent in the home. And there are other spheres of our lives and existence, outside the home, where the State should not be a dominant presence. Freedom extends beyond spatial bounds. Liberty presumes an autonomy of self that includes freedom of thought, belief, expression, and intimate conduct. This, as a general rule, counsels against attempts by the state to define the meaning of [an intimate] relationship or set its boundaries absent injury to a person. . . . When sexuality finds overt expression in intimate conduct with another person, the conduct can be but one element in a personal bond that is more enduring. The liberty

> protected by the Constitution allows homosexual persons the right to make this choice. Persons in a homosexual relationship may seek autonomy for these purposes, just as heterosexual persons do.[185]

Rejecting the high court's warning, and despite North Carolina already having a statute on the books banning same-sex marriage,[186] in September 2011 the Republican-controlled General Assembly passed Senate Bill 514, placing a proposed "Defense of Marriage" constitutional amendment on the 2012 primary ballot.[187] Amendment One's terse language caused some confusion. It appeared to not only ban same-sex marriage but also deny legal recognition of any relationship other than heterosexual marriage. Thus fears arose that the proposed amendment would erase legal protections for all unmarried couples in domestic partnerships and civil unions.[188] Polling responses varied notably, depending on whether respondents were reading the text of the amendment or reading a ballot summary of what the amendment purportedly would do.[189]

Proponents sought to focus on traditional marriage while opponents concentrated not only on gay rights but, often, on the impact of the amendment on unmarried couples broadly as well. Church congregations, perhaps as anticipated, participated heavily in the election. Political observers reported significant opposition to gay marriage in African-American religious communities—splitting some traditional Democratic constituencies (though Rev. William Barber, the state's leading civil rights activist and leader of the powerful Moral Monday movement, mounted massive and racially united opposition to the amendment).[190]

Still, ballot confusion or not, Amendment One passed with 61 percent voter approval.[191] A constitutional ban on same-sex marriage doubled down on the state's long-recorded statutory prohibition. Legal recognition of same-sex domestic partnerships in the North Carolina municipalities (such as Durham and Carrboro) that offered them was seemingly invalidated. Despite a broad and rising swell of national support for the recognition of gay marriage, North Carolina became the country's last state to outlaw it by constitutional amendment.[192] Cynically, Republican Speaker of the House Thom Tillis explained to a skeptical group of North Carolina State University students a few weeks before the election that his GOP-backed amendment would likely be repealed within twenty years because young people were more supportive of gay rights than folks his age were.[193] "Not to worry—my efforts will be gone in a generation," Tillis seemed to say. Some theory of constitutional enactment.

However, a twenty-year reign wasn't in the cards. In 2014 the U.S. Court of Appeals for the Fourth Circuit struck down Virginia's same-sex marriage ban—which mirrored much of Amendment One. The court relied heavily on the Supreme Court's earlier declarations in *Lawrence v. Texas*.[194] But, particularly noteworthy for Amendment One, the judges also quoted extensively from a mainstay of the canon of American constitutional law—Justice Robert Jackson's classic World War II opinion in *West Virginia State Bd. of Education v. Barnette*:

> The very purpose of a Bill of Rights was to withdraw certain subjects from the vicissitudes of political controversy, to place them beyond the reach of majorities and officials and to establish them as legal principles to be applied by the courts. One's right to life, liberty, and property, to free speech, a free press, freedom of worship and assembly, and other fundamental rights may not be submitted to vote; they depend on the outcome of no elections.[195]

Shortly after the Fourth Circuit's ruling, the U.S. Supreme Court refused to take up a challenge to the invalidation of the Virginia same-sex ban, thus effectively finalizing the appeals court ruling. Two North Carolina federal district courts, also being in the Fourth Circuit, quickly ruled that the Tar Heel bans on same-sex marriage were unconstitutional, concluding there was "no substantial distinction" between the North Carolina amendment and the one invalidated in Virginia. Attorney General Roy Cooper ceased to defend North Carolina's laws further, saying, "It is the job of the Attorney General to argue for state laws, but also to recognize when there are no arguments left."[196]

Republican leaders Thom Tillis and Phil Berger railed against Cooper. They then announced that they would seek to intervene in the (now effectively completed) federal action on behalf of the state legislature, denouncing "liberal activist judges." The U.S. Supreme Court, as Tillis and Berger knew, had already ruled in the case. Pursuing intervention and appeal at this expired date would cost North Carolina taxpayers hundreds of thousands of dollars—to no possible constructive purpose. No matter. Tillis and Berger could still vividly demonstrate their principal aim—expressing to the people of North Carolina, yet again, their leaders' expensive disdain for LGBTQ+ people. There was no chance to prevail in court. But as the *New York Times* noted, "Mr. Tillis has his eye on a very different victory."[197] So much for fiscal conservatism.

Same-sex marriages, then, have been legal in North Carolina since October 2014—though Amendment One remains unrepealed, but unenforceable, in the state's constitution.[198] In 2015 the U.S. Supreme Court handed down its landmark ruling in *Obergefell v. Hodges*, protecting the constitutional right to same-sex marriage across the nation. Justice Anthony Kennedy, for the Court, wrote famously:

> No union is more profound than marriage, for it embodies the highest ideals of love, fidelity, devotion, sacrifice, and family. In forming a marital union, two people become something greater than once they were. Marriage embodies a love that may endure even past death. It misunderstands these [litigants] to say they disrespect the idea of marriage. Their plea is that they do respect it, respect it so deeply that they seek to find its fulfillment for themselves. Their hope is not to be condemned to live in loneliness, excluded from one of civili-

> zation's oldest institutions. They ask for equal dignity in the eyes of the law. The Constitution grants them that right.[199]

An array of North Carolina Republican legislators, however, continue to carry the torch for marriage exclusion. In 2017 state GOP representatives Larry Pittman, Michael Speciale, Carl Ford, and Mike Clampitt introduced H.B. 780, a bill that would have purported to (somehow) invalidate *Obergefell* in North Carolina.[200] A similar proposal, H.B. 65, was filed in February 2019. It, too, would ban *Obergefell*'s applicability within our borders—deeming it "unenforceable" in the face of North Carolina's "Marriage Amendment." H.B. 65 referred to same-sex marriages as "parody marriages" and insisted that "the United States Supreme Court respect the rights of each state and its people." The act was sponsored by Republican house members Pittman, Speciale, Kidwell, Carter, and Brody.[201]

Statutory Permission for State Officials to Discriminate against LGBTQ+ People

Republican Senate leader Phil Berger, however, was determined not to settle for mere symbolism. Nor would he let *Obergefell* stand unmolested in North Carolina. In 2015 Berger pushed through a groundbreaking law that allows magistrates to refuse to marry and registers of deeds to refuse to issue marriage licenses to any couple that the public official has "a sincerely held religious objection" to serving.[202] So a good-hearted and strong-believing North Carolina magistrate doesn't have to do his statutory duty if the tax-paying citizen standing before him is gay, lesbian, bisexual, or transgender. Perish the thought. The Fourteenth Amendment may require marriage equality for LGBTQ+ Americans, but not in North Carolina. We've got to have our "exemptions." Perhaps the equal protection clause should be given an asterisk.

A magistrate or register of deeds need only assert that serving a lesbian couple would violate his religious scruples. Once declared, the judicial officers are free, without public explanation, to refuse to do their jobs. The same would be true for an interracial couple, an interfaith couple, a Catholic couple, or a Muslim one. The law offers no limiting principle. I'm guessing that Berger and his colleagues only mean to grant state-declared permission for right-leaning Christians to turn away gays and lesbians, but that's not what the statute says. And if American history proves anything, it is certain that no idea is so strange that some folks won't claim a religious compulsion to pursue it. It doesn't matter that Republican legislators might subsequently protest that they only meant to endorse *some* forms of religious bigotry. Notably, under the law, a magistrate or register of deeds may wait until the moment a gay couple walks into the office to claim the trumping religious objection—increasing the potential humiliation of the tax-paying LGBTQ+ petitioner and effectively saying, "Sorry, you may pay my salary, and this may be the United States, but you'll receive no equal protection, dignity, or decency here."

The law contains various administrative contrivances to offer the pretense of constitutional compliance. Once a magistrate makes a religious objection, for example, he or she is prevented from all marriage-related duties for six months.[203] (Now there's some fairness.) And the statute requires at least one nonobjecting magistrate and register of deeds to be on hand in each county so the shunned couple won't be forced to travel to the next jurisdiction. "If we shame you, we at least won't make you drive a long way to find a government official who will comply with the Fourteenth Amendment. We're not brutes, just believers."

In the weeks following the law's enactment, only 2 percent of state magistrates (14 of 672) had exercised their recusal option, suggesting the measure was motivated by animus toward LGBTQ+ North Carolinians rather than broad demand from civil servants.[204] After the first two years, fewer than 5 percent of the judicial officers had requested exemption. Rep. Larry Pittman, a vocal supporter of the statute in the House had argued that "state employees should not be required to sanction something they consider perverted and morally unconscionable." Pittman added:

> There is no way anyone can support anything other than what [God] made marriage to be. We at least ought not to be forcing people to be participating when they believe that to do so would make them traitors against the kingdom of God.[205]

Take that, Anthony Kennedy.

An early challenge to the Berger exemption law was dismissed for technical jurisdictional reasons—having been brought as a federal taxpayer case.[206] But the trial judge warned that future successful challenges were not unlikely: "A law that allows a state official to opt out of performing some duties of office for religious reasons while keeping it secret is fraught with potential harm of constitutional magnitude."[207]

The judge could have gone further. Government officials cannot be excused from the obligations of the Fourteenth Amendment, even if they really, really believe it crucial to deny full equality to some citizens. We can't have two tiers of state-funded, state-empowered public officials—fundamentalist Christians for whom constitutional obligations are voluntary and then all the rest. Can anyone imagine the U.S. Supreme Court allowing a religiously motivated North Carolina magistrate to refuse to perform an interracial marriage, no matter how strong the purported "religious" desire to do so? There is no basis to reach a different conclusion for LGBTQ+ people.[208]

North Carolina's Bathroom Bill

If the North Carolina Republican General Assembly trailed most of the equality-denying states in proposing Amendment One and then led them with the enactment of Phil Berger's "special rights for religious government officials" law in 2016, the lawmakers then went where no American government had gone before by passing

H.B. 2, North Carolina's infamous "Bathroom Bill." In February of that year, the Charlotte City Council approved an ordinance offering an array of legal protections for LGBTQ+ residents and visitors. The local law sought to prohibit businesses, bars, restaurants, taxis, and the like from discriminating against gay and transgender customers. More controversially, the ordinance permitted transgender residents to use the public bathroom facilities designated for the gender they identify with, regardless of the designation reflected on their birth certificates. In Raleigh, conservative legislators expressed stunned outrage and threatened to override the Charlotte provision. Social engineering Queen City council members, the claim went, were allowing men into women's bathrooms and locker rooms—thus putting young people, especially young girls, at great risk of falling prey to sexual predators.[209]

Charlotte stuck to its guns despite the threats, and Republican legislators, in turn, sprang to action. A special session was launched. Within hours, a bill invalidating Charlotte's nondiscrimination ordinance was introduced and enacted. Governor McCrory quickly added his signature, saying the statute was needed to protect families concerned about their privacy and safety. North Carolina thus became the first state in the nation to require transgender persons to use the public bathrooms and locker rooms of the gender on their birth certificates.[210]

And it did more than that. H.B. 2 also prevented all North Carolina municipalities from enacting their own nondiscrimination policies and from setting minimum wage levels higher than the state standard. It also eliminated various state-based discrimination claims and passed a new statewide nondiscrimination policy that pointedly excluded protections for LGBTQ+ North Carolinians. Republican support for H.B. 2 was unanimous. Rep. Dan Bishop, a leading sponsor of the "emergency provision," claimed the sweeping statute was necessary because Charlotte's antidiscrimination ordinance was "an egregious overreach."[211] North Carolina joined Tennessee and Arkansas as the only states preempting local nondiscrimination laws and became the country's only state to require that bathroom use correspond to gender at birth.[212]

Maxine Eichner, a sex discrimination and family law scholar at UNC, said, simply, "No one has ever done this."[213] The two-day special session had produced no hearings. The House allowed only thirty minutes for debate. Democrats walked out of the Senate in protest.[214] "We choose not to participate in this farce," Senate Minority Leader Dan Blue reported.[215]

But the discussion wasn't over. Opposition—state, national, and international—erupted immediately. The *New York Times* declared H.B. 2 a groundbreaking work of prejudice:

> Officials in Charlotte, N.C., spent more than a year carefully considering and debating an antidiscrimination ordinance that was passed in February to promote the city's culture of inclusiveness. State lawmakers quashed it on Wednesday by passing an appalling, unconstitutional bill that bars transgender people from using public restrooms that match their gender identity and prohibits cities from passing antidiscrimination ordinances that protect gay and transgender people. Gov. Pat McCrory, who signed the bill into law late Wednesday, said it was necessary to undo Charlotte's ordinance because it allowed "men to use women's bathroom/locker room." Proponents of so-called bathroom bills . . . have peddled them by spuriously portraying transgender women as potential rapists. That threat exists only in the imaginations of bigots. Supporters of the measures have been unable to point to a single case that justifies the need to legislate where people should be allowed to use the toilet. North Carolina is the first state to pass such a provision. By promoting the ludicrous idea that transgender women are inherently dangerous, the law endangers citizens who are already disproportionately vulnerable to violence and stigmatization.[216]

North Carolina newspapers were similarly adamant in opposition. The *Charlotte Observer* expressed visceral disappointment in Governor McCrory, former moderate mayor of the Queen City, saying he had "joined a short tragic list of [southern governors] . . . Wallace, Faubus, Barnett, men who fed our worst impulses." The *Greensboro News & Record* lamented that "it is painfully obvious now that official state policy is hostile to the gay and transgender communities." The *Asheville Citizen-Times* said North Carolina had now "equated the LGBT community with child molesters." The *Raleigh News & Observer* said the destructive "special session illustrates the flaws of a legislature led by extremists," adding that it was highly ironic that "Republican lawmakers rushed to Raleigh to protect children in the bathroom after they've done so little to help them in the classroom, or in life in general."[217]

The business, educational, sports, and entertainment worlds widely and vocally repudiated the bathroom law. Corporations scheduled to move to North Carolina, bringing sought-after jobs, bailed. PayPal pulled out of a scheduled deal. Co-Star, Deutsche Bank, and Adidas soon followed.[218] Businesses responded with vehement opposition. Apple, Google, Facebook, Starbucks, Dow Chemical, Biogen, Red Hat, IBM, American Airlines, Lowe's, Apple, and hundreds of others expressed concern about the future of their ties to North Carolina. Studies revealed that billions of dollars and thousands of jobs were lost as a result of H.B. 2.[219]

The NCAA, NBA, and ACC cancelled lucrative tournaments in the state—including (astonishingly) basketball tournaments. Several states prevented their employees from travelling to North Carolina. The British government issued a travel advisory to its LGBTQ+ citizens who might plan to visit North Carolina.[220] Boston, Pearl Jam, Cirque du Soleil, Ringo Starr, Maroon Five, and Bruce Springsteen cancelled performances in the state. Tourism groups estimated that the state was losing hundreds of millions dollars of travel-based revenue as a result of the anti-LGBTQ+ statute. Even Duke's basketball coach Mike Krzyzewski called the law "embarrassing."[221]

Government officials, academics, and activists broadened opposition and perspective. Then attorney general Roy Cooper announced that he wouldn't defend the discriminatory provision, saying "enough is enough." President Obama said at a youth town hall in London that the new North Carolina law was "wrong and should be overturned." The U.S. Commission of Civil Rights issued a formal statement saying H.B. 2's requirement that transgender people use bathrooms that match the gender on their birth certificates "jeopardizes not only the dignity, but also the physical safety, of transgender people."[222] Rev. William Barber protested that the unfurling fight subsuming North Carolina was "not just about bathrooms; it's about whether you can codify hate and discrimination into the laws of the state." Harold Lloyd, a law professor at Wake Forest University, added, "This is really a devious bill that harms workers under the guise of regulating bathrooms."[223]

The national headquarters of the American Civil Liberties Union described H.B. 2 as the "most extreme anti-LGBT measure" in the country.[224] Gov. Pat McCrory, who had become a bumbling defender of H.B. 2, described the opposition as consumed by "a vicious nationwide smear campaign," and he claimed that President Obama's goal was "to force our high schools to allow boys in the girls' restroom." Most political analysts opined that McCrory lost his 2016 reelection campaign in no small part because of his enthusiastic and often embarrassing defense of H.B. 2.[225]

Most importantly, though, in May 2016, the U.S. Department of Justice sued North Carolina to stop H.B. 2 from going into effect.[226] In a speech accompanying the filing of the federal court action, Attorney General Loretta Lynch, a native North Carolinian, drew parallels between the bathroom bill and the dark southern legacy of Jim Crow laws and intense opposition to *Brown v. Board of Education*. "It was not so very long ago," Lynch said, "that states, including North Carolina, had signs above restrooms, water fountains and on public accommodations keeping people out based upon a distinction without a difference."[227] Vanita Gupta, head of the Department of Justice's Civil Rights Division, also elevated the federal government's claim: "[H.B. 2] speaks to all of us who have ever been made to feel like somehow we don't belong in our community, like we don't fit in. . . . Let me reassure every transgender individual, right here in America, that you belong just as you are."[228] The U.S. government formally charged North Carolina with targeting the most vulnerable of its citizens in violation of the Fourteenth Amendment.

Eventually, the economic, social, and governmental pressures became so intense that the Republican leadership yielded to a partial repeal of H.B. 2.[229] The bill, this time entitled H.B. 142, was passed on the same date the NCAA had set as its deadline to determine whether North Carolina would be ineligible to host the NCAA tournaments for six years.[230] Ultimately, on Tobacco Road, the desire to suppress the LGBTQ+ community would yield to basketball.

The partial-repeal bill, passed in May 2017, was limited in effect and drew resistance from many state progressive groups. H.B. 142 preempted H.B. 2, but it kept some of the earlier statute's features. The bathroom-by-birth-certificate requirement was eliminated, but cities were prevented from regulating bathroom use until 2020. The same moratorium was applied to local nondiscrimination and minimum wage laws.[231] The new Democratic governor, Roy Cooper, supported H.B. 142, saying, "It's not a perfect bill, but it repeals House Bill 2 and begins to repair our reputation."[232] The North Carolina ACLU disagreed, urging "lawmakers to reject [a] disgraceful backroom deal that uses the rights of LGBT people as a bargaining chip." The Human Rights Campaign, Equality North Carolina, and the Lambda Legal Defense Fund protested that it enshrined antitrans discrimination and provided few meaningful benefits. Slate called it "an unmitigated disaster for LGBTQ rights and North Carolina."[233] The *Guardian* deemed the substitute "cruel and insulting."[234]

H.B. 142, however, was seen as enough of a backpedal from "the bathroom bill" that businesses began returning to the state and the NCAA resumed scheduling tournament events in North Carolina.[235] Still, litigation continues over the replacement law's meaning, constitutionality, and propriety.[236] And North Carolina's tourist industry still suffers economic hardship from the multifaceted boycotts and the state's deeply blemished reputation.[237] In the 2019 legislative session, Democrats introduced an array of proposals aimed at attacking discrimination against the LGBTQ+ community. One bill sought to add "sexual orientation, gender, gender identity, gender expression, ethnicity, and disability" to the classes protected by the state's anti–hate crime laws.[238] Another would extend the state's antidiscrimination statute to sexual orientation and gender identity.[239] The director of Equality NC, Kendra Johnson, said, "This historic slate of legislation is a collective effort towards making life more equitable and safe for queer North Carolinians who deserve the basic dignity of living, loving and growing without fear of prejudice or violence."[240] Near uniform opposition from the majority Republican caucus, however, prevented the equality-driven slate from being meaningfully considered.[241]

John Bingham

July 2018 marked the 150th anniversary of the ratification of the most consequential provision of the U.S. Constitution—the Fourth Amendment. It famously grants citizenship to anyone born in America and ensures that state governments afford due process and equal protection of the laws to their residents. Rep. John Bingham, Republican congressman of Ohio, was the amendment's principal draftsman. He explained that he sought:

> A simple, strong, plain declaration that equal laws and exact justice shall be secured within every state for any person, no

matter whence he comes, or how poor, how weak, how simple, how friendless.[242]

The Fourteenth Amendment, along with its Civil War counterparts, sought to remedy the tragic defects of the 1789 framing and to bring egalitarian democracy to the United States. Of course, Bingham's words have been much ignored in our constitutional history. The Fourteenth Amendment was largely gutted in its first fifty years, except as a tool for corporate interests. And *Plessy v. Ferguson* cruelly buried its central meaning.[243]

But since 1954, the U.S. Supreme Court has frequently used the Fourteenth Amendment to demand that the American government stay true to its foundational promises. *Brown v. Board of Education* (school segregation), *Loving v. Virginia* (antimiscegenation laws), *Craig v. Boren* (sex discrimination), *Harper v. Virginia* (voting rights), *Goldberg v. Kelly* (right to hearing), *Roe v. Wade* (reproductive rights), *Graham v. Richardson* (immigrant rights), *Obergefell v. Hodges* (gay rights), and *Reynolds v. Sims* (equal political representation) are its principal markers.[244] Without the amendment and its progeny, the United States would be a tyrannous nation—anything but the land of the free.

I sometimes try to think of ways to encapsulate the defining and pervasive political war that consumes North Carolina these days. As previously mentioned, the *New York Times* refers to it as the Republican's "pioneering work in bigotry."[245] I'd be hard-pressed to disagree with that. But it is also accurate to characterize the struggle as a continuing, never-yielding fight over Bingham's Fourteenth Amendment. "Equal and exact justice . . . for any person, no matter whence he comes, or how poor, how weak, how simple, how friendless." Remarkable, remarkable words. Republican words. There is, today, of course, no John Bingham. No Thaddeus Stevens. No Charles Sumner. Republicans in 1868 may have drafted and muscled the amendment into ratification, but today they don't seem to like it.

North Carolina initially voted against the Fourteenth Amendment in 1866. Eventually it yielded to the high pressures of the Reconstruction Congress. Echoing that early rejection, the aggressive social and political agenda of today's North Carolina Republican Party is impossible to square with the due process and equal protection mandates of the last half century. As I've indicated in these opening chapters, the North Carolina Republican General Assembly has repeatedly moved, in every manner it could fathom, to restrict the political participation of black Tar Heels, governing via an all-white caucus. It has boasted of its efforts to quash political electoral equality. It has waged a nation-leading crusade against impoverished North Carolinians. The statehouse has suppressed the intimate and egalitarian rights of women, seeking to push back frontiers thought long conquered. It has treated the LGBTQ+ community with derision, threatening their dignity, opportunity, and safety—even giving government officials free license to discriminate against them. They legislate for the powerful and burden the powerless. If John Bingham were alive today, he would not be welcome in the North Carolina Republican Party.[246]

As Faulkner put it: "The past is never dead. It's not even past."[247]

CHAPTER SIX

Taking the Public Out of Public Education

Private schools that receive scholarship [voucher] funds are (1) not required to be accredited by the State Board of Education or any other state or national institution; (2) not required to employ teachers or principals who are licensed or have any particular credentials, degrees, experience or expertise in education; (3) not subject to any requirements regarding the curriculum that they teach; (4) not required to provide a minimum amount of instructional time; and (5) not prohibited from discriminating against applicants or students on the basis of religion. See N.C. Gen. Stat. sec. 115C-562.1. The General Assembly fails the children of North Carolina when they are sent with taxpayer money to private schools that have no legal obligation to teach them anything.
—Trial Court Findings, Judge Robert Hobgood, *Hart v. State*, 2015, lawsuit challenging North Carolina voucher program[248]

I am no fan of hyperbole, but I mean it when I say this: North Carolina is waging war against public education. —James Hogan, Mitchell Community College, former North Carolina teacher, 2015[249]

When Republicans took control of the General Assembly in 2011, they moved swiftly to begin to change the character of public education in North Carolina. They're still at it.

Commitment to public education is deep in the bones here. It's also fair to say that, for decades, North Carolina leaders have been at or near the frontlines of efforts to reform the public schools. Governors, at least from the 1990s on, have professed strong rhetorical and, often, meaningful financial and programmatic commitments to pre-K–12 education. In the eyes of many, North Carolina became a leader in standards-based accountability—supplementing overarching assessment programs with additional early childhood regimes. Efforts were made to assess and reduce achievement gaps, professionalize the teaching force, and meaningfully raise teacher pay.

Achievements were surely uneven. And it may be overdoing it to claim that "North Carolina was once viewed as the shining light for progressive education policy in the South."[250] Or maybe not. But there was little doubt that the state experienced a profound and continuing governmental and citizen-based commitment to public education.[251] And for much of the last three decades, lawmakers in other states often looked to North Carolina education policies when seeking to lift student prospects.[252] When Republicans gained ascendancy, though, they were explicit and adamant that they intended to go in a different direction.[253]

In their first session, they offered modest opening moves, aiming principally at their adversaries.

North Carolina law bars public school teachers from unionizing, but the North Carolina Association of Educators (NCAE) had long served, with some effectiveness, as an advocacy group for the state's teachers. In 2011 the General Assembly passed a measure restricting how the NCAE collected dues from its members.[254] It was, unsurprisingly, vetoed by then (Democrat) governor Beverly Perdue. The next year, legislators tried a second time—triggering a second veto. This time the veto was overridden in what the local press deemed "an unprecedented midnight session."[255] A state court judge quickly ruled, however, that the dues deduction law "constitutes[d] retaliatory viewpoint discrimination against the NCAE." No other organization of active employees had been prohibited from using payroll deductions to collect dues under the statute. Thus the NCAE ban was held to violate the First Amendment.[256] Of course the General Assembly was, by this time, getting used to courts ruling that its longed-for interventions were unconstitutional.

The next pass at political retaliation was less direct but more profoundly wounding. Despite a continuing and problematic shortage of teachers in the state, the General Assembly, without explanation, defunded and then abolished the nationally recognized North Carolina Teaching Fellows Program.[257] The scholarship program had been in place since 1986—encouraging top students, from every corner of the state, to become and remain teachers. In return for the scholarship aid, fellows committed to spend at least four years in the classroom. More than eight thousand program students graduated and received teaching jobs in all one hundred counties. Retention rates (as teachers) were high. In its final year, there were more than two thousand applicants for the five hundred scholarships.

The Fellows Program was created by the Public School Forum, a nonprofit organization of business and education leaders, but activist groups on the right complained that the Teaching Fellows Program was closely identified with former Democratic governor Jim Hunt. So, teacher shortage or not, it had to go.[258] The following year's North Carolina teacher of the year, Keana Triplett, an alumna of the Fellows Program, said that ending the noted and highly successful recruiting tool was "one of the biggest mistakes that has ever been made in public education."[259]

The last move of 2011, though, was more predictive of the future.

Until then, families who wanted their children to attend a public charter school often had a relatively tough time of it. The state had placed a one-hundred-school limit on charters—that is, public schools that are taxpayer funded but exempt from many of the requirements that govern traditional public schools, such as offering school meals and transportation. Waiting lists at some charter schools could be long. So, in 2011, Republicans abolished the cap on charters. Since then, enrollment has more than doubled, reaching 100,000 students as the state's number of charter schools had risen to 173 by 2018.[260] Subsequent years would bring notable questions about diminished oversight and accountability in charter schools, for-profit management of charters, and their relative lack of racial and economic diversity. But the General Assembly seemed anxious to offer a pathway out of the traditional public schools, which they apparently deemed responsive to "competition" and "parental choice." There would be much more to come.[262]

The next legislative session (2013), with both Republican supermajorities and a newly elected Republican governor, brought more radical change. First, the General Assembly introduced a broadscale A to F grading system for all public schools, announcing that high percentages of schools were failures and massively disparaging public schools, their teachers, and students—especially those serving low-income families. Republican lawmakers then moved to abolish tenure for public schoolteachers, diminishing the status of the profession, chiding the quality of the state's teaching corps, and chilling the effective criticism of legislative policies by teachers. Lawmakers also determined to stop giving salary increases for teachers who obtained advanced degrees, again removing long-struggled-for teacher incentives. Historically, teachers obtaining a master's degree received a 10 percent raise from the state, but Republican leaders said teachers should be paid based on their performance, not their credentials.[263]

Finally, the General Assembly adopted a generous and aggressive voucher program significantly subsidizing the growth of private and religious education in the state and, along with the expanded charter program, draining much-needed resources from traditional public education. The unholy combination led *Education Week* to call the North Carolina General Assembly "the most backward legislature in the country."[264] Our lawmakers had, apparently, grown accustomed to the title.

By the end of 2013, the Republicans' K–12 education agenda had become clear. Legislators would first disparage, diminish, and deplete traditional public schools, even as the crucial importance of education became more obvious and indispensable and the ever-burgeoning enrollment demands of a fast-growing state rapidly increased. The trend became sufficiently pronounced that by late 2019 a nonpartisan court-ordered study would conclude that North Carolina per-pupil funding was the sixth lowest in the nation and had dropped, in real terms, by 6 percent under Republican leadership—moving "the state further away from meeting its constitutional obligation to provide every child with the opportunity for a sound, basic education."[265]

Second, dramatic levels of funding would be directed to private schools through the newly created state voucher program—expenditures going to private and religious schools that were required to comply with virtually no regulations, transparency demands, standards of training or rigor, or the commands of equality long thought inherent in public education. Charter schools would also be expanded and allowed to operate more like private entities. Weaken and diminish the traditional public system, the pattern suggested, and then provide attractive exit strategies to the private/religious sector.

Third, as the dynamic unfolds, feed it—thus providing increased carrots for private schools and sharper sticks for publics. The final result will be the destruction of the public school system through the allegedly neutral mantra of "parental choice." Though there would be nothing neutral about the agenda deployed to dismantle the public schools.

Rating Public Schools Based on the Economic Status of Their Students' Parents

The A to F public school report card system launched in 2013 and 2014 based the lion's share of a school's grade (80 percent) on "student achievement"—including performance on standardized tests. Twenty percent of a school's mark was tied to improvement in student performance year to year. In the initial reporting year, more than seven hundred North Carolina public schools received a score of D or F, nearly 30 percent of all N.C. public schools. More than 80 percent of the schools where four out of five students qualified for free and reduced lunch subsidies received a D or F. Over 90 percent of schools with less than 20 percent low-income students secured an A or B.[266] Eighty-seven percent of schools that got an A had less than 50 percent of their students eligible for free and reduced meals. One hundred percent of schools receiving an F had more than 50 percent food-subsidy-eligible students.

In other words, almost all "failing" schools were high-poverty institutions, and almost all stellar schools were high-wealth domains. The vaunted Report Card measured the socioeconomic status of a school's enrolled student body, not the quality of the institution. Virginia, which had begun a similar reporting system previously, repealed its requirement because its legislative sponsors concluded it stigmatized students at low-income schools and made it difficult to recruit teachers.[267] That apparently did not bother the Republican North Carolina General Assembly.

The North Carolina Report Card doesn't provide many surprises. The economic achievement gap is the most consistently documented shortcoming of American public education.[268] But it does disparage. Mark Jewell, head of the North Carolina Association of Educators, says the F grade is a "scarlet letter" inappropriately applied to schools that face the most daunting obstacles and students who have the greatest need for support. Instead, they get salaries and resources far below national averages, and legislators tag them as failures. Jewell calls it "a false narrative that public schools are failing when they are not; instead our politicians are failing our public schools." If anyone "deserves an F," Jewell says, they do.[269] I have interviewed many North Carolina teachers from Title One (high poverty) schools, engaged in doing our toughest and most vital work in what they describe as "a calling within a calling."[270] They believe our unsupportive General Assembly is piling on.[271] As the nonpartisan Public School Forum reports:

> What would you think if state legislators created a new A–F school grading system based on poverty, giving A's and B's

to the schools that serve the fewest poor students while tagging the highest-poverty schools with D's and F's? Unfortunately, the current grading scheme produces the same result. A is for Affluent.[272]

Taking Away Teacher Tenure

Before the changes of 2013, North Carolina teachers who completed a four-year probationary period and obtained a favorable vote from their school board received "career status"—a form of tenure that assured them various legal rights before they could be fired.[273] The Current Operations and Capital Improvements Appropriations Act of 2013 repealed the Career Status Law.[274] It revoked career status for all North Carolina teachers as of July 1, 2018. Under the new system it launched, teacher contracts for tenured faculty were no longer open-ended, but would extend "for a term of one, two or four school years." A decision not to renew a teacher could be based on any reason, not "arbitrary, capricious or discriminatory, for personal or political reasons, or any basis prohibited by state or federal law." A rejected teacher could petition the school board for a hearing, but the board could refuse at its discretion. Any teacher "who had not achieved career status prior to 2013 is no longer eligible to receive career status in the future and would, instead, be employed primarily through one-year contracts."[275]

Senator Berger explained that he had heard too many stories of ineffective teachers who couldn't be fired because of "career status."[276] Sen. Jerry Tillman, a Republican from Archdale, added, "I think it's much better when you make it easier to get rid of someone who isn't doing their job."[277] The General Assembly had, as indicated, also reduced teacher advanced degree compensation. And, later, lawmakers decreed that teachers hired after 2021 would no longer be eligible for state health insurance.[278] Legislators argued that teachers should need no greater job security than other professions. Rep. Craig Horn, a Union County Republican and House education leader, explained:

> It's my belief that not everyone in any profession should be in that profession. There are lawyers who should not be lawyers. There are doctors who should not be doctors. There are legislators who should not be legislators, and there are teachers who should not be teachers.[279]

Oddly, House Speaker Tim Moore later indicated that the abolition of tenure was part of his effort to "focus on recruiting and retaining the best teachers for our classrooms."[280] Teachers, unsurprisingly, didn't agree. As Akisha Bailey-Martin, a third-grade teacher from Wake County, put it:

> Tenure shows us we're valued as teachers. I know that some people think that tenure keeps the bad teachers, but I don't think that's true. We're losing a lot of good teachers because they don't feel they are valued and so the good teachers are leaving.[281]

Melissa Noel, an AP (advanced placement) English teacher in Johnston County, echoed Baily-Martin's overarching claim:

> It feels like we're being encouraged to leave the profession. Sending money to private schools in the form of school vouchers, reducing public school budgets, telling us our advanced degrees are not appreciated, and now our governor says experience is not appreciated. I know a lot of my colleagues will leave.[282]

Speaker Moore's plan for recruiting teachers appears to create the opposite effect.

Three years after the tenure repeal was enacted, the North Carolina Supreme Court ruled unanimously (both Republican and Democratic justices) that it was unconstitutional for the legislature to simply abolish tenure for teachers who had already received it.[283]

Once again, the troublesome constitution intervened. Republican justice Robert Edmunds wrote for the high court that the repeal obviously interfered with the vested property and contract rights of teachers. "Teachers rely on their career status rights in making employment decisions," and such protections substitute for diminished "monetary compensation." They were "promised career status protections in exchange for meeting the requirements of law" and "relied on the promise in exchange for accepting their teaching positions and continuing their employment with their school districts." Accordingly, the "elimination of these benefits substantially deprives current career status teachers of the value of their vested contractual rights," the state justices concluded.[284]

The North Carolina Supreme Court also dismissed the General Assembly's claimed justification for attacking teachers' tenure rights:

> We fully agree that maintaining the quality of the public school system is an important public purpose. Nevertheless, while alleviating difficulties in dismissing ineffective teachers might be a legitimate and justifying change to the Career Status Law, no evidence indicates that such a problem existed. Instead, the record is replete with affidavits from teachers and administrators who relate that the Career Status Law did not impede their ability to dismiss teachers who failed to meet the academic standards necessary to properly educate students in public schools. Instead, these affiants indicate that the [tenure] law was an important incentive in recruiting and retaining high quality teachers. Inadequate teachers could be and were dismissed under the Career Status Law. . . . Accordingly, we fail to see a legitimate purpose for which it was necessary to impair the vested contractual rights of career status teachers.[285]

Once again, the Republican General Assembly's asserted basis for violating protected constitutional rights was found to be a sham. The North Carolina Supreme Court invalidated the retroactive application of the tenure repeal. It rejected the claimed, but illegitimate, foundation of the entire statute. Teachers were, no doubt, getting the message. As Lee Quinn, a teacher at Broughton High in Raleigh put it:

> School administrators and teachers are still doing good work, but we are fighting against a state leadership that is hostile to our public education system. We all know that and a lot of teachers are becoming attuned to how state politics that are hostile to public education affect our daily lives.[286]

Vouchers: Public Money to Private and Religious Schools

The stoutest blow against the future of public education in North Carolina delivered by the Republican General Assembly in the 2013 session was the creation of the "Opportunity Scholarship" voucher program. The financial assistance vouchers, offering students $4,200 a year, was touted as a way to help low-income students by providing access to private schools that would be closed to them otherwise. There was no small irony in the asserted rationale since the North Carolina General Assembly has waged such a spirited crusade against poor children on every other front. And, predictably, Republican voucher sponsors have, since enactment, sought to lift the economic eligibility standards to higher-income families. Still, the "Opportunity Scholarship" scheme opened the door to sending huge amounts of taxpayer funding to private schools, 70 percent of which, in North Carolina, are religious.[287]

The North Carolina Constitution requires that the General Assembly fund a "uniform system of schools for primary and secondary education."[288] Article I, section 15, declares, "The people have a right to the privilege of education, and it is the duty of the State to guard and maintain that right." The North Carolina Supreme Court's landmark ruling in *Leandro v. State* had held, years earlier, that "public funds spent for education must go to institutions that will provide meaningful educational services—specifically, to institutions with a sufficient curriculum and competent teachers."[289] It was no surprise, then, that the voucher plan was quickly challenged in the state courts. The entire program was initially ruled unconstitutional by one of North Carolina's most respected and independent trial judges, Robert Hobgood. But the North Carolina Supreme Court upheld the voucher program under a straight-line 4–3 partisan vote in *Hart v. North Carolina* (2016). The Republican majority, however, could offer no rebuttal to the remarkable, uncontroverted findings by the trial court. They make for unusual reading.

> Private schools that receive scholarship (voucher) funds are (1) not required to be accredited by the State Board of Education or any other state or national institution; (2) not required to employ teachers or principals who are licensed or have any particular credentials, degrees, experience or expertise in education; (3) not subject to any requirements regarding the curriculum that they teach; (4) not required to provide a minimum amount of instructional time; and (5) not prohibited from discriminating against applicants or students on the basis of religion. See N.C. Gen. Stat. sec. 115C-562.1.
>
> Of the 5,556 scholarship applicants, 3,804 applicants identified 446 private schools they planned to attend. Of those 446 schools, 322 are religious schools and 117 are independent schools. Of the 322 religious schools scholarship recipients planned to attend, 128 are accredited by some organization, and 194 are not accredited by any organization. Of the 117 independent schools scholarship recipients planned to attend, 58 are accredited by some organization and 59 are not accredited by any organization. The General Assembly fails the children of North Carolina when they are sent with taxpayer money to private schools that have no legal obligation to teach them anything.[290]

After all of the legislature's demands for accountability, transparency, responsiveness, and widely published grading schemes for North Carolina's traditional public schools, the "Opportunity Scholarship" program unleashed the most unregulated, nontransparent, and standardless voucher program in America. As Justice Robin Hudson put it in dissent, "The main constitutional flaw in this program is that it provides no framework at all for evaluating any of the participating schools' contribution to public purposes; such a huge omission is a constitutional black hole into which the entire program should disappear."[291]

Rather than allowing the ruleless voucher program to disappear, the General Assembly has, of course, dramatically expanded it. Almost $11 million was freed up for "Opportunity Scholarships" with the Hart decision in 2016. The allocation for the following year was $17.6 million. Remarkably, a spending plan approved in 2017 calls for increasing the voucher budget by $10 million a year through 2027. And in 2019 the North Carolina Senate moved to lift the qualifying family income level for the voucher program to $71,456 per year—as critics had long predicted they would. Sen. Jeff Jackson (D-Mecklingburg) protested that the "original rationale" for vouchers, which "was about providing educational options to low-income children, is gone." "This is," he argued, "full-fledged subsidizing private schools with public funds."[292]

Thus far, the North Carolina voucher program has proven unable to spend all the money allocated; student demand has been insufficient. Still, Sen. Phil Berger was undeterred. "We've got substantial demand," Berger recently said. "I think the growth that's currently built into the program is something that we don't need to go backwards on." No need to rein in spending now. It may be vital to starve the public schools. But completely unaccountable, discriminatory, and nontransparent taxpayer funding for religious schools is nonproblematic. "We'll even throw in barrels of walking-around money for good measure," Berger seemed to suggest. And, unlike the trial judge in the *Hart* case, Republican lawmakers don't mind that tax dollars will go to private institutions that are charged with no legal demand to teach students anything.[293]

The Impact of Privatization

I went to visit this school. It's in the back of a church and has 10–12 students—and one teacher or one and a half teachers. I think you need to go slow with Opportunity Scholarships [vouchers]. From what I saw, it didn't seem to be a school that we would want to send taxpayer dollars to. —Rep. Leo Daughtry (R-Johnston), 2015[294]

The massively expensive and utterly unaccountable "Opportunity Scholarship" program obviously drains huge resources from the underfunded public school system in North Carolina. Large numbers of students who obtain voucher payments would attend, or are already attending, private schools without the subsidy.[295] Fundamentalist Christian schools get the bulk of the funds from the North Carolina voucher scheme.[296] But a careful study by the League of Women Voters found that most of the subsidized schools fail to provide the "sound basic education" the North Carolina Constitution promises to our children. The League studied the curriculum used at the one hundred schools receiving the highest number of voucher payments over the program's first four years. The report found that "77% of the private schools receiving vouchers are using curricula that do not comply with state standards, leaving many students unprepared for college-level coursework or careers in certain fields."[297]

The League study determined that three out of four of the voucher schools used something called the Abeka curriculum or other "Christian Biblical world view" instructional materials. Students using the Abeka books learn that God created the world six thousand years ago in six days, that Noah's Ark is a true story that occurred around 2500 BC, and that runoff from the flood formed the Grand Canyon.[298] The University of California has rejected an array of high school courses that use Abeka texts. The former chair of UNC's Asian Studies Department, upon reviewing the Abeka world history materials, "found multiple errors in every page; it was nonsense." A professor in the UNC Department of Neurology said the Abeka science textbook laces religious teachings interchangeably with scientific texts in a manner "that has no place in a science textbook." Overall, the League of Women Voters study concluded:

> We found that 76.7% of voucher funding is going to schools with a literal biblical world view that affects all areas of the curriculum. This amounts to an estimated $997.1 million over fifteen years. Expert educators have concluded that this biblical worldview curriculum does not prepare students for 21st century colleges or careers.[299]

So, we pay astonishing amounts of taxpayer money to mislead, disadvantage, and handicap our children in order to please religious and political ideologues.

We also tax all North Carolinians in order to pay for religious schools that disparage and discriminate against some North Carolinians.[300] The "Opportunity Scholarship" program allows recipient schools to discriminate on the basis of religion in hiring and student admission. Testimony in the voucher challenge case revealed that various voucher schools require that applicants (and sometimes their parents) "receive Jesus Christ as their Savior" and are recommended by a pastor. Others exclude students from "non-Christian religions . . . Mormons, Jehovah's Witnesses, Muslims, Jews, Hindus, Buddhists, etc." Others bar those who participate in cults, naming not only most of those above, but adding "Christian Scientists, Unitarians, Unificationists, and United Pentecostals." Impressive. Not stopping there, some exclude students from "families that engage in illicit drug use, sexual promiscuity, homosexuality (LGBT) or other behaviors that Scripture defines as deviant and perverted."[301]

The people of North Carolina aid and abet this work. We pay for it. We assure that it can continue. We ease its path. We force gay Tar Heels to pay for schools that announce they are abominations. No decent government would bathe in this stream.

And the combination of charter schools and these voucher admission restrictions increases racial segregation in North Carolina schools. Duke University scholars found that from 1999 to 2012, our charter schools have become increasingly racially homogenous—sometimes predominantly serving white students, sometimes students of color. A North Carolina Justice Center found that more than 70 percent of counties with at least one charter school have increased the degree of racial segregation in the public schools of the district.[302] Of course, charter schools are public and voucher schools are private institutions, now receiving hefty taxpayer dollars. But neither helps in our broad social mandate to have racially integrated educational institutions.

The wide, unrelenting, and radical campaign being waged by the Republican North Carolina General Assembly against public education in the state is said to be driven, fundamentally, by an overarching deference to "parental choice." As Senate leader Phil Berger puts it, "Parents—not education bureaucrats or politicians—ought to be able to choose the educational pathway best suited to their children's needs."[303] I should be candid to say that, personally, I don't buy it. I'm much more inclined to believe that the aggressive anti–public school agenda is rooted in antagonism toward schoolteachers and the NCAE, opposition to the egalitarian values that tend to dominate the culture of public education, an aversion to the public sphere more broadly, and a near-religious conviction that everything the private sector does is better than anything ever done in the public sector. But, admittedly, I don't know that my predispositions are true. So, for the moment, let me take Senator Berger at his word: the key driver for public education policy should be parental choice.

I, for one, don't believe this. In my old age, I don't believe that parents always know best. Or, maybe more accurately, I don't believe, as a university teacher and administrator for forty years, that the highest goal of an education system should be satisfying the wishes and predispositions of parents. I don't think that is any more the case for public K–12 education than I think that the highest goal of a university should be satisfying the wishes of its undergraduates or that the highest goal of a law school should be satisfying the preferences of law students.

Popular approval, in this broad sense, can't be the answer. Or, again, maybe more precisely, I think it is very tough work figuring out what a strong state system of public education should do in 2020 and beyond. I'm not sure I know the answer to that question. Or that I ever will. But I am pretty certain that those charged with helping to craft and implement the solution can't simply punt to "parental choice." That's too easy. It's almost certainly wrong and ill-informed. And it is an abdication of one of our hardest jobs as a people—figuring out how to best educate our society's next generation.

Let me give an example removed from North Carolina and its hyper-tendentious politics to try to at least hint at the point. When I was a young law professor, I enjoyed teaching my constitutional law students the landmark free exercise of religion case *Wisconsin v. Yoder.*[304] In that case, in 1972, the U.S. Supreme Court ruled that Wisconsin's compulsory education law was unconstitutional as applied to the Amish community. Three Amish fathers, who according to their religious convictions refused to send their children to school past the eighth grade, sued the State of Wisconsin. The Court ruled that Amish beliefs rooted "in fundamentals for centuries" could not be made to give way to Wisconsin's purportedly "compelling interest in its system of compulsory education." As a result, the Amish fathers' free exercise of religion required that an exemption be provided from the reach of the compulsory Wisconsin system. Parents prevailed.

In my comparative youth, I believed this to be an inspiring result. The dissenters prevailed against the heavy hand of the state. They weren't part of the mainstream of American society, but the mainstream couldn't just roll over them. Maybe most powerfully of all, the broader society couldn't tell these autonomous and equal adults how they should raise their kids. That special liberty was protected from the government's intrusive hand. We can't all be forced into the same path. Hear, hear.

A lot of me, in my dotage, still feels that way. But now I also have a great hesitation to conclude that parents ought to be readily given power to inflict such a daunting and perhaps unrecoverable wound upon their children. I don't know exactly what it does to kids in 2020 to be told that their education stops at fourteen. But I fear it could cramp the possibilities for one barely even a teenager in a way that I wouldn't happily determine ought to be allowed, even for a parent. If it were up to me, I'd make the Amish go to school like everybody else. I think the United States owes its children that.

I realize that my now-altered view of *Wisconsin v. Yoder* likely leaves me outside of respectable liberal and conservative camps. And it may be that I am wrong and will be thought so even into succeeding generations. But I use the example to try to suggest that parental choice isn't everything, and even if it is foundationally important, it can't substitute for our broad-ranging obligation to decide as a society how we ought to try to educate our next generation of citizens.

North Carolina's fascinating 1868 constitution stated that the General Assembly must "provide by taxation and otherwise, for a general and uniform system of public schools, wherein tuition shall be free of charge to all the children of the State."[305] That broad charge remains one of this state's highest missions. For the last eight years, the Republican General Assembly has betrayed it.

CHAPTER SEVEN

Trashing the Natural World

These aren't small tweaks. —Molly Diggins, director, Sierra Club, commenting on changes to North Carolina's environmental policy[306]

The Philistines have come over the walls. —Derb Carter, Southern Environmental Law Center, 2015[307]

It's rarely good news to hear that your efforts have captured the attention of Stephen Colbert. Think of McCrae Dowless, North Carolina's "election fraud sasquatch," newly employed Tar Heel "bathroom junk checkers," or Colbert's message to the General Assembly members who brought us H.B. 2: "You guys are the real weirdos." (Not to mention Colbert's shameful tendency to throw shade on North Carolina barbecue.) It is a tough competition, to be sure. But I doubt Mr. Colbert ever had more fun at Tar Heel expense than with our (again) internationally famous moves to legislate against the ocean's rise.

As WUNC radio put it a few years later, "North Carolina became forever known around the world as the state that outlawed climate change a few minutes after 11:30 p.m. on June 4, 2012. . . . That's when satirical newsman Stephen Colbert boiled down" the General Assembly's actions:[308]

> If your science gives you a result you don't like, pass a law saying the result is illegal. Problem solved. Bravo North Carolina. By making this bold action on climate change today, you're ensuring that when it actually comes, you'll have plenty of options, or at least two: sink or swim.[309]

ABC News joined in, announcing, "New law in North Carolina bans latest scientific predictions of sea level rise." The *Guardian* in London piled on "North Carolina didn't like the science on sea levels . . . so passed a law against it."[310] The *Washington Post*, ever at the ready, reported, "[S]cary climate-change predictions prompt a [North Carolina] change of forecast."[311] Republican lawmakers proved, once again, that there is more than one way to wound a state. You can make the world believe your commonwealth is comprised of ten million idiots. And the opportunities to demonstrate loopiness are apparently endless.

North Carolina lawmakers voted, through H.B. 819, the sea level legislation, to quash a March 2010 report from scientists of the Coastal Resources Commission that projected a 20-to-55-inch sea level rise on the state's coast by the end of the century. The statute also banned local communities from using the report to pass new regulations. The U.S. Geological Survey had also indicated that the sea level rise from North Carolina to Massachusetts was accelerating at three to four times the global rate. But North Carolina politicians said they weren't convinced by science. Intense opposition rose from fears of costlier home insurance and accusations of antidevelopment alarmism among residents in the state's Outer Banks region.[312]

Republican Rep. Pat McElraft, who drafted the statute, is a former real-estate agent who lives on Emerald Isle. She claimed the measure was "just a breather"—requiring the state to "step back" and continue studying sea level rise until a more accurate prediction model could be developed. It would also protect developers and homeowners, she said, against an overactive state government that sought to take away their right to build on their own property. According to the National Institute on Money in State Politics, McElraft's largest campaign contributor since she was elected in 2007 has been the North Carolina Association of Realtors. The North Carolina Association of Home Builders came in second. "Most of the environmental side say we are ignoring science, but the bill actually asks for more science," she announced. "We're not ignoring science; we're asking for the best science possible."[313] We need to use "some science we can all trust when we start making laws in North Carolina that affect property values on the coast."[314] Realtor science perhaps.

Rep. Deborah Ross (D-Wake) compared McElraft's bill to burying your "head in the sand." When she goes to the doctor, Ross argued, "[I]f I'm not fine, I'd rather know now than in four years. . . . [T]his is like going to the doctor and saying you are not going to get a test on a problem."[315] Orrin Pikey, retired Duke University coastal geologist, would write later that North Carolina had failed to take the essential steps that Virginia and New Jersey had taken to prepare for changing sea levels. "Instead coastal development flourishes as more beachfront buildings, highways and bridges are built to ease access to beaches. . . . [T]he unspoken plan is to wait until the situation is catastrophic and then respond."[316]

A couple of years later, the state produced a second report, examining much shorter time lines and producing less-alarming conclusions.[317] But as destructive storms have continued to roil the North Carolina coastline, many worry that the decision to deep-six the report has had a long-term impact. And in August 2019, a national nonprofit's study concluded that North Carolina is a leader among states where new homes have been built in areas where the sea level rise will increase flood risk.[318]

Stanley Riggs, a retired research professor at East Carolina University who helped write the 2010 report, claims that "we were ready to step up to the plate and take a hard look at this long-term problem and we blew it."[319] Geoffrey Gisler, a lawyer at the Southern Environmental Law Center, argues that North Carolina was a "leader in really thoughtful coastal management" until the Republicans took over in 2011. But a "lot of folks who have interests in developing areas that are currently vulnerable, and would become more vulnerable with sea level rise, objected to the public finding out that there was this projected significant sea level rise . . . so the legislature decided to prohibit looking that far out."[320]

An Ag-Gag Law

The radicalized General Assembly had set January 1, 2016, as the prized day when a number of its most potent enactments would take effect. The vaunted new voter ID requirement was to be launched, beginning with the upcoming March primary. Of course, as discussed in chapter 2, the federal courts were to have a say in the matter. A separate measure now required that abortion providers send an array of documents to the state Department of Health and Human Services for all abortions after the sixteenth week of pregnancy "for statistical purposes only," but many had their doubts. Melissa Reed, director of Planned Parenthood Votes, said, "The true intent of the law is clear—to shame women and intimidate the doctors that care for them." The "Protect North Carolina Workers Act," which banned immigrants from using documents issued by their country's consulates as a valid ID, was extended to insurance companies, and technology data centers got new, generous exemptions from paying sales taxes on equipment and electricity. And then North Carolina's now-famous ag-gag law went into effect.[321]

North Carolina is a huge pork-producing state. According to the U.S. Department of Agriculture, we trail only Iowa. Pig sales are reportedly worth more than $2.5 billion annually and constitute almost 15 percent of the entire national market.[322] Duplin County is often the highest hog-producing county in the country.[323] Ag-gag laws have developed in a handful of states as a response by the pork, poultry, and slaughterhouse industries to undercover investigations revealing the brutality of their operations. As the *New York Times* has put it:

> Factory farm operators believe that the less Americans know about what goes on behind their closed doors, the better for the industry. That's because the animals sent through those factories often endure an unimaginable amount of mistreatment and abuse. Cows too sick to walk are dragged by

> the neck across cement floors. Pigs are stabbed and beaten with sledgehammers. Chickens are thrown against walls and stomped to death. And accepted practices, like confining animals in impossibly small cages, are just as brutal. Nearly always, the treatment comes to light only because courageous employees—or those posing as employees—take undercover video and release it to the public. The industry should welcome such scrutiny as a way to expose the worst operators. Instead, the lobbyists have taken the opposite approach, pushing for so-called "ag-gag" laws, which ban undercover recordings on farms and in slaughterhouses. . . . [No state] has gone as far as North Carolina.[324]

H.B. 405, the N.C. ag-gag bill, originally singled out factory-farm exposés, but the narrowed "special rights" notion failed to pass twice in the face of stiff opposition. North Carolina legislators then passed a generalized version—purportedly covering everyone equally. Gov. Pat McCrory, to the surprise of many, vetoed the measure, expressing concern about its impact on valid whistle-blowers. Powerful big-agriculture lawmaker Sen. Brent Jackson (R-Autryville) exploded, saying, "I am extremely disappointed in [the governor's] decision to veto a bill that defends private property rights and puts teeth into trespass laws." One of the bill's other principal sponsors told a Senate committee that the whole point of the statute was to stop people "who would go running to a news outlet." In June 2015 the offended General Assembly overrode the governor's veto.[325]

The "North Carolina Property Protection Act" provides a private right of action against any person who "exceeds the scope of authorized access" to the property of an owner or operator.[326] More specifically,

> [a]n employee who intentionally enters the non-public areas of an employer's premises for a reason other than a bone fide intent of seeking or holding employment and who thereaf-

> ter without authorization records images or sound occurring within an employer's premises and uses the recording to breach the person's duty of loyalty to the employer . . . or intentionally places an unattended camera or electronic surveillance device to record images or data [is subject to] damages, costs, attorney fees and exemplary damages in the amount of $5,000 for each day the person has acted in violation of [this] Act.[327]

Matthew Dominguez of the Humane Society of the United States protested that H.B. 405 is "deceitful." It is "a broad and dangerous ag-gag bill because it doesn't just affect agriculture, it affects nursing homes, day cares, veteran facilities, anywhere you have people who are vulnerable." The law was designed, Dominguez said, "To chill the ability to do whistle-blowing exposés into facility farms, it was expanded into other businesses to provide a talking point, saying, 'Oh, this isn't just about agriculture.' "[328] The broader sweep, of course, only makes it more dangerous.

The *Charlotte Observer* called H.B. 405 "boneheaded." It noted that an animal rights group had earlier videotaped a worker at one of Perdue poultry's suppliers kicking, stomping, and throwing chickens against the wall. Perdue had publicly thanked the activists for disclosing "clear animal abuse." The abusive worker was later convicted of animal cruelty. "Too bad for him," the *Observer* wrote, "that he didn't commit his misdeeds" after the statute passed.[329] Then the supplier would have been allowed to go to state court and sue the activist who had videotaped the crimes—running up, perhaps, an incredible tab. No more exposés. No PR problem. Vandhana Bala, counsel for Mercy for Animals, the group who carried out the Perdue investigation, said their "exposés are now in peril" because "a corrupt legislature" had surrendered to pressure from corporations. But everything—from food safety, to worker safety, to the welfare of kids and seniors—is at greater risk as well. Bala's group and an array of others have sued in federal court, challenging H.B. 405 under the First Amendment.[330] Precedent suggests they'll win.[331] The *New York Times* wrote that "the secrecy promoted by the (General Assembly's) Ag-Gag law should have no place in American society."[332]

I reread Upton Sinclair's *The Jungle* last summer—exploring both human nature and the grotesque Chicago meat-packing plants of the early twentieth century.[333] I'm guessing the North Carolina General Assembly thinks Sinclair should have been driven into bankruptcy to assure that the meat-packers' property rights were never again jeopardized.[334]

The ag-gag law, combining egregious fines with all-encompassing application, is accurately described as the worst in the nation.[335] Nevertheless, it is within the sweet spot for the Republican North Carolina General Assembly. It uses the power of law to protect and bolster the advantages of the wealthy and powerful and, in this instance, the cruel, while it jeopardizes, penalizes, and endangers the weak and marginalized. It rewards big donors and handicaps their adversaries. It is premised upon dissembling justifications. It attempts to use the North Carolina courts to further hamper equality and access to justice. And it carries out its suppressive agenda by violating the most fundamental American constitutional norms—freedom of expression and freedom of the press. And, of course, it wounds and threatens the broad majority of Tar Heels as it shelters a small and abusive economic elite. It reflects, our Republican lawmakers hope, the new North Carolina.

The North Carolina Farm Acts

When Gov. Pat McCrory vetoed the Ag-Gag Act, the North Carolina Senate's strongest advocate for agricultural interests, Brent Jackson (R-Autryville), successfully rallied his troops to override the veto, speaking fervently about defending private property rights and strengthening trespass laws.[336] A few short months later, Senator Jackson had to learn to speak just as passionately out of the other side of his mouth when he became the cosponsor of the North Carolina Farm Act.[337] Centuries-old property and tort rights of private real-estate owners allowing them to sue industrialized hog operations for nuisance were ignominiously stripped by the Jackson-sponsored Farm Act. Suddenly, when poor African-American neighbors obtained a series of large damage awards against massive hog operations causing great and pervasive injuries to their health, well-being, and property, Jackson and other state legislators decided that "defending private property rights" was not all it was cracked up to be. Apparently, for the North Carolina Republican General Assembly, the sanctity of traditional property rights depends upon who is attempting to assert them.

In April 2018 a North Carolina jury awarded $50 million in damages to neighbors of a fifteen-thousand-hog farm in eastern North Carolina. The lawsuit, brought against Murphy-Brown/Smithfield Foods, the largest pork producer in the world, was filed by ten neighbors of the industrial-scale hog operation who claimed that the open-air sewage pits on the property were the source of noxious, sickening, and overpowering odors. The smell produced was so thick, they asserted, it was impossible to remove from their clothes. The plaintiffs focused particularly on the continuing use of "anaerobic lagoons," where hog waste was stored near livestock pens and then liquefied and sprayed onto surrounding fields.[338] The jury readily determined that the farm had unreasonably prevented the complaining neighbors from the full use and enjoyment of their property—the core premise of nuisance law.[339]

The massive punitive damages component of the award was later reduced notably by the federal judge. But a few months later, a second jury gave $25 million to another eastern North Carolina couple in a nuisance case filed against Smithfield Foods. There, the Duplin County property owners complained of injury resulting from the swarms of flies, stench, rumbling trucks and machinery, and, again, the lagoons and waste spray coming from the huge hog farm next door. This time, also, punitive damages were limited by the court, but the message was clear: industrial-scale hog farms were not to be given free license to destroy the quality of life of their neighbors.[340]

The Republican North Carolina General Assembly responded clearly and quickly as well. In late June 2018, lawmakers passed the North Carolina Farm Act, which notably circumscribed a neighboring property owner's ability to file a nuisance action against hog farms. A separate restricting version (H.B. 467) had been enacted a year earlier (in response to the filing of various nuisance claims), limiting the sorts of injuries that could be encompassed by such actions when directed at agricultural or forestry operations. Personal discomfort, annoyance, injuries to health and mental health, and loss of enjoyment were constrained—though they are traditionally countenanced in nuisance suits. Various restrictions on negligence actions and punitive damages were included as well. The 2018 act, passed just weeks after the first verdict was handed down, pressed harder. It required that potential plaintiffs live within a half mile of the offending nuisance and file the suit within a year of the date the hog farm began operating. Another provision said the farm can't be sued for certain classifications of damages if state regulators hadn't assessed civil or criminal penalties on the operation within the last three years.

Rep. Jimmy Dixon had conceded, in the earlier House debates, that the purpose "of the bill is clear. We're trying to limit lawsuits." Sen. Brent Jackson, the bill's cosponsor, who represents parts of the nation's largest hog-producing counties—Duplin, Sampson, and Johnston—openly acknowledged that the statute was a response to the Murphy-Brown/Smithfield losses in federal court. Jackson explained, "The latest court ruling is why I'm so passionate about the bill." Nuisance actions have been afforded by English common law since the 1600s and given credence in North Carolina since even before the adoption of our first state constitution.[341] Protecting toxic polluters had apparently now become more crucial than "defending [traditional] private property rights" (in the ag-gag law) for Senator Jackson. Perhaps it depends on who the plaintiff is.

The Farm Act went so far that even some stalwart Republican leaders objected. Ex–House majority leader Paul Stam wrote to his former colleagues, saying the measure trampled on neighbors' crucial private property rights. Rep. Michael Special (R-New Bern) complained that "if we're going to limit compensatory damages, we ought to do it for everybody.[342] Rep. John Blust (R-Guilford) warned his colleagues not "to rush to bail out a particular defendant." And Democratic governor Roy Cooper objected that "special protection for one industry opens the door to weakening our nuisance laws in other areas which can cause real harm to homeowners, the environment, and everyday North Carolinians." Still, Senator Jackson and his friends pushed on, unimpressed.

Devon Hall, director of the Rural Empowerment Association for Community Help in Duplin County, lives near dozens of industrial hog operations. He objected to the North Carolina Farm Act:

> This is my family's homeplace. I believe that the North Carolina General Assembly overstepped its constitutional grounds to block me or anyone else from seeking justice in court from anyone that has caused unreasonable harm to a neighbor. How is it that the state can take away my community's ability to protect our homes and health? How can that be right?[343]

Article II, section 24, of the North Carolina Constitution bars the legislature from enacting "special laws"—special rights "for a special class or a favored few."[344] North Carolina Central University law professor Brenda Reddix-Smalls objected that "the constitution is very clear that special laws create unreasonable classifications, [and yet legislators] are carving out a business interest against [North Carolina] citizens." The legislature is saying, she added, we "don't give a damn what the courts say."[345] For Professor Reddix-Smalls, the North Carolina Farm Act also presents a potent equal justice concern:

> Here we have a location issue—farms, landfills, prisons—they tend to locate in less dense areas, on cheaper land. That's

> where black people live and gather. It is underestimated how important environmental concerns are in our community.[346]

Of course, the Republican General Assembly has hardly shown itself to be congenial to such racial concerns, unless they are pressed by white people.

"Dismantling"

I'm not an environmental lawyer. The North Carolina "sea level censoring" statute, the ag-gag law, the Farm Act—these are environmental measures in a broad sense, but I've studied them because they are just like the legislative transgressions in every other chapter of this book. They are straightforward, intentional, and brutal abuses of power in which government authority is deployed by the privileged to feather their own nests and to further wound and marginalize the disadvantaged, the impoverished, and the powerless. They are, in this sense, like powerful appropriation chair Sen. Brent Jackson's quiet steps to zero out the state appropriation for Legal Aid of North Carolina in 2014 because a couple of its lawyers had the gall to win cases on behalf of poor farmworkers in eastern North Carolina.[347] Just bully work. Old school.

But the North Carolina General Assembly's environmental agenda is decidedly more overarching, ambitious, and complex than these isolated interventions. And those who do knowledgeably follow the particulars find the same vexing patterns cast on the broader canvass.

Derb Carter, the highly regarded executive director of the Southern Environmental Law Center (SELC), gave a much-noted speech at Duke University in 2015 entitled, "This Is Not My State." He began by saying:

> Many of us, including many present here, have worked for years to protect what is special about North Carolina: our coast and mountains, streams and rivers, water quality and

> air quality, and natural areas. It is hard to even imagine this has happened in North Carolina, in our state. The Philistines have come over the walls. It is not the North Carolina I know, and I want it back.[348]

Carter's address made its way into papers across Carolina.[349] It was later expanded by SELC into a scathing 2016 report, "Dismantled: The North Carolina Government Attack on Environmental Protections."[350] It concluded, perhaps by now unsurprisingly:

> Since 2011, when the current majority took control of the North Carolina General Assembly, every legislative session has seen new laws and amendments to existing laws that have eroded and dismantled important protections for the state's environment. North Carolina's water, air, land, energy, and coastal policies have been assaulted by the state's current leadership. The results have been catastrophic.[351]

I won't rehearse the changes in detail here, but here's a summary: Massive cuts to regulatory agencies and funding for land and water conservation and state parks. Repealing protections for public beaches. Reducing water quality enforcement. Prohibiting environmental commissions and agencies from adopting more stringent regulations than the federal government. Fast tracking fracking and offshore drilling. A changed environmental regulatory mission to one of "customer service." Inadequate regulation and sweetheart deals on leaking coal ash pits. Passing what has been dubbed a "Polluter Protection Act," which would give companies a free pass on enforcement penalties who self-report pollution incidents. And more.[352]

It is important to emphasize, finally, that as the General Assembly has moved to take the state in a dramatically different direction environmentally, it has employed many of the same practices of governing that appear in other arenas—gathering power to itself and restricting the traditional authorities of other government actors.

One of the first general bills passed in 2011 barred North Carolina administrative agencies from enacting more stringent environmental regulations, on various fronts, than the federal government.[353] Every state, of course, must comply with minimum federal regulatory standards. Regardless of local needs, therefore, such "handcuffing" laws assure that North Carolina will be lodged at the bottom of the class in its protecting of air and water quality. For almost thirty years, North Carolina agencies previously had been given the authority, when appropriate, to move to the forefront in environmental stewardship. When the Republicans took over the statehouse, that was abruptly ended. On many fronts, local government environmental authority has been curtailed as well—leaving independent power only in the General Assembly.[354]

The power-grabbing methodology played out stoutly in the General Assembly's controversial treatment of fracking.[355] After many years protecting North Carolina citizens from the perils of hydraulic fracturing for natural gas, in 2012 the legislature lifted the ban on horizontal drilling, as used in fracking.[356] S.B. 786, the "Energy Modernization Act," fast-tracked fracking, authorized permits for exploration, and created the N.C. Oil and Gas Commission to oversee the process. Oddly, legislators not only opened the door to the worrisome procedure; they provided $2 million in taxpayer subsidies to market the practice to energy companies who were apparently reluctant to invest here. The law did little to ensure the safety of North Carolinians from fracking, but it did protect the mix of chemicals and materials drilling companies used to carry out their fracking operations from disclosure—effectively criminalizing the revelation of companies' brew of toxic fluids in a strange reversal of the usual premises of public health.

S.B. 786 also barred counties and municipalities from enacting ordinances that would regulate or prohibit oil and gas exploration in their jurisdictions. Additionally, cities and counties were stopped from imposing a "franchise, privilege, license, income or excise tax on the severing, production, treating, processing, ownership, sale, storage, purchase, marketing or transportation on any energy minerals produced in the state."[357]

Finally, the General Assembly took upon itself the power to appoint the majority of the members of the new N.C. Oil and Gas Commission. So, despite widespread apprehension about the dangers of fracking, the Republican-dominated lawmakers legalized it in the state, forced unwilling taxpayers to subsidize it, protected the harmful concoctions from disclosure, stopped local governments from safeguarding the health of their residents, preempted municipal regulatory powers, and robbed the governor of executive authorities in order to woo and placate the fracking industry. None but the General Assembly should decide upon and regulate fracking. And submission to frackers would be the only response from the General Assembly.

The invasion of executive authority was eventually challenged in the courts by Governor McCrory, placing North Carolina's most powerful Republicans on opposite sides of an important constitutional law dispute.[358] Former governors Jim Hunt (Democrat) and James Martin (Republican) joined McCrory in the suit. They argued that the state constitution and North Carolina separation of powers principles require that the governor retain the capacity to control, through appointment and retention, the makeup and operation of such an executive commission. Accordingly, they said the General Assembly's appointment power grab ought to be deemed impermissible. Legal challenges, opposition by Governor Cooper, and, likely most telling, a dramatic drop in the price of natural gas have combined to keep fracking from taking significant hold in the Tar Heel State. The General Assembly's usurpations of authority, however, have expanded enthusiastically.[359]

The North Carolina Supreme Court agreed. In *State v. Berger*, the justices wrote:

> A frequent recurrence to fundamental principles is absolutely necessary to preserve the blessings of liberty, and the principle of separation of powers is a cornerstone of our state and

> federal governments. In the current constitution, Article III, Section 5(4) gives the Governor the duty to take care that the laws be faithfully executed. The Governor must have enough control over [the contested commission] to perform his constitutional duty. When [the legislatively appointed] officers form a majority on a commission that has the final say on how to execute the laws, the General Assembly, not the Governor, can exert most of the control over the executive policy that is implemented in any area of the law that the commission regulates. As a result, the Governor cannot take care that the laws are faithfully executed in that area. The separation of powers clause plainly and clearly does not allow the General Assembly to take this much control over the execution of the laws from the Governor and lodge it with itself.[360]

The General Assembly, in other words, has the power to enact the laws of North Carolina but not the power to enforce them. Not only did the fracking red-carpet package introduced by the Energy Modernization Act impose a dangerous policy upon North Carolina; it violated the fundamental structures of state government in the process. It was an abuse of powers for destructive ends. It crippled governing norms as it altered substantive policies. As the following three chapters demonstrate, that combination—violating centuries-old traditions of North Carolina and American governmental practice to gather power to itself and to privilege its policies from democratic constitutional review—has become a hallmark of the Republican-dominated North Carolina General Assembly.

CHAPTER EIGHT

Attacking the Independence of the Courts

The Republican majority has a right to initiate radical reform. Everybody else has a right to sue them. That's why Supreme Court races are critical for long-term Republican dominance. Lose the courts, lose the war. —John Davis, North Carolina Republican political consultant, 2013 report, "How the NC Republican Party Can Maintain Political Power for 114 Years"[361]

That reaction could be re-amending the Constitution, censure, adding positions to the court and/or impeachment. —Dallas Woodhouse, executive director, N.C. Republican Party, August 2018, announcing the likely Republican legislative response to disfavored judicial decisions[362]

The North Carolina judiciary is under siege as Republicans seek to rip the blindfold of impartiality from Lady Justice. —Rep. Joe John (D-Wake), elected in 2016 after serving twenty-five years as a state judge[363]

Since Roy Cooper was elected governor in 2016—breaking the Republican lock on at least one branch of North Carolina government—he has twice delivered a traditional State of the State address. On each occasion, Cooper was conciliatory and consensus-building; he is generally moderate and thoughtful by temperament. Over a long career, he has been bipartisan, congenial, agreeable, and almost definingly responsible. I am, sadly, sometimes referred to as a "firebrand." To his strong credit, no one has ever called Roy Cooper that.

After each of Cooper's thoughtful, unifying, and hopeful State of the Union addresses, North Carolina Republicans have chosen

Senate leader Phil Berger—clearly the most politically powerful man in the state—to offer the loyal opposition's reply. Here the tone is notably different. Berger isn't much of an orator. And he is existentially angry and disagreeable. So, it's an understatement to say that when he replies to Cooper's address, the mood changes.

To be candid, I've never understood what Senator Berger has to be so mad about. He gets his way on almost everything. But, I suppose, Berger's disposition is ultimately none of my business. And more relevant to this project, my real objection to Berger's approach is the oddity of what he says, not how he says it.

Phil Berber has developed the strange habit of making sweeping, generalized, overarching statements about the Republican General Assembly's agenda and legislative record that are comically inaccurate—almost as if he takes bold pride in declaring, "We gather tonight to celebrate the fact that, as we've demonstrated, the sun rises in the west and descends happily in the east." Here are some examples.

In March 2017 Berger said that the entire revolutionary Republican platform of the past six years was guided by a single maxim—Henry David Thoreau's adage "that government is best which governs least."[364] Most folks shook their heads, as if perhaps they'd misheard. There are a lot of ways to characterize the bathroom bill, the forced abortion sonogram/legislatively mandated doctor script bill, the ban on LGBTQ+ people marrying their chosen partners, the new license for magistrates to discriminate against North Carolina taxpayers they don't like, and the endless cascade of hurdles passed by Republicans to make it harder to vote. But letting folks chill isn't one of them. If Thoreau were alive, he'd drown himself in Walden Pond.

Next time, in 2019, just as remarkably, Senator Berger explained, "We came into power in 2010 with a simple philosophy, providing an equal opportunity for success to everyone willing to work for it." Republicans believe "every person deserves a fair shot, regardless of zip code, color, or family income."[365] No kidding. He said that.

Equal opportunity was apparently the defining mission when Republicans took to their closed-door, all-white caucuses in the House and Senate to repeal the Racial Justice Act, deliver the most racially punitive electoral districts in American history, alter election rules with precision to handicap black voters, eliminate state race discrimination suits, further racially segregate the public schools, and protect police camera footage from public disclosure. I guess it was a good thing the White People's Party was on equality's side.

Then, as if to test the traditions of the English language, Berger protested that Governor Cooper and the Democrats have attacked the North Carolina judiciary, "which should be the least political branch of government, to frustrate the will of the people of our great state." The jaws of all within earshot fell to the basement. This claim—that it's the Democrats who are going after the judiciary in North Carolina—will be the focus of this chapter. I begin with a simple assertion: no one in North Carolina, including Berger himself, could possibly believe that what he said is true. Even beyond that, the entire country understands that the Republican General Assembly of North Carolina has, in the last eight years, unleashed an attack on the independence of the state courts unparalleled in modern American history. Berger speaking up for judicial independence is no more farcical than Donald Trump speaking up for honesty.

A quick spoiler alert: Berger's boys have required that judges' races be partisan, they have abolished public funding of judicial campaigns, they've limited judicial review of legislative acts, manipulated the size of the Court of Appeals for partisan gains, passed (an invalidated) law to try to protect an incumbent Republican justice from being required to stand for reelection, attempted to dramatically constrict the governor's judicial appointment powers, threatened disobedient judges with impeachment, interfered with individual supreme court justice elections, gerrymandered disfavored Wake and Mecklenburg county judges' districts, moved to intimidate judges from protecting the rights of low-income criminal defendants as the constitution requires, threatened all 403 state judges with two-year electoral terms (shortest in the country), cancelled the judges' 2018 primary election, and intervened statutorily to put Phil Berger's son at the top of the ballot in a Court of Appeals race.[366] Who knew the majority leader believed in judicial independence and the rule of law? Certainly no lawyer or judge in North Carolina.

But I won't ask you to take my word for it. Not long after the 2019 State of the State address, Berger again attacked Cooper's record on the judiciary. Highlighting a headline in the local papers reporting, "North Carolina Republican legislative leader Phil Berger Criticizes Democratic Governor Cooper for Not Appointing Republican to State Supreme Court," the country's leading election law scholar, Rick Hasen of the University of California, Irvine, wrote of Berger's astonishing "chutzpah":

> This coming from someone who has done more (than anyone) to make North Carolina a partisan battleground is too, too rich. . . . From an extreme partisan gerrymander which was defended solely on grounds that it helps Republicans, to voter ID amendment put on the ballot after the last law was struck down as unconstitutional (targeting African-American voters "with almost surgical precision") to multiple attempts to deprive the Democratic governor of the power governors have had to multiple attempts to try to change the partisan power of state election boards in Republicans' favor, Berger has had a hand in all of them. Just wow.[367]

The Republican Assault on the Courts

As the brief listing above suggests, the Republican General Assembly's agenda to dominate the North Carolina state courts has been an extraordinarily fulsome one. It has also become as extensive as it is relentless. Too extensive, in candor, to be fully explored in a book of this length. So, I'll limit myself to a few of the major categories of legislative intervention: tampering with judicial elections, limiting the powers of and altering the structure of the courts, attempting to affect the selection process and terms of judges, and, somewhat distinctly, forcing North Carolina judges to criminalize poverty—bringing together two of the General Assembly's favored pastimes, bullying judges and targeting poor people.

As a package, the record reveals an astonishing rejection of judicial independence. It reflects an energetic move to destroy traditions of judicial review central to both the rule of law and the American constitutional experience. It is also testament to the Republican General Assembly's broad attempt to draw all authorities to itself, despite historic commitments to separated powers.

Tampering with Judicial Elections

I suppose the most obvious way to control state courts is to control who gets elected to the judiciary. In 2013 the General Assembly ditched a popular, successful, and nationally lauded public financing system for judicial elections that had been in place for roughly a decade.[368] Art Pope, right-wing mega-funder and McCrory administration budget director, played a central role in ending public financing. The system was initially defunded; then the General Assembly repealed it outright, unsurprisingly, as part of the massive voter suppression law of 2013.[369]

Two years later, Republican legislators undertook a bizarre step to protect incumbent Republican supreme court justice Robert Edmunds from being defeated at the polls. Since Edmunds was the only high court member up for reelection, the General Assembly passed a statute providing for retention elections for state supreme court justices (at least, most folks thought, temporarily).[370] The law was declared unconstitutional as a direct, straightforward textual violation of the North Carolina constitution.[371] Justice Edmunds was then defeated by African-American Democrat Michael Morgan at the polls.[372]

Markedly unhappy with this result, the Republican General Assembly passed a statute requiring that party affiliation be listed in all future state appellate and supreme court elections.[373] Partisan affiliation was extended to district and superior court races in March 2017. North Carolina thus became the first state in nearly a century to switch from nonpartisan to partisan judicial elections. Experts had noted, unsurprisingly, that choosing judges in expensive, partisan elections "discourages many highly qualified lawyers from aspiring to the bench."[374] Late 2016 was also flooded with rumors that the Republican legislators planned to expand and pack the North Carolina Supreme Court, though no actual bill was introduced. A statute was passed, however, to insert the Court of Appeals, which maintained a Republican majority, into the constitutional litigation process, making it more difficult for constitutional questions to reach the state supreme court with a new Democratic majority.[375]

In 2017 the legislature continued the onslaught. In April a statute was passed reducing the size of the Court of Appeals by preventing Governor Cooper from appointing replacements for the next three retiring appellate judges. The move was seen as so egregiously partisan that it prompted Republican Court of Appeals judge Doug McCullough to retire early, before the provision took effect, to allow Cooper to appoint a replacement, keeping the court at its full complement.[376] Months later, hoping to improve incumbent Republican judges' electoral prospects, the General Assembly eliminated primary elections for judges running for office in 2018, ostensibly due to time constraints associated with proposed judicial redistricting plans.[377] Governor Cooper, however, wasn't buying it, calling the action yet another "part of an effort to 'rig the system.' "[378]

Soon after, the General Assembly passed a statute attempting to prevent a disfavored Republican supreme court candidate from being listed as a Republican on the ballot. Republican leaders also changed ballot order listing rules to ensure that Senator Berger's son would be listed on the top line in his (eventually unsuccessful) Court of Appeals race. By 2018, North Carolina judicial races were subject to constantly shifting rules and constantly moving goalposts. All were designed with a sole purpose: electing Republican judges.

In October 2017 the Republican leadership sought to apply the unconstitutional gerrymandering practices they had mastered in the legislative redistricting processes to judicial elections. The House Judiciary Committee passed a judicial redistricting bill pressed by Stanly County bail bondsman Rep. Justin Burr.[379] He announced the bill by Twitter, providing less than forty-eight hours' notice, seeking swift passage. When asked if judges or the state bar or the administrative office of the courts had been consulted about the redistricting plan, Burr responded, "No, I am the legislator, I make the laws."[380] The bill would have "double-bunked" one quarter of incumbent district court judges. More than 40 percent of all black judges were placed in a district with another incumbent. The state's only Latina judge and its only Native American Superior Court judge received the same treatment. (Once again, people of color happened to receive wildly disparate treatment from secretly developed, Republican, white-caucus-hatched redistricting plans. I'm sure there was some "neutral" reason. They always have one ready.)

Maps were designated to give Republican candidates the majority of Buncombe County's judicial seats, though most Buncombe voters pick Democrats according to the *Asheville Citizen-Times*.[381] Such distortion was apparently thought necessary to ensure a clean sweep of the North Carolina government. One person, one vote is old-school. And apparently so is the Voting Rights Act. Burr's plan stirred such virulent opposition from judges and the legal community that it failed to achieve passage in the Senate. Apparently there are some limits, even in the Republican Party—but not until the entire state erupts. In June 2018 the General Assembly did manage to override Governor Cooper's veto to redraw the districts of disfavored judges in Wake and Mecklenburg counties prior to the November elections. Cooper complained that such "piecemeal attempts to target judges show contempt for the North Carolina judiciary."[382] That apparently was the goal.

Michael Crowell, former associate director of the Institute of Government at the University of North Carolina, who is not affiliated with either party, explained:

> Anybody who has been around for a while will tell you what's happened in the last few years is on a different level than anything done before. The common feature is that so much of it seems to be designed to manipulate the election process. The legislature doesn't like the courts, doesn't like the judges on the courts. It wants to change who they are, and they don't seem to care how they go about it.[383]

Altering the Structure of Judicial Review

Of course, trying to change who gets elected to the courts is not the only way to mess with the judiciary. It is also possible to alter the powers of the courts, the rules under which they operate. Here the Republican General Assembly has been active as well. In 2014, apparently unhappy with a string of early superior court decisions invalidating several of their statutes, legislators changed the process for litigating constitutional challenges to their work product. The new provision required determination of such cases by a three-judge panel appointed by the chief justice of the state supreme court.[384] Because then–chief justice Mark Martin was a reliable and enthusiastic Republican partisan, legislative leaders no doubt felt assured of more congenial outcomes.[385] The American constitutional system has long recognized the dangers that can arise when legislators seek too bold a control over the powers of judicial review. Lawmakers can be inclined to attempt to shield their own constitutional transgressions—in effect performing the combined roles of legislating and adjudicating. North Carolina Republicans were apparently anxious to accomplish the fusion, thus crushing the rule of law.

Soon, however, other urgent demands entered. In 2016 Democrats won a thin majority of seats on the North Carolina Supreme Court despite Republican legislative efforts to interfere with the election.[386] As a result, the General Assembly reinserted the Court of Appeals, which still maintained a Republican majority, into the constitutional litigation process, thus making it more difficult for constitutional questions to reach a state supreme court with a new and apparently unwelcome Democratic majority.[387] Different rules for different times. One supposes that if the Republicans regain control of the supreme court, they will simply change the standards yet again. All yields before partisan legislative ascendancy. Thank God that Phil Berger and his boys stand ready to ensure that the courts are independent from politics.

Threatening Judges

It is also apparently thought to be effective, or at least irresistible, for the state's most powerful legislators to threaten purportedly wayward judges. Senate leader Phil Berger and House Speaker Tim Moore warned ominously in 2017, when a lower court issued an unfavorable order in another constitutional challenge:

> Judges are not legislators and if these three men want to make laws, they should hang up their robes and run for a legislative seat. Their decision to legislate from the bench will have profound consequences, and they should immediately reconvene their panel and reverse their order.[388]

One of the judges on the panel was sufficiently moved to file a complaint with the state ethics board.[389] Berger and Moore, both of whom are lawyers, were surely unmoved. Small wonder that months later, when Dallas Woodhouse, executive director of the North Carolina Republican Party, suggested that legislators might well impeach any judges or justices who ruled against the General Assembly on challenges to constitutional amendments placed on the ballot, neither Berger nor Moore condemned him.[390] Bullying is contagious.

There is also more than one way to threaten. Seemingly taking up the Berger-Moore dicta, Senate Rules Chair Bill Rabon introduced S.B. 698, entitled the "Increase Voter Accountability of Judges Resolution."[391] It called for the enactment of a constitutional amendment to end every North Carolina judge's term at the close of 2018. Thereafter, all 403 state judges—district court, superior court, court of appeals, and supreme court—would have their terms reduced to two years. Presently, North Carolina district court judges are elected to four-year terms. All others serve for eight. Unsurprisingly, no American state has adopted two-year terms for its judges—believing it would crush judicial independence and effectiveness.

Clearing the whole offending slate and forcing them to run constant, expensive, relentless, and hyperpartisan campaigns was thought, somehow, to be the answer. No matter that judges take oaths to be accountable to the law and the constitution, not to the voters. Or that jurists would be left with little time to do their actual jobs, given the demands of perpetual campaigning. Party fealty, again, was all that mattered. Independent, professional, reasoned judicial decision-making—the rule of law—is apparently passé. Who needs it in New Carolina? Nation-leading gerrymander artist State Rep. David Lewis explained, "If you are going to act like a legislator, [we're going to] make you run like one."[392]

Caryn McNeill, president of the North Carolina Bar Association, explained her organization's staunch opposition:

> Nowhere in America do voters elect their general jurisdiction judges for two-year terms of office. This is as it should be. Electing judges for two-year terms would force judges to campaign and raise money constantly, and would disrupt the ad-

> ministration of justice. Judicial terms of office are longer than executive and legislative terms of office because judges have a different function. Judges are accountable, first and foremost, to the federal and state constitutions and the law. They apply the law uniformly, and equal justice under law is the ultimate goal of any court system. The people of North Carolina should have a meaningful role in the judicial selection and retention process, just as citizens do around the country. But two-year terms are not the answer.[393]

Rep. Marcia Morey (D-Durham), a former chief district court judge, called it "an unprecedented power grab by the zealous GOP leadership to control the judiciary."[394] Former Republican state supreme court justice Robert Orr described the whole venture as "a punitive threat,"[395] a "continued effort to try to intimidate the judiciary": "There is this sense of 'we have all the power, so if we want to shaft you, we'll shaft you.' I appeal to my fellow Republicans: Let's be the party of good government. Let's not be the party of coercive government."[396]

Appointing Judges

In fall 2017 Senate leader Berger appointed a commission to draft proposals to reform the process of judicial selection. All four of the commission plans submitted gave the General Assembly itself broad authority in the selection of judges.[397] On June 20, 2018, Berger's office announced the result of months of "deliberation" over judicial appointments and elections. Under Berger's proposal, which would require voters to approve a constitutional amendment, vacant judicial seats would no longer be filled by the governor. Instead, the General Assembly would choose two candidates, one of whom the governor would select. The proposed system would leave in place judicial elections, as earlier proposals to move all judicial selection to a system dominated by the General Assembly drew very intense public criticism. Legislative sponsors issued a joint public statement indicating, "It is clear that North Carolinians want to elect their judges."[398]

Retired Wake County Chief Judge Donald Stephens had sounded the alarm about legislative overreach. "Although they will call it 'merit selection,' I assure you it will be partisan selection; it would be a disaster." They "plan to take over the courts to appoint their own judges . . . so when we challenge them, we won't have anywhere else to go." State Rep. Joe John (D-Wake), who was elected to the state House after serving twenty-five years as a judge, warned that "the North Carolina judiciary is under siege. Republicans seek to rip the blindfold of impartiality from Lady Justice."[399]

As the November 2018 elections approached, North Carolina's six living former supreme court chief justices took the unprecedented step of joining forces to publicly oppose the judicial selection amendment. The former chief justices—two Republican and four Democrats—said the amendment purported to introduce a "non-partisan, merit-based system" for judicial appointments but was, instead, "partisan and not merit-based." Chief Justices Rhoda Billins, I. Beverly Lake, James Exum, Henry Frye, Burley Mitchell, and Sarah Parker said, "All of us will vote against" the amendment; "we urge you to vote against" it; and "we urge you to join us in advocating for [its] defeat."

Unrepentant, House Rules Committee Chairman David Lewis of Harnett County dismissed the chief justices' concerns: "I hope that when I'm retired in my eighties I don't have to seek relevance in this way."[400] North Carolina voters defeated the judicial selection amendment handily at the polls, apparently siding with the chief justices rather than Lewis, the nation's most famous electoral gerrymanderer.[401]

Bullying Judges to Criminalize Poverty

I add one final category of legislative interference with judicial independence, though it is different in kind, if not in motivation.

These moves are not designed to remove or replace judges, to limit their terms, to formally alter judicial powers, or to make judges more overtly partisan. They are, however, potently aimed at intimidating judges from doing what their jobs demand and, often, from enforcing the constitution. They are less noted and perhaps less notorious than the bullying measures previously described. They are worthy of examination, however, because they bring together two of the North Carolina Republican General Assembly's favored themes—interfering with judges and crushing poor people.

Over the past two decades, North Carolina has created one of the country's most robust and extensive schedules of "user fees" to help pay for the operation of the criminal justice system. A guilty plea for even a modest nonviolent offense is often accompanied by hundreds or thousands of dollars in fee-based financial obligations—for court costs, lawyers, witnesses, experts, probation, community service, sheriffs' fees, law enforcement retirement plans, and the like. Since almost all criminal defendants are indigent, the fees represent a formidable set of hardships for most litigants. Huge numbers become trapped in a cycle of poverty. Increased debts and ancillary punishments—probation extensions, license revocations, and sometimes even incarceration—often result. Constitutional rights are routinely sacrificed. And a Kafkaesque bureaucratic scheme develops whereby the criminal courts, meant to benefit us all, are purportedly sustained through exactions from the least plausible set of economic actors—impoverished, heavily sanctioned, often unemployed, and prospectless defendants.[402]

North Carolina has joined its impressive list of judicial user fees with what is likely the nation's most aggressive enforcement scheme.[403] Both the federal constitution and North Carolina law frequently require, or at least allow, that most fees and costs be waived in instances where their imposition would criminalize litigants for their poverty or effectively annul constitutionally protected liberties. Since 2011, the General Assembly has worked steadily to restrain this traditional judicial authority. Though waiver occurs in only a tiny percentage of cases—less than 5 percent statewide—legislators have moved repeatedly to close the door even further.

The push to curtail waiver was initiated by a procedural requirement mandating that judges issue a "written finding of just cause" before granting relief. The next year, 2012, the requirement was expanded to include fully elucidated "findings of fact and conclusions of law." Well enough, I suppose. But in 2014, legislators doubled down, mandating an administrative report listing the number of waivers granted for every judge and judicial district. We're apparently the only state to demand such a published roster. Judges call it the "shaming report."

In 2017 the legislature piled on. It amended the court fees law to prohibit any waiver unless "notice and opportunity to be heard" are presented to all government entities potentially receiving court fee funds. The notice must proceed by first-class mail to a massive number of agencies at least fifteen days before any granted waiver. This too is a first-in-the-nation hurdle—eating up time and money and requiring secondary hearings. State judges believe the goal is to "make the process so burdensome [we] simply won't bother."[404]

The "shaming report" and purposeless notice requirement unconstitutionally interfere with the independence and integrity of North Carolina tribunals. It is impermissible to grant courts the authority to decide waiver issues—especially ones of constitutional import—and then place a legislatively crafted thumb on the scale of determination. Federal courts have held such coercive schemes to be unacceptable efforts to intimidate a coequal branch of government. Last year, the American Bar Association passed a formal resolution declaring "no law or rule should limit a judge's ability to waive or reduce any fee when payment would cause substantial hardship."[405]

Our General Assembly tells judges: You have the power to issue waivers in cases of potent economic hardship, but if you use it, we'll punish you by making you step through massive procedural hurdles and your name will be published on a blacklist. If, on the other hand, you deny a requested waiver, we'll smile, nod our approval, and let you be. We're holding down the scales for a reason. We don't want judges to grant waivers. Even when the law demands it. Wise up, your honor, or pay the cost.

It is bad enough to, yet again, interfere with the independence of the North Carolina judiciary. It's even worse to abuse your power to force judges to further criminalize poverty.

Independent judicial review is one of the historic cornerstones of American government. A written constitution is essential. Restricting government authority through a bill of rights is vital. But unless these measures are made meaningfully enforceable through a system of independent courts, they broadly fail. The foundationally American notion of judicial review has been repeatedly proven to be a sine qua non (an essential part) of successful constitutional democracy.

Marbury v. Madison, the most important judicial decision in Western history, concluded that it is "emphatically the province of the judicial branch to say what the law is."[406] Without the constraining power of independent courts, *Marbury* ruled, our prized Constitution becomes a "mere parchment barrier." If independent legal constraints do not actually bind legislative adventurism, the constitution becomes whatever ambitious and powerful lawmakers say it is. Power becomes boundless. Liberty dissolves.

When newly retired Wake County chief judge Donald Stephens—likely North Carolina's most respected trial judge—was scheduled to testify before a legislative committee dealing with judicial selection in late 2017, the chairman, Republican Dan Bishop, author of H.B. 2, refused to allow him to appear. Stephens's proposed written remarks included the following:

> I believe in a fiercely independent judiciary. A judiciary elected by the people. A judiciary that has no constituency except its duty to the constitution of this state and to the Constitution of the United States, and to the laws enacted in conformity with those mandates. North Carolina is entitled to have judges who make decisions without regard to partisan politics or any improper pressure or influence. That is how the judicial branch of government should work.[407]

It is no wonder the North Carolina Republicans tried to shut him up.

CHAPTER NINE

An Assault on Democracy

I think electing Republicans is better than electing Democrats, so I drew this map to help foster what I think is better for the country. We used [redistricting] criteria to gain [political] advantage. [I sought] to give partisan advantage to 10 Republicans and 3 Democrats because [I] didn't believe it possible to draw a map for 11 Republicans and 2 Democrats. —Rep. David Lewis, architect of redistricting laws in North Carolina House of Representatives, cited by federal court as reflecting "extreme partisanship bias of historic magnitude, not just relative to North Carolina history, but that of the United States"[408]

Once partisan goals trump democratic commitments, everything is on the table. —Brendan Nyhan, political science professor, University of Michigan[409]

Over a half century ago, the U.S. Supreme Court ruled emphatically in *Harper v. Virginia Board of Electors* that the right to vote is fundamental to the American democracy and subject to the most searching judicial protection.[410] The right to vote, the justices further explained in *Reynolds v. Sims*, is "preservative of all rights," so any infringement strikes at the heart of the substantive rights and privileges guaranteed by the Constitution.[411] The 1965 Voting Rights Act was passed on a broad bipartisan basis.[412] Its 1972 amendments were passed on almost unanimous votes by the Congress.[413] All of this is to say that, two decades ago, I would not have thought it possible that a major American political party, much less North Carolina's dominant political party, would embrace as a central tenet of its policy agenda the suppression of the voting and electoral rights of some of its citizens. But that is precisely what the North Carolina Republican General Assembly has done over the last decade.

Nor have the Republican generals been satisfied with mere voter and representational suppression—though many would reasonably cast a crusade against the electoral franchise as among the worst transgressions conceivable in a democracy. American constitutional traditions are chock-full of less concretely defined but equally crucial and hard-won standards—notions like an appropriate separation of powers, the independent enforcement authorities of elected attorney generals and prosecutors, deference to local elections and decision-makers, respect for defining limits on the exercise of legislative powers, and the like. Here, too, as we saw was the case with interference with state courts and judicial review, usurping legislators have thrown aside deeply established and essential standards in the pursuit of an all-encompassing demand for expanded power.

If constitutional law embraces both hard legal norms and sometimes softer restraining conventions to protect against tyranny, the North Carolina Republican General Assembly, since 2011, has flattened both to accumulate and further entrench its powers. Dominating lawmakers have not been satisfied to use the tools of democracy to alter the substantive rules that govern life in the state. They have moved, repeatedly, to dismantle democratic traditions themselves to punish their adversaries and expand their burgeoning authorities. All that has mattered, literally, is an emboldened and ahistorical zeal for power.

Literal, Old-School Voter Suppression

As soon as North Carolina Republicans secured all three branches of state government in 2013, they enacted what national election law experts deemed the most ambitious voter suppression statute passed by an American state government in a half century.[414]

Three years later, yet another unanimous federal court invalidated the statute in a sweeping ruling.[415] The Fourth Circuit panel determined that the North Carolina General Assembly's "omnibus" election statute selectively chose voter ID requirements, reduced the number of early voting days, eliminated same-day registration and out-of-precinct voting, and changed voter registration procedures in ways explicitly designed to harm its electoral adversaries. That was the case, the court ruled, even though the state "failed to identify even a single individual who has ever been charged with committing in-person voter fraud in North Carolina." The judges did find evidence of past "fraud in absentee voting by mail," a method of voting used heavily by Republicans but "exempted" from the strictures of the new law.

The crafted regulations were not designed to ensure electoral integrity, as the General Assembly claimed, the judges ruled. "The asserted justifications cannot and do not conceal the State's true [suppressive] motivation," the court held. The new rules "impose cures for problems that do not exist." Upon receiving various arrays of voting data, "the General Assembly enacted legislation that restricted voting and registration in five different ways," each of which "disproportionately penalized" their adversaries. The moves intentionally violated both the U.S. Constitution and the federal Voting Rights Act. The legislative history of the 2013 act "cumulatively and unmistakably reveals that the General Assembly used the law to entrench itself." Once again, amassing and retaining power guided Republican efforts, not any neutral effort to secure fair elections. When legislators said otherwise, the judges determined, they purposefully misled the people of North Carolina.

The attorney general of the United States, North Carolina native Loretta Lynch, praised the court's ruling: "The ability of Americans to have a voice in the direction of their country—to have a fair and free opportunity to help write the story of this nation—is fundamental to who we are and who we aspire to be."[416]

Republican governor Pat McCrory whined that the intruding federal judges were "undermining the integrity of our elections while also maligning our state."[417] The U.S. Supreme Court refused to overturn the Fourth Circuit ruling. Dale Ho, the national director of the ACLU's Voting Rights Project, cheered that "an ugly chapter in voter suppression is finally closing." Turns out Mr. Ho spoke too soon.[418]

More ominously, and more accurately, Sen. Phil Berger and Speaker Tim Moore issued a statement saying they'd not yet begun to fight: "All North Carolinians can rest assured that Republican legislators will continue fighting to protect the integrity of our elections." The federal courts again deployed a different definition of *integrity* than the Republican leviathan.[419] Some months later, the Republican suppression agenda would be highlighted on the front page of the *New York Times* with a story entitled, "Arrested, Jailed and Charged with a Felony. For Voting." A young black man named Keith Sellars had been arrested, handcuffed, and taken to jail, while his two daughters cried in the back seat of his car, for voting in the 2016 election while still on parole. "I didn't know," Sellars said. "I thought I was practicing my right."[420] "That's the law," Pat Nadolski, the Republican district attorney from Alamance County said coldly. "We're going to prosecute." Nadolski had, apparently, received the message. So had the people of North Carolina.

Crushing Democrats

North Carolina conducted two congressional elections under a plan developed in 2011 (as discussed in chapter 2), which was later declared to be an unconstitutional racial gerrymander. In 2016, with both chambers of the General Assembly still controlled by Republicans and, as the federal courts noted, elected under one of the most widespread gerrymanders ever confronted by a federal court,[421] Rep. David Lewis and Sen. Bob Rucho again took charge of Republican congressional redistricting efforts. The result, this time, was the enactment of what scholars, historians, and once again, the federal courts concluded was the most blatant, pervasive, biased, and unapologetic political gerrymander in American history.[422] Rick Hasen, a professor at the University of California, Irvine, called the new North Carolina gerrymander "the most brazen and egregious" political electoral distortion yet seen in the United States. North Carolina leaders, he wrote, "admitted the practice but argued it should be seen as perfectly legal."[423]

Representative Lewis was stunningly candid in describing his purposes. The goal "in drawing this map is to gain partisan advantage." This was, he said openly, "a political gerrymander," which, he opined, "is not against the law": "I think electing Republicans is better than electing Democrats. So I drew this map to help foster what I think is better for the country."

The reviewing federal court was unsuccessful in keeping its jaw from dropping. Rarely had venality been so pointedly embraced, cheating so enthusiastically disclosed. Putting a cap on it, Representative Lewis added that he drew the maps to give a partisan advantage to ten Republicans and three Democrats "because [he did] not believe [it would be] possible to draw a map with 11 Republicans and 2 Democrats." The "goal" of the whole effort, the map's author explained, was "to elect 10 Republicans and 3 Democrats."[424] Welcome to the new North Carolina. If you don't like it, move to Massachusetts.

The federal court ruled Lewis had gotten it badly wrong: "Partisan gerrymandering—the drawing of legislative district lines to subordinate adherents of one political party and entrench a rival party in power—strikes at the heart of foundational constitutional principle." Partisan gerrymanders "raise the specter that Government may effectively drive certain ideas or viewpoints from the marketplace." That is precisely, the judges held, what the Republican-controlled North Carolina General Assembly sought to do with the 2016 congressional plan:

> [Rucho and Lewis] drew a plan designed to subordinate the interests of non-Republican voters not because they believe doing so advances any democratic, constitutional, or public interest, but because, as the chief legislative map drawer openly acknowledged, *the General Assembly's Republican majority* "think[s] electing Republicans is better than electing Democrats." But that is not a choice the Constitution allows legislative map drawers to make. Rather, "those who govern should be the *last* people to help decide who *should* govern." Indeed, "the core principle of [our] republican government [is] that the voters should choose their representatives, not the other way around.[425]

Accordingly, the General Assembly's plan, yet again, was ruled unconstitutional:

> In sum, we find that Plaintiffs' statewide evidence establishes that the General Assembly drew and enacted the 2016 Plan with a predominant intent to subordinate the interests of non-Republican voters and entrench Republican control of North Carolina's congressional delegation. [The Constitution] does not permit the government "to restrict the political participation of some in order to enhance the relative influence of others." A common thread runs through the restrictions on state elections imposed by Article I, the First Amendment and the Equal Protection clause: the Constitution does not allow elected officials to enact laws to intentionally favor certain political beliefs, parties or candidates and disfavor others.[426]

Michael Li, senior counsel for the Brennan Center for Justice's Democracy Program, summed the case up this way:

> If the North Carolina map isn't constitutionally problematic, it's hard to see what would be. North Carolina Republicans didn't just get caught red-handed robbing the bank, they had

a press conference beforehand and said, "We are going to rob the bank."[427]

Representative Lewis also proved that at the outermost extreme, arrogance can become so pronounced that it accidentally leads to candor.

The U.S. Supreme Court eventually decided that there was no federal court jurisdiction in the *Rucho* case—it represented a political question. Chief Justice Roberts indicated that such "excessive partisanship leads to results that reasonably seem unjust," and he cited a previous ruling calling political gerrymandering "incompatible with democratic principles"—but such evils should be directed to the Congress, not the courts.[428] Justice Elena Kagan responded in dissent that political gerrymandering is "anti-democratic in the most profound sense" because it deprives people of the ability to fully choose who represents them. The "practices challenged in [this] case imperil our system of government . . . the foundation of free and fair elections." Kagan expressed "deep sadness" that the conservative majority of the court had determined not to do its job. "Of all times to abandon the law, this was not the one," she complained.

> The partisan gerrymanders in these cases deprived citizens of the most fundamental of their constitutional rights: the rights to participate equally in the political process, to join with others to advance political beliefs, and to choose their political representatives. In so doing, the partisan gerrymanders here debased and dishonored our democracy, turning upside down the core American idea that all governmental power derives from the people. These gerrymanders enabled politicians to entrench themselves in office as against voters' preferences. They promoted partisanship above respect for the popular will. They encouraged a politics of polarization and dysfunction. If left unchecked, gerrymanders like the ones here may irreparably damage our system of government.[429]

Since the U.S. Supreme Court rejected the *Rucho* case on federal jurisdictional grounds, that left open the possibility that state courts would come to the opposite conclusion about the legality of extreme partisan gerrymandering under the provisions of the North Carolina Constitution. That is precisely what occurred in *Common Cause v. Lewis* in September 2019.[430] There, a unanimous three-judge court (with both Republican and Democratic judges) explained:

> The issue before the Court is distilled to simply this: whether the constitutional rights of North Carolina citizens are infringed when the General Assembly, for purposes of retaining power, draws district maps with a predominant intent to favor voters aligned with one political party at the expense of other voters, and in fact achieves results that manifest this intent and cannot be explained by other non-partisan considerations.[431]

The judges found that the 2017 state legislative maps had been drawn by the General Assembly with the partisan aim of perpetuating Republican control, that lawmakers had deployed that intention "with surgical precision," and that their efforts reflected "extreme outliers" of partisanship. Accordingly, "it [was] the carefully crafted maps, not the will of the voters, that dictated the election outcomes in a significant number of legislative districts and, ultimately, the majority control of the General Assembly." Such purposeful and pervasive cheating, the judges held, violated the central tenets of the North Carolina Constitution.[432] A few months later, another state court ruled that North Carolina's congressional districts were unconstitutional political gerrymanders as well—taking the explicit step the United States Supreme Court had avoided in *Rucho*. Eric Holder, former United States attorney general, wrote that "for nearly a decade, Republicans have forced the people of North Carolina to vote in districts that were manipulated for their own partisan advantage. . . . [N]ow, finally, the era of Republican gerrymandering in the state is coming to an end."[433]

Delaying to Avoid Compliance—Breaking the Bonds of Consent

In 2016 the federal courts held that the North Carolina Republican General Assembly's state redistricting plan violated the equal protection clause of the Fourteenth Amendment (discussed in chapter 2). The ruling was summarily affirmed, without dissent, by the U.S. Supreme Court.[434] After various legislative delays and excuses, the successful plaintiffs petitioned the federal court to order a special election to remedy the constitutional violation. Ultimately, the district court determined that the constrained time frame made such a remedy impractical. But the impatient jurists also made clear that the massive constitutional violation—when accompanied by repeated (successful) legislative attempts to delay implementation—effectively broke the bonds of consent between the Republican General Assembly and the people of North Carolina.

> These harms have persisted for over six years, tainting three separate election cycles and six statewide elections. Even after the Court deemed the existing maps unconstitutional, it granted the State's request to conduct the November 2016 election using the invalidated maps due to the infeasibility of enacting remedial districting plans. This constitutional violation has infected so many elections and deprived North Carolinians of constitutionally adequate representation during numerous state legislative sessions [that it] enhances the severity [of the violations].[435]

The Covington court made clear that the gerrymanders affected nearly 70 percent of all state House and Senate districts, touched more than 75 percent of the state's counties, and encompassed 83 percent of North Carolina's entire population—almost eight million people. Lawmakers had thus jeopardized the foundational premise of popular sovereignty—denying "the mechanism by which the people ensure that elected officials have a habitual recollection of their dependence on the people." The "true principle of a republic is that the people should choose who they please to govern them," the court reminded.[436]

The Covington judges also noted the arrogance of the General Assembly defendants. Republican lawmakers argued against the implementation of a remedy "because the constitutional violation, at a minimum, is certainly subject to rational disagreement." That, Judge James Wynn responded, "is patently wrong":

> There is no "rational disagreement" as to whether the districting plans at issue in this case violated the Constitution. This Court unanimously held that the challenged districts violate the Constitution. The U.S. Supreme Court affirmed that conclusion without argument and without dissent. Thus, there is no disagreement between this Court's and the Supreme Court's conclusion that the challenged districts are unconstitutional.
>
> We recognize that legislatures elected under the unconstitutional districting plans have governed the people of North Carolina for more than four years and will continue to do so for more than two years after this Court held the districting plans unconstitutional. . . . But at this juncture, with only a few months before the start of the next election cycle, we are left with little choice but to conclude that a special election would not be in the interest of [the people of North Carolina].[437]

It was hard to avoid the conclusion that the federal court believed that the North Carolina General Assembly had conclusively forfeited its electoral validity.

Overturning Local Elections: Sore Loser Laws

It is unconstitutional to use traditional legislative authorities to suppress the right to vote and the right to equal political representation. But it is at least generally true that state legislatures possess the power to regulate aspects of the franchise and to create or alter legislative electoral districts. They don't, on the other hand, have the license to simply overturn the results of municipal and county elections because they disagree with the outcome. But that hasn't stopped the North Carolina Republican General Assembly from doing precisely that.

Stepping wildly outside its role, our legislature has recast electoral processes in school district and county commission races in Wake County and in city council elections in Greensboro because the voters chose too many Democrats. Republican lawmakers did so largely without consultation with local authorities, without following normal committee and hearing processes, and without even arguably defensible justifications. When pressed, they have simply lied about their goals or, at least, so the courts have concluded. They interfered to elect Republicans and defeat incumbent Democrats. They did so, apparently, because they thought they could get away with it—attempting, in the process, to teach voters that there will be consequences for electing Democrats. Lawlessness literally unmasked.

Republican legislators' antidemocratic, even despotic, efforts have usually been swiftly invalidated by the federal courts—who have no reason to fear the leaders of the North Carolina General Assembly. Still, these are steps rarely seen in American government, and they reveal how little tied North Carolina Republican lawmakers are to the norms of constitutional government. They remind us that autocratic tendencies can still live in political hearts. And that, even after two centuries, democratic traditions are not notably assured. I will concentrate here, for illustration purposes, on the General Assembly's interference with Wake County commissioner elections. But the same tactics, sentiments, and objections apply to the Wake County school board and Greensboro city council interventions.

In March 2015 Republican General Assembly leaders pushed through a plan to remake the Wake County Commission by redrawing its districts and adding two new seats to the commission.[438] In the most recent Wake election, the four Republican candidates had been trounced by their four Democratic opponents. Thus the (then) seven-member Board of Commissioners became entirely Democratic. Republican senator Chad Barefoot (Wake Forest) apparently found the result intolerable. He secured passage of a "local bill" (not subject to the governor's veto) radically redrawing all the districts. Wake County Republicans Paul Stam and Gary Pendleton pushed the measure through the House.

Local government officials had not requested the change. The Wake County Commission unanimously passed a resolution opposing it. Republicans blocked a vote on amendments, proposed by local Democratic senators, requiring county residents to approve the structural changes through referendum. An independent analysis found that, had the new boundary plan been in effect for the 2014 election, Republicans would have captured five of the nine seats despite Democrats securing thirty thousand more votes than Republicans. The *Raleigh News & Observer* called the scheme the "nefarious sore loser plan."[439]

A three-judge panel of the Fourth U.S. Circuit Court of Appeals invalidated the Barefoot-Stam-Pendleton measure under the Fourteenth Amendment equal protection clause.[440] The judges scoffed at the array of purported justifications lawmakers offered to support the changes. Increased representation, reduced campaign costs, and elevated voter turnout were mere "pretexts" for the actual goal of the statute, which was political partisanship to help Republicans and hurt Democrats:

> Uncontroverted evidence at trial showed that the redistricting reflected the predominance of illegitimate reapportionment factors . . . the skewed, unequal attempt to guarantee Republican victory through the intentional packing of Democratic

> districts. Rather than seeking proportional representation of the two main political parties, the evidence shows that the challenged plans under-populated Republican-leaning districts and over-populated Democratic-leaning districts in order to gerrymander Republican victories. In other words, the challenged redistricting here subverts political fairness [in favor of] partisan gamesmanship.[441]

The Fourth Circuit noted, as well, that "the legislators who hatched the redistricting plans claimed legislative immunity"—refusing to testify or be cross-examined about their motives in passing the statute. The record did, however, "contain several emails including third parties that revealed partisan motives behind the redistricting plan." For example, the court indicated, "the Wake County Republican Party chair exchanged several emails with, and apparently met with, key legislators involved in the redistricting, with a focus on 'how we would take five of the nine seats.' "[442] Once again, the federal courts determined that the Republican General Assembly said it was regulating for one purpose when it was actually acting for another, illegitimate, one. You can rely on them to cheat for partisan purposes but not to tell the truth about it.

Sen. Chad Barefoot, who sponsored the legislation, of course expressed great outrage at the ruling, calling the decision "unconscionable." According to Barefoot, "an unelected and unaccountable federal court has not only quashed an effort to increase representation and geographic diversity on the Wake County Board of Commissioners, but has effectively disenfranchised all Wake County voters."

He didn't explain why he felt compelled to lie a second time.

Breaking Democracy's Most Basic Rule

> North Carolina set a precedent in playing a kind of political hardball that we haven't seen in other places. Does it spiral out of control? This has been more asymmetrical with Republicans, but I don't think it would always stay that way. —Richard Hasen, University of California, Irvine, leading election law scholar[443]

The antidemocratic agenda of the North Carolina Republican General Assembly has, no doubt, been a radical one. Denying the right to vote, cheating in the drawing of electoral districts, governing through invalidly elected assemblies, overturning municipal elections, excluding racial minorities from effective political participation—these are serious, illegitimating transgressions. As an accumulation, they well exceed the oppressive patterns seen in even the most determined states. Likely few believe that more resolutely than I.

Still, there is one sense in which even these potent sins against democracy falter by comparison. It might be fair to say that the most basic principle of democratic government is that when you lose an election, you hand over power to your successful opponents.[444] As the scholars put it, the core democratic norm, reflected in the peaceful transition of governmental power, is that "the losers accept the results of an election and move on."[445]

In a democracy, you don't burn down the buildings when the vote doesn't go your way. You might contest the outcome through legal processes, ask for a recount, and the like. But when the legal reviews are exhausted, you don't seize the armies or the police force. You certify the results and move forward. You'll get 'em next time around. You don't bomb the governor's mansion. Astonishingly, the Republican North Carolina General Assembly has experimented with rejecting this defining premise of self-government.

In November 2016 Democrat Roy Cooper defeated incumbent Republican governor Pat McCrory in a very close election.[446] The margin was less than 1 percent, with roughly ten thousand votes separating the candidates. McCrory was exceedingly slow to concede. The weeks after the election were filled with speculation—given the track record of the General Assembly—that the legislature might intervene and simply declare McCrory the winner. McCrory almost seemed to expect it. Yet, the vote margin held, the General Assembly did not act, and, eventually, on December 5, 2016, Governor McCrory conceded.[447] Most Tar Heels were relieved to have a decision.

The drama, however, did not conclude. Three weeks before Cooper was to be sworn in on January 27, the General Assembly was called into a special session to provide storm relief following a deadly snowstorm. When that one-day session ended, however, the legislature called an immediate second special session. This time the agenda was much more ambitious. Anita Earls had also been elected in November to the North Carolina Supreme Court, giving the Democrats a 4–3 majority on the high court. Republican leaders introduced a bold slate of legislative proposals to diminish the power of the soon-to-be-incoming Democratic governor and the newly Democratic-dominated North Carolina Supreme Court.

General Assembly leaders moved to require that the governor's cabinet members, for the first time, be confirmed by the Senate. The number of state employees to be appointed by the governor was to be dramatically reduced by 1,200. The governor's power to name university trustees was stripped. Other appointment powers were lost. Both local and state election boards were to be reconstituted, giving massive advantages to the Republican Party. The state ethics commission was altered. North Carolina Supreme Court races were to be made partisan. And the now-disfavored state high court had limits placed on its jurisdictional authority. Sweeping governmental changes were passed in a moment. To his eternal discredit, Governor McCrory signed into law powerful constraints on his successor.

Sen. Jeff Jackson (D-Mecklenburg) pointed out that "to pull off an ambush like that, all the Republicans had to be in on it, they started immediately filing bills that were forty pages long, they had been working on this [secretly] for weeks."[448] Incoming governor Roy Cooper said, "Most people think this is a partisan power grab, but it is really more ominous than that"; it is an effort "to nullify the vote of the people." Longtime North Carolina congressman David Price, a trained political scientist, warned, "American democracy may be more fragile than we realized."[449] And, of course, all this occurred in "emergency" special session, with an electorally defeated lame-duck governor, passed by a legislature that had been repeatedly held to be illegally constituted because of its own impermissible racial gerrymanders. National commentators were quick to label it a "legislative coup":

> What's happening in North Carolina is not politics as usual. It is an extraordinarily disturbing legislative coup, a flagrant effort to maintain one-party rule by rejecting democratic norms and revoking the will of the voters. It is the kind of thing one might expect to see in Venezuela, not in a U.S. state. It should terrify every American citizen who believes in the rule of law. This is so much more than a partisan power grab. This is an attack on democracy itself.[450]

The North Carolina legislative coup may have been a first, but two years later, Republicans lost the governor's office while retaining control of the statehouse in Wisconsin and Michigan. Both then followed what was called "the North Carolina playbook"—passing power-stripping bills after Democratic gubernatorial victories. Wisconsin lawmakers took away various executive and implementation powers traditionally held by the governor and the new (Democratic) attorney general. The Wisconsin Republican speaker explained, candidly, "We are going to have a very liberal governor who is going to enact policies that are in direct contrast to what many of us believe."[451] In other words, the Republicans didn't like who got elected governor so they decided to dramatically diminish the governor's power. If you lose an election, demolish the office you lost, even if it has to be done in a lame-duck session. Wisconsin's new governor, Democrat Tony Evers, replied, "Power-hungry politicians rushed through sweeping changes to our laws to expand their own powers and to overrule the people of Wisconsin."[452] Michigan at least partially played out similarly.

Both states explicitly looked to North Carolina for lessons in the antidemocratic abuse of power. North Carolina legislators taught them that perhaps you are not required to actually turn over the keys to the governor's mansion. It is not necessary to respect the results of an intervening election. "Consent of the governed" is not all it's cracked up to be. Maybe the people don't actually have the right to choose who governs them if incumbents don't like the results.

Following the foundational traditions of democracy is for suckers—like Democrats. Republicans—now in North Carolina, Wisconsin, and Michigan—apparently think the more powerful course, when you lose a governor's race, is to spend the last moments in office undermining the future authority of the winner. North Carolina senator Jeff Jackson (D-Mecklinburg), speaking of Wisconsin and Michigan, said, "We've lived through this in North Carolina, I feel for them."[453] Again, the Tar Heel State acted as pathbreaker in constitutional transgression.

Let me end with a distinction.

I detest a wide array of the choices made by North Carolina's General Assembly over the past nine years. I think it despicable, for example, to have refused crucial health care to low-income Tar Heels to show disdain for a president. I believe it loathsome to force unemployed workers into destitution to subsidize wealthy donors and businesses. I'm confident kicking people off food stamps to show your constituents that you'll give poor folks the rough treatment deserves unrelenting contempt. I could go on.

But I make no claim that these choices, no matter how villainous, are beyond the understood and accepted authorities of an American state government. We opt, broadly speaking, for majority rule. The preferences of the bulk of the people, enacted through their representatives, prevail. They are not necessarily invalid, even if they are vicious or stupid or vile. An action of government isn't rendered impermissible just because it's wrong.

Still, of course, there are acts, according to our governing framework, that are seen as beyond the legitimate authorities of a state. In order to make "consent of the governed" operational, to open securely channels of political participation, and to ensure the full dignity and opportunity of the commonwealth's membership, we prohibit government from distorting or debilitating the effective functioning of democracy. Majority rule demands a policing of access, a constraint on the ability of the "ins" to unfairly exclude the "outs"—lest the commitment to self-governance itself be defeated.

Many of these foundational restraints are written directly into the text of the Constitution. It's impermissible, for example, to deny someone's right to vote because of her race, or her sex, or because she's only nineteen, or because she can't pay a poll tax. Americans are assured rights to speak, to publish, to assemble, and to petition their governments for redress of grievances.

Other constraints, though less overtly textual, are thought to arise from the structure of government itself—the celebrated independence of the judiciary, the enforced demand for a workable separation of powers, the residual sovereignty necessary for required leeway in the states, and, assuredly, the full and peaceful transitions of government power.

And some limitations, at various governing levels, have been developed through traditions and practices meant to check and balance worrisome distortions of power—our predilections for municipal and county prerogative, our customs of academic and religious independence, our deference to institutions of civil society, and the like.

We have believed these safeguards and structures necessary for the implementation of American liberty. We've maintained those requisites, knowing that, on occasion, they make the animation of government less smooth and efficient than it might be otherwise. We recognize higher values than speed and momentary political dominance. We'd rather check government than forfeit freedom.

These ancient constraining lessons are now being tested, and sometimes lost, in North Carolina.

The Republican General Assembly has not been content to merely enact its substantive policy choices to stamp its imprint on life in North Carolina. It has moved repeatedly to reject the pillars and infrastructure of democratic governance.

The legislature has, notably and officially, deployed its redistricting powers to distort both state and federal elections in favor of incumbent Republicans. It has forced identification and polling practices that it admits are designed to put a thumb on the electoral scale in its favor. It has effectively charged election boards to act like party functionaries.

It has repeatedly attacked the independence of the courts—shielding Republican justices from the electoral process, opening the door to purchased judicial elections, and narrowing the processes of constitutional review to protect its own statutes from invalidation.

It has moved to overturn municipal elections that didn't yield its preferred results. It has stripped local governments of traditional prerogatives, even before the breathtaking usurpations of H.B. 2. It has regularly forced campus leaders in Chapel Hill to cower like frightened children.

Although it should stun us, we are now unsurprised that a governor would seemingly conceive it possible (even if temporarily) to stay in office despite losing his race, or that a supreme court election would be threatened by a floated court-packing plan. All gives way before bare, unbridled, radical, and arrogant assertions of power.

And once constraining democratic standards are discarded, it becomes impossible to say what is not called into question.

Phil Berger, Tim Moore, Thom Tillis, David Lewis, Bob Rucho, Pat McCrory, and others have sought not only to make North Carolina the most politically conservative state in America; they've also worked to make it the most autocratic. Arthur Schlesinger wrote, decades ago, that a "totalitarian regime crushes all autonomous institutions" in its drive to wield authority.[454] Hail the new totalitarians.

I have an odd affection for Huey Long. He did much for the poor and marginalized of Louisiana (and, to be sure, for himself). Long can't been seen as a hero, though, because he laid waste to the democratic processes of his state to do it. He would have detested the "lickspittle" of the Republican North Carolina General Assembly. But he would have admired their antidemocratic prowess and their totalitarian style.

CHAPTER TEN

Abandoning Truth

"When *I* use a word," Humpty Dumpty said, in rather a scornful tone, "it means just what I choose it to mean—neither more nor less."

"The question is," said Alice, "whether you *can* make words mean so many different things."

"The question is," said Humpty Dumpty, "which is to be master—that's all." —Lewis Carroll, *Through the Looking Glass* (1872)[455]

The law requires that agencies offer genuine justifications for important decisions, reasons that can be scrutinized by courts and the interested public. Accepting contrived reasons would defeat the purpose of the enterprise. —Chief Justice John Roberts, *Department of Commerce v. New York* (2019)[456]

I have argued, in the preceding chapters, that since 2011 the broad and radicalized agenda of the North Carolina Republican General Assembly betrays our most fundamental constitutive values as a people. Assaults on the participatory rights of African Americans, on the dignity and opportunity of poor Tar Heels, on the full autonomy of women, and on the equal humanity of the LGBTQ+ community violate the ideals of equal protection and status that bind us as a nation. Dismantling ancient commitments to public education and to the shared enjoyment and obliged protection of our natural wonders and resources also tread upon legally stated and embraced public duties. Violations of our long-developed norms of governance—separation of powers, judicial independence, the rule of law, and the centrality of democratic decision-making—also reject our agreed-to defining obligations as a people. When we discard them, as the North Carolina General Assembly has so easily and eagerly done over the past decade in pursuit of expanded powers, we cast aside what we have promised to be, what we have claimed (through hard-constructed convictions) that it means to be an American and a North Carolinian. This Republican program is a betrayal of who we have been, who we say we are, and who we will be.

I mean this to be a claim of transgressed agreement, of violation of compact. I don't press it as a naked moral claim—though surely turning one's back on what we have said ourselves to be carries a powerful moral component. But I'm a constitutional lawyer, not a philosopher or an ethicist. I seek to direct my attentions to what we have pledged ourselves to do, not to what the components of the good life might be said to prescribe. That is surely beyond my ken or conceivable warrant. It is true that as I explore the General Assembly's broad-ranging war on equality, if I were to attempt to open up a front based in morality itself, it would likely begin with Scout's lesson from Atticus in *To Kill a Mockingbird*:

> "First of all," he said, "if you can learn a simple trick, Scout, you'll get along a lot better with all kinds of folks. You never really understand a person until you consider things from his point of view . . . until you climb into his skin and walk round in it."[457]

And if I became more ambitious, I'd turn to Galatians 5:14: "For the entire law is fulfilled in keeping this one command, 'Love your neighbor as yourself.' "[458]

Still, I refuse the temptation, certain that if I can't convince of our joint undertakings, I can't possibly prevail on claims of life's meaning. I'll stay closer to my home turf.

I mention all this because I close with something that sounds, I'll concede, more like a direct assertion of moral failing—abandoning accuracy in discourse, losing truth. To exaggerate, governing by perjury.[459] But, even here, I make the claim as a sin against democracy, not against the beneficent soul. As Andrew Young put it when he was nearly eighty, "There can be no democracy without truth."[460]

I know in some ways that sounds childishly naive. Truth is always contested—particularly truth about how we should govern ourselves, what policies we should embrace. Democracy itself requires the contest. As historian Sophia Rosenfeld puts it,

> Democracy insists on the idea that truth both matters and that nobody gets to say definitively what it is. That's a tension that's built into democracy from the beginning, and it's not solvable, but intrinsic to democracy. I think both things matter.[461]

I'm saved from the dilemma—if I am—by having in mind a very modest vision of truth. I mean, here, only "truth" that should prohibit the speaker from saying things he knows to be factually untrue but that, for either legal or political purposes, he finds, nonetheless, convenient to say. Known falsehoods uttered because, if the speaker admitted the truth, the proffered policy would be defeated—either legally or politically.

For example, in the early summer of 2018, the North Carolina Senate passed a measure that would require all public schools to display the phrase "In God We Trust" in "a prominent place." Headlines read, "NC Lawmakers Back 'In God We Trust' Sign in Schools, Say It's Not Promoting Religion." The bill was sponsored and introduced by Senate members of the N.C. Prayer Caucus who denied, by statement, that the new law would "promote religion in general or Christianity in particular." Rep. Larry Pittman explained that the law wasn't religious; it "merely acknowledges a very important factor of our national history." Pittman, who a year earlier had explained that "Lincoln was the same sort of tyrant [as] Hitler," is always ready with a history lesson.[462]

"In God We Trust" certainly sounds like a religious declaration to me. When Treasury Secretary Salmon Chase introduced the motto onto coins during the Civil War, he said, "No nation can be strong except in the strength of God." And when President Eisenhower endorsed the adage as our motto in the 1950s, he indicated it would "constantly strengthen those spiritual weapons which will forever be our country's most powerful resource in peace and war." Why the disingenuous disclaimer?

It turns out that the U.S. Supreme Court held decades ago that a state law must have "a secular purpose" and cannot "promote religion" to pass constitutional muster.[463] So, a law that is designed precisely and singularly to promote religion has to become something else—a history billboard perhaps. Deceit is demanded lest the sought-after result be foreclosed. Better to lie than to tempt a verdict of unconstitutionality. Even if it seems odd to lie for God.

This methodology lies behind a good deal of the North Carolina Republican General Assembly's battle with truth. Much of what they have sought to accomplish violates the constitution—or seems to. A dozen or more of the legislature's principal enactments have been invalidated by the courts in the last seven years. Our leaders seem to be in a constant and fierce battle against the Fourteenth Amendment. That frequently makes it impossible to confess what they are actually up to.

We now have more famous examples.

North Carolina's "Bathroom Bill," H.B. 2, was said to be necessary because Charlotte's nondiscrimination ordinance allowed men into women's bathrooms and locker rooms, thus putting young girls at great risk from sexual predators.[464] Governor McCrory described it as a necessary "safety measure, a common sense privacy law that keeps predatory men out of women's restrooms."[465] He reportedly stood strong, allies indicated, "in protecting the privacy and safety of women and young girls in bathrooms, locker rooms, and showers" from a "dangerous ordinance that would have allowed any man to enter a woman's bathroom at any time merely by claiming to be a woman that day."[466] Rep. Dan Bishop, H.B. 2's principal author, said the new law was absolutely required because "the safety of women was being subverted and sacrificed."[467] Republican senator Buck Newton said H.B. 2 was necessary to protect women and children from assault by keeping men out of women's bathrooms, arguing, "This is the day the Lord has made, and [we won't] bow and kiss the ring of their political correctness theology."[468] The *New York Times* explained:

> Proponents of so-called bathroom bills have peddled them by spuriously portraying transgender women as potential rapists. That threat exists only in the imagination of bigots. Supporters of the measures have been unable to point to a single case that justifies the need to legislate where people should be allowed to use the toilet. North Carolina is the first state to pass such a provision. By promoting the ludicrous idea that transgender women are inherently dangerous, the law endangers citizens who are already disproportionately vulnerable to violence and stigmatization.[469]

The nation's leading organizations dedicated to stopping violence against women signed a letter saying that argument is flatly untrue:

> [H.B. 2] utilizes and perpetuates the myth that protecting transgender people's access to restrooms and locker rooms endangers the safety and privacy of others. As rape crisis centers, shelters, and other service providers who work each and every day to meet the needs of all survivors and reduce sexual violence throughout society, we speak from experience and expertise when we state that these claims are false.[470]

Advocates for H.B. 2 tended to cling to the predator and assault myths, despite being unable to find or reveal any factual support for them. That, apparently, could more readily be squared with a Fourteenth Amendment demand for equal protection of the laws than a declared desire to push transgender North Carolinians around and humiliate them in their intimate moments.

North Carolina's monster voter ID law was almost as famous as the Bathroom Bill. It was repeatedly tagged as the most suppressive electoral measure in a half century. The statute's proponents said, incessantly, that the photo ID measure was simply designed to eliminate voter fraud and ensure the accuracy of the ballot. Again, it was a "common sense" measure. (Lots of "common sense" going around.) The federal courts found, however, that the Republican lawmakers' proffered justification was, again, a lie. The "state failed to identify even a single individual who has ever been charged with in-person voter fraud in North Carolina."[471]

So, lots of folks would be disenfranchised by a photo ID requirement to no good end, serving no actual purpose. On the other hand, the judges said, there is apparently all kinds of "fraud in absentee voting by mail," but the General Assembly exempted that from regulation. Huh? The justifications, the court concluded, "cannot and do not conceal the state's true motivation." Neither this "legislature, nor any other legislature in the country, has ever done so much, so fast, to restrict access to the franchise." The asserted interest in "ballot integrity" was, instead, a ruse. A lousy one. The law "imposes cures for problems" that don't exist. The real goal of the statute, instead, was to handicap black voters. That was demonstrated repeatedly with "surgical precision." But, of course, that's an objective that can hardly be admitted. It is explicitly prohibited by the text of the constitution. Better to lie about the whole undertaking. And then holler about activist judges.[472]

North Carolina's "motorcycle vagina bill" was much the same. An entire cascade of Republican antiabortion leaders explained, for perhaps the first time in their lives, that they had no intention whatsoever, through the provision, to deny women access to abortion procedures. They were exclusively concerned with the health of women seeking to terminate a pregnancy. As a result, they hoped to more heavily regulate, and perhaps even close, abortion facilities. But that was only to ensure the well-being of women seeking to exercise their right to terminate a pregnancy.

The newly discovered health-oriented attentions, however, were apparently regarded with an imposing skepticism on the floor of the General Assembly. The antiabortion Republicans' opponents seemingly were not buying the claim.[473] Folks like Rep. Sarah Stevens (R-Surry) felt compelled to respond defensively: "Don't tell me this isn't about health and safety; that's exactly what it's about. I'm sorry if you don't believe me." Sorry indeed. Sen. Trudy Wade (R-Guilford) proclaimed, "This whole bill is about making abortion safer for women." Sen. Warren Daniel protested the new statute was "about safety, first to last," nothing more. Noted abortion opponent Republican Rep. Ruth Samuelson made it clear that "we're not going to wait until women die in abortion clinics before we raise standards." Certainly not. All this newly expressed fretting over the effective health care of women seeking abortion was necessary because the Supreme Court had long ago held that it is unconstitutional to simply try to make it harder for women to get previability abortions.[474] A state can regulate the abortion process to protect a woman's health, but not merely to hinder the exercise of the privacy right.[475] So, you use the claim remaining available to restrict abortion, even if you have to lie to get there. Surely lying to stop abortions, the theory goes, is God's good work.

Chad Barefoot (R-Wake Forest) and his Republican colleagues apparently didn't worry about the purportedly worrisome makeup of the Wake County commissioners electoral districts until all four Republican candidates lost their seats to Democrats—entirely sweeping the seven-member governing body for the Democratic Party. So, as discussed in the last chapter, in 2015, Senator Barefoot pressed and passed a local bill redrawing all the districts and expanding the commission. Barefoot said, of course, that he wasn't concerned about politics—far from it. Instead, he wanted to ensure elevated voter turnout, achieve more effective representation, and reduce electoral campaign costs. Thus what his critics called the "sore loser plan" was necessary. The federal courts explicitly determined, though, that Barefoot's story was just "pretext." The actual goal, of course, was to give Republicans an advantage and set Democrats at a disadvantage. And that goal, the court held, was simply illegal. Senator Barefoot hid behind an asserted legislator's privilege to avoid testifying and being cross-examined about his motives. Nonetheless, the reviewing court found that he wasn't being truthful.

Even more formally, in 2018 a panel of state judges took the unusual step of ruling that the Republican General Assembly's crafted description of two constitutional amendment ballot initiatives was so deceptive the judges would not allow the proposals to even be placed on the ballot.[476] The proffered amendments would have altered the way judicial vacancies were filled and members of state boards and commissions were appointed. The challengers argued, however, that the "legislature had made a deliberate attempt to perpetuate a fraud with the ballot language." The state court concluded, in response, that the legislatively fashioned ballot questions did not accurately inform voters of the changes that would occur if the measures eventually passed.[477]

The ballot questions, the judges ruled, "were not stated in such a manner as to enable [the voters] intelligently to express their opinion." The language also made "no mention of [the negative] effect of the Amendment upon the veto powers of the Governor." Accordingly, the ballot language failed to meet the "constitutional standards [of accuracy demanded] for submission to the voters." Lawyers for Speaker Tim Moore and Sen. Phil Berger argued that courts had no power to nix the ballot submissions, regardless of how deceptive they might be. And the executive director of the Republican Party threatened that disobedient judges might well be impeached. But the judges refused to yield, sticking to their traditional duties of constitutional enforcement. It wasn't Moore's and Berger's job to say what the law is. Or to be allowed to deceive the voters of North Carolina.[478]

Governing by Pretext

It is no doubt extraordinary to be governed by a General Assembly that state and federal courts have so regularly and repeatedly concluded misleads the citizenry about the goals and purposes it pursues as it legislates the rights and responsibilities of its membership. The judicial findings of deceit are repeated and expansive. They reveal a design, surely, to fundamentally delude and hoodwink the electorate. And it is not unreasonable to assume that where there is so much judicially identified and declared smoke, there is also likely ample fire.

The Republican North Carolina General Assembly has refused to accept Medicaid expansion—excluding nearly a half-million poor Tar Heels from health care coverage. And its leaders have been extraordinarily inarticulate in explaining the odd decision (three-quarters of the states have decided otherwise). The legislators' penchant for dissembling at least makes it more reasonable to ask whether, despite the simplistic denials, the Medicaid refusal is based on continuing aversion to President Obama and his agenda or simply on a straightforward disdain for poor people. That would surely be more challenging to explain to the families of a thousand or more impoverished North Carolinians who, studies show, die each year as a result of the decision.[479]

Perhaps the proffered justifications, slippery as they appear, are simply more needed "pretexts" to avoid admitting yet another impermissible motivation. Unlike any other state in the nation, North Carolina Republican legislators—even with then-soaring unemployment rates—withdrew from central aspects of the national unemployment compensation program, slashing the benefits of more than 170,000 out-of-work residents and, again, turning away funds from Washington. Why did they do it? We know our leaders can't be taken at their word. So did they crush unemployment compensation to teach poor Tar Heels a lesson? To further reward and cozy up to the Republican donor class? They have repeatedly cut the income tax obligations of the very wealthiest North Carolinians under the tired and inaccurate assertion that such dollars will trickle down to low-income workers. Really? Do Republican lawmakers, all history to the contrary, actually believe that? Or, perhaps more likely, is it simply too politically untenable to announce that their sole focus is the welfare of the top 5 percent of North Carolinians? That can be a tough sell, no doubt, in a democracy.

We became the only state in American history to end its earned income tax credit—actually raising the tax bill of working families making about $35,000 a year. Does something not actually count as a tax increase if it only raises the taxes of the bottom third of citizens? Why? Perhaps because they aren't actually part of the constituency? If it's so important to create tax incentives for millionaires, what about those barely able to get by? Is it possible that our legislative leaders merely operate in service and obeisance to their wealthiest funders and actually aim to target and penalize impoverished Tar Heels? That's got to be hard to press in a thirty-second ad. Should we believe Republican legislators' declarations to the contrary?

And what does this do to government officials when they seem to so regularly dissemble to their constituents? Do they, as one suspects, simply get in the habit? Surely they don't only deceive in important constitutional cases. Why limit their mendacity to such foundational matters? It doesn't usually work that way. If folks will lie on one front, they are typically in for the others as well. And at some point it becomes clear that leaders are untroubled to say things that they know to be untrue. What does it do to political discourse when speakers think it unnecessary to believe in the accuracy of the claims they propound? How do they keep track? Why bother to keep track? Where does democracy go in such darkness?

And, more vital, what are North Carolina citizens to do in the face of such democracy-draining practices? What is the expected response to a government that stacks the political deck against its adversaries, its racial minorities, its most marginalized members, and those most needing fair educational opportunities? Against the rule of law, the vital norms of democracy, and, finally, even against truth itself? Is the citizen still to engage in thoughtful and civic-laden discourse? Is there a meaningful contest of ideas and policies under such a framework? What do we call such a government? How do we name it? Are we willing to deem it our own?

In August 2019 *Common Cause v. Lewis* was tried before a three-judge state court in Raleigh. It posed yet another challenge to the districting plans for the North Carolina General Assembly.[480] This one explored whether the extreme political gerrymandering deployed by Republican General Assembly members in crafting their own districts violated the North Carolina constitution—after the U.S. Supreme Court had decided there was no jurisdiction in the federal districting political gerrymandering challenge (*Rucho v. Common Cause*).[481] The plaintiffs alleged, unsurprisingly, that Rep. David Lewis and his colleagues' political line drawing—again, among the most biased ever witnessed—was legally impermissible. They eventually won readily and unanimously on the political gerrymandering claim.

The allegations made by Common Cause, though, were additionally telling. A large portion of the trial focused on a set of files produced by the Republicans' nationally noted gerrymandering expert, Thomas Hofeller. After Mr. Hofeller died, his daughter had turned the trove of documents over to Common Cause—much to the consternation of North Carolina Republican leaders. The state court, nonetheless, allowed the Hofeller files to be disclosed.[482] As the trial ended, Common Cause asked not only that the existing maps be declared unconstitutional, but that new maps be drawn and that the North Carolina General Assembly be effectively removed from the line-drawing process for the upcoming election cycle.

Common Cause argued that not only had the legislative delays and constitutional transgressions repeatedly violated their members' representational rights, but that the Hofeller files demonstrated that "representations made by legislative leaders" earlier in various proceedings, leading the court to at least temporarily leave the districts in place, were "untrue" and constituted "a charade."[483] Common Cause charged Republican dissembling on two fronts. The General Assembly defendants had argued that even if the districts were unconstitutional, there was insufficient time to implement a new districting plan before the next election. Common Cause said the Hofeller files refuted that assertion—almost all of the work had already been done by the storied consultant. Second, legislative leaders had represented earlier in the suit that race had not been used in the previous district line-drawing process, now under challenge. The files also showed, Common Cause claimed, that simply wasn't so. The legislators lied.

Republican leaders disputed the Common Clause claims of misrepresentation enthusiastically, arguing that the "plaintiffs were attempting to create a bogeyman out of a dead map drawer to distract from the weakness of [their] case."[484] The court flatly rejected the proffered defenses of Lewis and the Republican leaders and sided with Common Cause on essentially all fronts. The suit itself, though, stands as a unique marker for the democracy-destroying efforts of the North Carolina Republican General Assembly over the past decade. Common Cause had claimed that the partisan-obsessed lawmakers drew district lines in order to hinder and burden the free operation of the democratic process, working to entrench Republican majorities. They also asserted that lawmakers had again used racial data to discriminate against black voters. Next, Common Cause asserted, Republican leaders had knowingly misled the court about their efforts—showing contempt for the judiciary. And finally, the plaintiffs claimed, the Republican defendants failed to speak truthfully to the people of North Carolina about what they had actually done in the redistricting process.[485]

Accordingly, the suit suggested, the North Carolina Republican General Assembly had lodged potent attacks on democracy, on African Americans, on the courts, and, finally, on the truth itself.[486] The unanimous, bipartisan court issued a potent judgment on behalf of Common Cause. The judges did not appoint a special master, but showing impatience, they put the legislative defendants on an exceptionally brief, two-week leash, to redraw the state districts.[487] The court also concluded that the lawmakers' claims that they had not lied to the tribunal were "highly improbable" and "unpersuasive."[488]

Tellingly, as this book was being edited, North Carolina again burst into national headlines when the Republican House leadership, breaking a months-long stalemate, seemed to turn to deception to override Gov. Roy Cooper's veto of the state budget. Cooper had insisted the budget include Medicaid expansion. As the *Wall Street Journal* headline put it, "North Carolina House GOP Overrides Budget Veto with Few Democrats Present."[489] Democrats, who had only a handful of members on the floor, explained that (alas, again) Republican leader David Lewis had assured them there would be no morning votes taken at the session. When Speaker Tim Moore proceeded despite the assurances, a righteously indignant Deb Butler (D-New Hanover) screamed from her seat, "How dare you do this, Mr. Speaker. It's a travesty and you know it." Moore sneered in response, cutting off her microphone. Sen. Terry Van Duyn (D-Buncombe) called on Moore to resign.

Governor Cooper said during a press conference that the move was a literal assault on democracy: "There was no confusion about what happened here; this was a lie." Cooper is among the most cooperative, accommodating, moderating leaders in North Carolina history. No one had ever heard him speak that way.[490] It was difficult to tell whether Cooper was madder because he believed the Republicans had lied or because they had crushed democratic norms in order to keep 500,000 poor Tar Heels off of Medicaid.

CHAPTER ELEVEN

An Agenda of Oppression

> We've come too far and worked too hard. Too many good people have paid too high a price, paid with their lives, to allow this to happen now. There has been too much hard work done. What we're seeing now is another hard chapter in the long, ongoing battle for the soul of the nation.
>
> —Bruce Springsteen, "The Ghost of Tom Joad (Introduction)"[491]

It is a long, breathtaking, and fundament-destroying list.

The North Carolina Republican General Assembly has, since 2011, enacted a bold and historically stunning agenda to diminish the political, judicial, and dignitary rights of African Americans. The program has been launched, without embarrassment or hesitation, from all-white Republican House and Senate caucuses. Through redistricting plans held to be among the largest racial gerrymanders "ever presented to an American court," intentionally biased voter ID laws, ballot access limitations, polling place restrictions, threatened criminal prosecutions, and public accusations of voter ineligibility, Republicans have sought to reembrace Jim Crow electoral schemes. Lawmakers also repealed a groundbreaking Racial Justice Act, curtailed state discrimination actions, increased school segregation, and demanded idolatrous protections for Confederate statues. They seek to build a bridge to 1953.

They have offered similar treatment to poor Tar Heels. A half-million low-income citizens have been denied health care through a long-standing refusal to expand Medicaid—costing the state billions of dollars and thousands of lives. Republican lawmakers initiated the largest cut to a state unemployment compensation program in American history and made North Carolina the only state ever to cancel its earned income tax credit—raising tax bills for poor working families. They kicked thousands of kids off food stamps, though the federal government paid the fare; abolished the appropriation for legal aid; and sharply cut child care subsidies. In the meantime, they've disparaged poor people as unworthy and reprehensible—effectively excluding them from the constituency.

North Carolina Republicans have also pushed frontiers in the denial of human dignity to LGBTQ+ Tar Heels. Through animus-driven constitutional amendments, licenses to discriminate in government services, and internationally denounced bathroom regulations meant to humiliate and endanger the vulnerable, legislators have declared thousands of our fellow North Carolinians officially diminished.

Republican lawmakers have also arrogantly violated the personal liberty, constitutional privacy, and bodily integrity of North Carolina women. They have not only passed an array of impermissibly restrictive abortion laws, but also enacted a shocking mandatory sonogram law—enlisting a woman's body, physician, and pocketbook in a coercive campaign to intimidate her from the exercise of her constitutional rights. They have required doctors to mouth a state-mandated consent script, like Stalinist apparatchiks, contrary to their perception of the best interests of their patients. A caucus that one female Republican House member called the "middle-age white man's club" has repeatedly and enthusiastically instructed women about how to order their lives.

Senate and House leaders have also systematically and pervasively moved to diminish, and perhaps eventually dismantle, public schools. Through teacher and teaching assistant layoffs, the elimination of tenure, the shuttering of the N.C. Teaching Fellows program, the expansion of charter schools, a gigantic investment in an unaccountable and discriminatory school voucher program, the creation of an absurd and stigmatizing A–F school grading system, and the adoption of achievement school districts, the General Assembly has worked to lay waste to traditional public schools. Our state constitution says the legislature must "provide by taxation or otherwise, for a general and uniform system of public schools, wherein tuition shall be free of charge to all children of the state."[492] Republican lawmakers have repeatedly violated that command.

Doors have been widely opened to the degradation of the environment and natural resources. Lawmakers have effectively limited research on climate change, embraced fracking and offshore drilling, crushed funding for state parks and environmental enforcement, repealed state rules more protective than their federal counterparts, and preempted various forms of local environmental regulation. Overtly protecting the wealthy and powerful from even the traditional legal rights of the marginalized—through gag laws and limitations on nuisance actions—the General Assembly has cast aside public interests in favor of private ones.

Republican lawmakers have unleashed an energized and multifaceted assault upon the independence of the North Carolina courts as well. They ended public funding of judicial campaigns, reintroduced partisan judges' races, curbed and manipulated jurisdiction in constitutional cases reviewing their own laws, intervened by statute to try to ensure the election of a Republican supreme court incumbent, altered the size of the Court of Appeals for partisan purposes, temporarily eliminated judicial primaries in hopes of helping Republican judges, directly tampered with yet another supreme court election, redistricted disfavored Wake and Mecklenburg county courts, sought to reduce gubernatorial judicial appointment powers, threatened all state judges with two-year terms (the shortest in the country), and introduced a constitutional amendment to secure dominant judicial appointment powers for the legislators (which failed at the ballot box). Republican lawmakers have found independent judicial review to be a troublesome inconvenience when carrying out their zealous legislative initiatives. They've indicated that in North Carolina it has to go.

And, as if attacking judicial independence and the rule of law wasn't bad enough, the North Carolina General Assembly has moved to thwart and distort democracy itself. Lawmakers have delivered the most ambitious voter suppression law and the most extreme political gerrymander in modern American history—to secure political ascendancy for themselves. They have effectively overturned city and county elections won by Democrats. They diminished the traditional powers of the governor and attorney general because Republicans lost the elections. Basic democratic norms and practices have been cast aside in favor of ever-expansive demands for Republican power. As one commentator put it, "What is happening in North Carolina is an extraordinarily disturbing legislative coup, a flagrant effort to maintain one-party rule by rejecting democratic norms and revoking the will of the voters." It is "the kind of thing one might expect to see in Venezuela, not in a U.S. state."[493]

Rarely have so few inflicted so much, so quickly, on so many, with so little justification. This is revolution born in malice and greed.

North Carolina: Outlier or Pathbreaker?

North Carolinians, no doubt, continue to face a battle that few expected. It is not just a struggle for liberalism or conservatism, progress or stasis, generosity or cruelty, pluralism or tribe. It is, rather, a defining, unyielding fight for equality itself, and for the essential foundations of American government—democratic accountability, limited and separated governmental powers, the overarching rule of law, the rejection of one-party legislative supremacy, the sanctity of rights to representation and the vote. Guarantees and commitments centuries in the making. Guarantees that we have long thought defined us as a people. If philosopher Richard Rorty were alive, he would remind us that we are called upon—even in 2020—to contribute our chapter to "achieve our nation."[494] We could wish, perhaps, that it was otherwise, that the fight was not as astounding as it is, that less was at stake, or that success was more certainly assured, but that wouldn't change a thing. It is what it is.

But will North Carolina's battle become the rest of the country's battle too? Is North Carolina an outlier or a bellwether? For me, at least, the answer is decidedly unclear. Many of the state's political grievances and resulting overreactions can seem singular. I certainly hope they are—though I understand, in my old age, that is likely naive. And the stunning impact of Donald Trump's presidency has made it almost impossible to envision a comprehensible future for our politics anywhere, even at the state level.

I mentioned earlier that some Republican state assemblies are now said to be "following the North Carolina playbook." National commentators also refer to the state as "a laboratory" for extremism or a "poster child for regressive conservative policies"[495]—all of which suggest at least some role as guidepost for North Carolina, even if a temporary or troubling one.

It is perhaps easier to make the claim that we are experiencing the country's largest or most brutal split—its most intense form of polarization. Election law scholars conclude that "North Carolina [has] set a precedent in playing a kind of political hardball [not] seen in other places."[496] The *New York Times* has written, "Nowhere is the battle between liberal and conservative visions of government fiercer than in North Carolina."[497] Others describe the state as "Exhibit A of the partisan self-sorting that has defined national politics in recent decades." Or temporally, some national folks have claimed, "North Carolina experienced its political cataclysm a few years ahead of the rest of the country."[498]

Without doubt, there has been some borrowing from a North Carolina game plan. Wisconsin and Michigan officially experimented with North Carolina's worst habits when incumbent Republican governors lost their races. Thom Tillis argues, or boasts, that the federal government now follows North Carolina's regressive economic strategies. And since the U.S. Supreme Court has said it will permanently stay its hand, even in the face of North Carolina's production of the most extreme, purposeful partisan gerrymandering abuse in our national history, there can be little doubt other legislatures (of both parties) will seek to follow Tar Heel leadership in abusive redistricting efforts.[499]

But apart from these more obvious side shots, it is possible to see North Carolina, as Karen Cox has written, less as an outlier and more as "the distillation" of potent nationwide trends.[500] North Carolina is often described as a "purple" state, but that shouldn't be mistaken for "moderate" or tepidly "undecided." Having long been involved in political life here, I think it is more accurate to say North Carolina is a deeply divided, somewhat evenly split, state politically.

Our elections are more about organizing than persuading. And we are divided in a particularly polarizing but not singular way. Democratic voters tend to be concentrated in faster-growing, economically potent, racially diverse metropolitan areas—often linked to powerful research universities, high-tech industries, or booming commercial sectors. A large percentage of the state's growth occurs in a relative handful of the state's one hundred counties. In rural communities, tobacco, textile, and manufacturing industries have largely collapsed. Despite potent statewide growth, most counties actually lose population with each succeeding census. Cities are securely, even expansively, blue, while rural areas are blood red.

Gerrymandering helps give rural communities largely disproportionate power, at least for a time. Polarizations are vivid and intense. Small towns cordial to H.B. 2, for example, seemed to care little if Charlotte lost NBA games to boycotts or if Bruce Springsteen chose not to come to some large and distant city. Democrats and Republicans agree on less and less and, increasingly, carry out a scorched earth politics impervious to compromise and little interested in niceties like separation of powers, traditions of governing deference, or the bulwarks of the rule of law. Perceptions of tribe and purported lost ascendancies can make more theoretical constitutive values weaken or vanish. Politicians want, principally, to vanquish their adversaries, come what may. And to keep them vanquished.

As my Duke friend Mac McCorkle puts it, the evenness of the political split increases its intensity: "If it was clear [this was] an overwhelmingly Republican state, Republicans would be more relaxed."[501] As it is, the close divide contributes to the meanness and paralysis of North Carolina politics. And, unfortunately for the future, I doubt that the tight but vivid and often debilitating schism appears only here.

I close, therefore, with Robert Kennedy's declaration at the University of California at Berkeley in 1966: "The future belongs to those who can blend passion, reason, and courage [in] a personal commitment to the ideals and enterprises of the American [democracy]."[502]

What was for Kennedy a description of the world he saw unfolding around him becomes for us a manifesto and prayer.

ACKNOWLEDGMENTS

I'm most grateful to my students Julia Prieto, Aaron Dalton, Jaaz Catterall, and Emily Monnett for the strong research they contributed to this effort. Robin Miura and Lynn York of Blair also did a great deal to improve the final product. I'm particularly grateful to my friend and colleague, Ferrel Guillory, for providing a close and thoughtful read of the manuscript. My late friend Charlie van der Horst, as always, provided inspiration.

NOTES

1. Michael Fletcher, "An Unimpeded GOP Veers North Carolina to the Right," *Washington Post*, May 26, 2013; Katrina Vanden Heuvel, "The Third Koch Brother Hits North Carolina," *Washington Post* (May 26, 2013).

2. Editorial, "The Decline of North Carolina," *New York Times* (July 9, 2013), https://www.nytimes.com/2013/07/10/opinion/the-decline-of-north-carolina.html.

3. Karen L. Cox, "What's the Matter with North Carolina?," *New York Times* (December 19, 2016), https://www.nytimes.com/2016/12/19/opinion/whats-the-matter-with-north-carolina.html.

4. Kim Severson, "G.O.P.'s Full Control in Long Moderate North Carolina May Leave Lasting Stamp," *New York Times* (December 11, 2012), https://www.nytimes.com/2012/12/12/us/politics/gop-to-take-control-in-long-moderate-north-carolina.html.

5. N.C. Policy Watch, "Altered State: How 5 Years of Conservative Rule Have Redefined North Carolina" (December 2015), http://www.ncpolicywatch.com/wp-content/uploads/2015/12/NC-Policy-Watch-Altered-State-How-5-years-of-conservative-rule-have-redefined-north-carolina-december-2015.pdf (hereinafter "Altered State").

6. Severson, *supra* note 4. See also Chris Kardish, "How North Carolina Turned So Red So Fast," *Governing Magazine* (July 2014), https://www.governing.com/topics/politics/gov-north-carolina-southern-progressivism.html.

7. James Oliphant, "GOP Wonderland: Inside North Carolina's Conservative Makeover," *The Atlantic*, September 23, 2013 (calling McCrory "compliant"). See also Mary Curtis, "Abortion Restrictions in North Carolina Senate Bill Set Up Political, Moral Standoff," *Washington Post*, July 5, 2013.

8. Jason Zengerle, "Is North Carolina the Future of American Politics?," *New York Times Magazine* (June 20, 2017), https://www.nytimes.com/2017/06/20/magazine/is-north-carolina-the-future-of-american-politics.html.

9. Editorial, "Transgender Law Makes North Carolina Pioneer in Bigotry," *New York Times*, March 25, 2016.

10. Jason Zengerle, *New York Times Magazine*, "Is North Carolina the Future of American Politics?" (June 20, 2017), https://www.nytimes.com/2017/06/20/magazine/is-north-carolina-the-future-of-american-politics.html.

11. Fletcher, *supra* note 1; Vanden Heuvel, *supra* note 1.

12. Ari Berman, "The 2015 Moral Monday Movement: 'North Carolina Is Our Selma,'" *The Nation* (February 12, 2015), https://www.thenation.com/article/2015-moral-monday-movement-north-carolina-our-selma.

13. Katrina Van Heuvel, "The Power of Moral Mondays," *The Nation* (December 1, 2015), https://www.thenation.com/article/the-power-of-moral-mondays.

14. Dan T. Carter, "North Carolina: State of Shock," *Southern Spaces* (September 24, 2013), https://southernspaces.org/2013/north-carolina-state-shock.

15. Cleve R. Wootson, "Rev. William Barber Builds a Moral Movement," *Washington Post* (June 29, 2017), https://www.washingtonpost.com/news/acts-of-faith/wp/2017/06/29/woe-unto-those-who-legislate-evil-rev-william-barber-builds-a-moral-movement/?noredirect=on.

16. Kim Severson, "Budding Liberal Protest Movements Begin to Take Root in South," *New York Times* (March 18, 2014), https://www.nytimes.com/2014/03/19/us/protest-disrupts-georgia-senate-session-on-bill-to-block-medicaid-expansion.html.

17. Michelle Boorstein, "'Closest Person We Have to Martin Luther King Jr.': Pastor-Activist William J. Barber Wins $625,000 'Genius' Grant," *Washington Post* (October 4, 2018), https://www.washingtonpost.com/religion/2018/10/05/closest-person-we-have-martin-luther-king-jr-pastor-activist-william-j-barber-wins-genius-grant/.

18. Zengerle, *supra* note 8.

19. Craig Jarvis, Colin Campbell, and Lauren Horsch, "Democrats Break Supermajority," *Raleigh News & Observer* (November 6, 2018), https://www.newsobserver.com/news/politics-government/article221033465.html.

20. Zengerle, *supra* note 8.

21. Gene Nichol, "In North Carolina All the Diversity on One Side of the Aisle," *Raleigh News & Observer* (January 20, 2019), https://www.newsobserver.com/opinion/article224507140.html.

22. Carter, *supra* note 14.

23. Gene Nichol, "The 14th Amendment's Unhappy Birthday," *Raleigh News & Observer* (July 18, 2018), https://www.newsobserver.com/opinion/article214960195.html.

24. "Fundament," *Merriam-Webster* (2019), https://www.merriam-webster.com/dictionary/fundament.

25. Chris Hedges, "Warning from a Student of Democracy's Collapse," *New York Times* (January 6, 2005), https://www.nytimes.com/2005/01/06/nyregion/warning-from-a-student-of-democracys-collapse.html.

26. Timothy Snyder, "Donald Trump and the New Dawn of Tyranny," *Time* (March 3, 2017), https://time.com/4690676/donald-trump-tyranny.

27. Zengerle, *supra* note 8. See also Maggie Astor, "Wisconsin, Limiting Governor, Borrows a Page from North Carolina's Book," *New York Times* (December 5, 2018), https://www.nytimes.com/2018/12/05/us/politics/wisconsin-governor-legal-challenge.html.

28. David Graham, "How North Carolina Became the Wisconsin of 2013," *The Atlantic* (July 1, 2013), https://www.theatlantic.com/politics/archive/2013/07/how-north-carolina-became-the-wisconsin-of-2013/277007.

29. Tara Golshan, "North Carolina Wrote the Playbook Being Used by

Michigan and Wisconsin," VOX (December 5, 2018), https://www.vox.com/policy-and-politics/2018/12/5/18125544/north-carolina-power-grab-wisconsin-michigan-lame-duck.

30. Zengerle, *supra* note 8 (quoting Congressman David Price).

31. Golshan, *supra* note 29.

32. Gene Nichol, *The Faces of Poverty in North Carolina: Conversations with Our Invisible Citizens* (University of North Carolina Press, 2018), 143.

33. Lyndon Johnson, President of the United States, "Special Message to Congress" (March 15, 1965), http://www.lbjlibrary.org/lyndon-baines-johnson/speeches-films/president-johnsons-special-message-to-the-congress-the-american-promise.

34. National Park Service, "Martin Luther King, Jr., Memorial: Quotations," https://www.nps.gov/mlkm/learn/quotations.htm.

35. *N.C. Const.* art. I, § 2.

36. Rob Christiansen, *The Paradox of Tar Heel Politics* (University of North Carolina Press, 2008), 307.

37. Robert Korstad and James Leloudis, *To Right These Wrongs: The North Carolina Fund and the Battle to End Poverty and Inequality in 1960s America*, (University of North Carolina Press, 2010), 1–2, 54–55.

38. Christiansen, *supra* note 36 at 307.

39. See Timothy B. Tyson and David D. Cecelski, *Democracy Betrayed: The Wilmington Race Riot of 1898 and Its Legacy* (University of North Carolina Press, 1998).

40. Equal Justice Initiative, *Lynching in America: Confronting the Legacy of Racial Terror* (3rd ed., 2017), https://lynchinginamerica.eji.org/report.

41. *Bob Jones and the North Carolina Ku Klux Klan*, Public Broadcasting Service (PBS), https://www.pbs.org/wgbh/americanexperience/features/klansville-gallery.

42. Christiansen, *supra* note 36 at 307.

43. Nichol, *supra* note 32 at ch. 9.

44. Gene Nichol, "Numbers Don't Lie: There Is Systemic Racial Subordination in North Carolina," *Greensboro News & Record* (April 22, 2018), https://www.greensboro.com/opinion/columns/gene-nichol-numbers-don-t-lie-there-is-systemic-racial/article_2a6e657d-a207-5ed1-a36b-8a3cf8a053ce.html.

45. Ibid.

46. See Nichol, *supra* note 32 at ch. 9.

47. Ibid.

48. Cooper v. Harris, 137 S. Ct. 1455 (2017).

49. Lynn Bonner, "Appeals Court Finds Racial Gerrymandering in North Carolina Districts," *Raleigh News & Observer* (August 11, 2016), https://www.newsobserver.com/news/politics-government/state-politics/article95080647.html; Covington v. North Carolina, 316 F.R.D. 176 (M.D.N.C. 2016), *aff'd*, 137 S. Ct. 2211 (2017) (mem.).

50. Covington v. North Carolina, 316 F.R.D. 176 (M.D.N.C. 2016), *aff'd*, 137 S. Ct. 2211 (2017) (mem.).

51. Covington v. North Carolina, 270 F. Supp. 3d 881, 897 (M.D.N.C. 2017).

52. See N.C. State Conference of the NAACP v. Moore & Berger, 18 CVS 9806 (Wake Cty. Sup. Ct. February 22, 2019) (order from Hon. G. Bryan Collins, Jr. ruling that N.C. constitutional amendments are invalid).

53. Covington v. North Carolina, 270 F. Supp. 3d.

54. Ann Blythe, "Federal Judge Invalidates Greensboro Redistricting Plan," *Raleigh News & Observer* (April 3, 2017), https://www.newsobserver.com/news/politics-government/article142454699.html.

55. Wesley Young, "Ward Plan Puts Three Black City Council Members into One District," *Winston Salem Journal* (March 29, 2019), https://www.journalnow.com/news/elections/ward-plan-puts-three-black-city-council-members-into-one/article_8cd889ea-90c2-5de2-832e-0b69c6b5ae5c.html.

56. See generally Vann R. Newkirk, "The Battle for North Carolina," *The Atlantic* (October 1, 2016), https://www.theatlantic.com/politics/archive/2016/10/the-battle-for-north-carolina/501257.

57. Shelby County v. Holder, 133 S. Ct. 2612 (2013).

58. "North Carolina Voter Bill Moving Ahead," WRAL (June 25, 2013), https://www.wral.com/nc-senator-voter-id-bill-moving-ahead-with-ruling/12591669.

59. Ari Berman, "North Carolina Passes the Country's Worst Voter Suppression Law," *The Nation* (July 26, 2013), https://www.thenation.com/article/north-carolina-passes-countrys-worst-voter-suppression-law.

60. *NAACP v. McCrory*, U.S. Court of Appeals for Fourth Circuit, July, 29, 2016, No. 16-1468, https://pdfserver.amlaw.com/nlj/7-29-16%204th%20Circuit%20NAACP%20v%20NC.pdf.

61. Associated Press, "Federal Judge to Block Latest North Carolina Voter ID Mandate" (December, 27, 2019), https://www.nbcnews.com/politics/elections/federal-judge-block-latest-north-carolina-voter-id-mandate-n1107896, and Will Doran, "Judge Temporarily Blocks NC Voter ID Law as Lawsuit Continues," *Raleigh News & Observer* (December 27, 2019), https://www.newsobserver.com/news/politics-government/article238747723.html.

62. Gene Nichol, "Given NC History, GOP's Black Suppression Gravest Sin," *Raleigh News & Observer* (September 17, 2016), https://www.newsobserver.com/opinion/op-ed/article102292057.html.

63. Michael Stone, "North Carolina Repeals Racial Justice Act," National Coalition to Abolish the Death Penalty (July 1, 2013), http://www.ncadp.org/blog/entry/north-carolina-repeals-the-racial-justice-act.

64. Bob Geary, "The Injustice of Repealing the Racial Justice Act," IndyWeek (November 30, 2011), https://indyweek.com/news/northcarolina/injustice-repealing-racial-justice-act.

65. Lynn Bonner, "Why NC Charter Schools Are Richer and Whiter," *Raleigh News & Observer* (October 10, 2017), https://www.newsobserver.com/news/local/education/article178022436.html.

66. Ibid.

67. T. Keung Hui, "NC Should Close Charter Schools That Aren't Diverse,

New Report Says," *Raleigh News & Observer* (March 16, 2018), https://www.newsobserver.com/article205190044.html. See also Hui, "Report Looked at Racial Impact of NC Charter Schools. That Section Is Being Removed," *Raleigh News & Observer* (January 3, 2020), https://www.newsobserver.com/news/local/education/article238936383.html.

68. Valerie Strauss, "North Carolina Passes Charter School Law That Critics Say Is Meant to Promote Segregation," *Washington Post* (June 14, 2018), https://www.washingtonpost.com/news/answer-sheet/wp/2018/06/14/north-carolina-passes-charter-school-law-that-critics-say-is-intended-to-promote-segregation.

69. James Ford, Editorial, "Matthews v. CMS: Yes, The Fight About Charter Schools Is About Race," *Charlotte Observer* (April 27, 2018), https://www.charlotteobserver.com/opinion/op-ed/article209884959.html.

70. Lauren Horsch, "It's Now Up to Judges to Release Police Body Cam Footage. Here's How That's Going," *Raleigh News & Observer* (March 9, 2018), https://www.newsobserver.com/news/politicsgovernment/state-politics/article204290209.html.

71. "Gov. McCrory Signs Bill That Keeps Police Camera Footage," ACLU of North Carolina (July 11, 2016), https://www.acluofnorthcarolina.org/en/press-releases/gov-mccrory-signs-bill-keeps-police-camera-footage-secret. See also Elaina Athans, "New Law Makes Police Cam Footage Off Limits to Public," ABC 11 (July 12, 2016), https://abc11.com/politics/new-law-makes-police-cam-footage-off-limits-to-public/1422569.

72. See Max Blau, Holly Yan, and Ryan Young, "Keith Scott Killing: Protestors Upset Over Lack of Charges," CNN (December 1 2016), https://www.cnn.com/2016/12/01/us/charlotte-protest-keith-scott-no-charges/index.html.

73. Peter Holley, "Congressman: Charlotte Protesters 'Hate White People Because White People Are Successful,'" *Washington Post* (September 23, 2016), https://www.washingtonpost.com/news/post-nation/wp/2016/09/22/charlotte-protesters-hate-white-people-because-white-people-are-successful-congressman-claims/?utm_term=.09f602c183c7.

74. Paul Specht, "Protections for Drivers Who Hit Protesters? 'No Plans' to Move Bill, NC Lawmaker Says," *Raleigh News & Observer* (August 14, 2017), https://www.newsobserver.com/news/politics-government/state-politics/article167100452.html.

75. See Craig Jarvis, "NC Legislature Adopts New Rules on Protests," *Charlotte Observer* (May 14, 2014), https://www.charlotteobserver.com/news/local/article9122084.html.

76. Colin Campbell, "NAACP's Rev. William Barber among Those Banned from NC Legislative Building," *Raleigh News & Observer* (June 16, 2017), https://www.newsobserver.com/news/politics-government/state-politics/article156649019.html.

77. See Chris Seward, "NAACP Activists Threatened with Arrest While Delivering Letter to House Speaker's Office," *Raleigh News & Observer* (February 8, 2018), https://www.newsobserver.com/news/politics-government/politics-columns-blogs/under-the-dome/article156146389.html.

78. See Joe Killian, "The Confederate Monuments Controversy: What the Law Says, What Historians Say," N.C. Policy Watch (August 23, 2017), http://www.ncpolicywatch.com/2017/08/23/confederate-monuments-controversy-law-says-historians-say.

79. Ibid.

80. Gene Nichol, "Lincoln's Words Haunt N.C. Law Protecting Confederate Monuments," *Raleigh News & Observer* (April 17, 2017), https://www.newsobserver.com/opinion/op-ed/article167729352.html.

81. Gene Nichol, "In NC, All Diversity Sits on One Side of the Aisle," *Raleigh News & Observer* (January 20, 2019), https://www.newsobserver.com/opinion/article224507140.html.

82. Ibid.

83. Brian Beutler, "GOP Senate Candidate Tillis Blows Lid Off Racial Politics," *The New Republic* (May 6, 2014), https://newrepublic.com/article/117672/gop-senate-candidate-tillis-divide-and-conquer-welfare-recipients.

84. See Phillip Alston, *Report of the Special Rapporteur on Extreme Poverty and Human Rights on His Mission to the United States of America*, UN Human Rights Council (2018), https://digitallibrary.un.org/record/1629536.

85. See John Cassidy, "Piketty's Inequality Story in Six Charts," *The New Yorker* (March 26, 2014), https://www.newyorker.com/news/john-cassidy/pikettys-inequality-story-in-six-charts.

86. "Quick Facts—North Carolina," *U.S. Census Bureau* (July 1, 2018), https://www.census.gov/quickfacts/fact/table/NC/PST045218.

87. North Carolina Justice Center, Brian Kennedy, "One Third of North Carolina Workers Make Poverty Level Wages," *Raleigh News & Observer* (November 6, 2017), at https://www.newsobserver.com/news/politics-government/article221033465.html.

88. Alexandra Sirota, *The Legacy of Hardship: Persistent Poverty in North Carolina* (N.C. Budget and Tax Center, January 2012); Sarah Willets, "Report: Poverty Entrenched," *The Robesonian* (April 15, 2018), https://www.robesonian.com/news/86584/report-ooverty-entrenched.

89. Maureen Berner, Alexander Vazquez, and Meagan McDougall, *Documenting Poverty in North Carolina* (University of North Carolina School of Government, March 2016), 8–10.

90. Alana Semuels, "Why It's So Hard to Get Ahead in the South," *The Atlantic* (April 4, 2017), https://www.theatlantic.com/business/archive/2017/04/south-mobility-charlotte/521763.

91. Nancy McLaughlin, "Greensboro, High Point Top Nationwide Hunger List," *Greensboro News & Record* (March 26, 2015), https://www.greensboro.com/news/local_news/greensboro-high-point-top-nationwide-hunger-list/article_88828c52-e568-11e4-9b5b-db55afd7f635.html; Gene Nichol, "In One of the Hungriest States—A Call to Cut Food Stamps," *Raleigh News & Observer* (May 24, 2017), https://www.newsobserver.com/opinion/op-ed/article152432659.html.

92. Raj Chetty et al., "'Where Is the Land of Opportunity? The Geography of

Intergenerational Mobility in the United States," National Bureau of Economic Research (June 2014), https://www.nber.org/papers/w19843; Allen Smith, "The 15 Cities Where Poor Neighborhoods Are Expanding Fastest," *Business Insider* (August 7, 2014), https://www.businessinsider.com/cities-poverty-soaring-2014-8. See generally Nichol, *supra* note 32 at 1–6.

93. See "America's Shrinking Middle Class: A Close Look at Changes within Metropolitan Areas," Pew Research Center (May 11, 2016); Michael Sauter et al., "America's Richest and Poorest Cities," *24/7 Wall Street* (October 8, 2015); Gregory Aisch, "The Best and Worst Places to Grow Up: How Your Area Compares," *New York Times* (May 4, 2015).

94. See Korstad, *supra* note 37.

95. See Nichol, *supra* note 32 at 180–81.

96. Editorial, *supra* note 2.

97. Jonathan M. Katz, "In North Carolina, Some Democrats See Their Grim Future," *Politico* (December 27, 2016), https://www.politico.com/magazine/story/2016/12/in-north-carolina-some-democrats-see-the-future-214553.

98. See Gene Nichol, Heather Hunt, and Matthew Norchi, "Putting a Face on Medicaid Expansion in North Carolina" (October 2016), http://www.law.unc.edu/documents/poverty/publications/medicaid_report_final.pdf.

99. Ibid.

100. Mark Binker, "Supreme Court Ruling Brings Medicaid Expansion for NC into Focus," WRAL (June 25, 2015), http://www.wral.com/supreme-court-ruling-brings-medicaid-expansion-for-nc-into-focus/14737591; Reid Wilson, "North Carolina Governor Weighing Medicaid Expansion," *Washington Post* (October 31, 2014), https://www.washingtonpost.com/blogs/govbeat/wp/2014/10/31/north-carolina-governor-weighing-medicaid- expansion.

101. Mark Hall, "Do States Regret Expanding Medicaid?," Brookings Institute (March 26, 2018), https://www.brookings.edu/blog/usc-brookings-schaeffer-on-health-policy/2018/03/26/do-states-regret-expanding-medicaid.

102. Justin Wolfers, "North Carolina's Misunderstood Cut in Jobless Benefits," *New York Times* (July 26, 2014), https://www.nytimes.com/2014/07/27/upshot/north-carolinas-misunderstood-cut-in-jobless-benefits.html?_r=0.

103. See Editorial, *supra* note 2. See also Jeff Linville, "McCrory's Great Triumph," *Mount Airy News* (December 15, 2016), https://mtairynews.com/opinion/46756/gov-mccrory-and-his-great-triumph; Kevin Rogers, "North Carolina's Unemployment Program Experiment Is a Failure," *Charlotte Observer* (February 23, 2016), http://www.charlotteobserver.com/opinion/op-ed/article62016117.html; Mike Evangelist, "One-Two Punch: As States Cut Unemployment Benefit Weeks, Jobless Also Lose Federal Aid, Even as Jobs Remain Scarce," National Employment Law Project (February 11, 2013), https://www.nelp.org/publication/one-two-punch-as-states-cut-unemployment-benefit-weeks-jobless-also-lose-federal-aid-even-as-jobs-remain-scarce; Editorial, *supra* note 2; Catherine New, "North Carolina Unemployment Benefit Cuts Harshest in the Nation," *Huffington Post* (February 1, 2013), http://www.huffingtonpost.com/2013/02/11/north-carolina

-unemployment-benefits-cuts_n_2662511.html; Colin Campbell, "NC Has Country's Smallest Unemployment Benefits—But a $3 Billion Fund," *Raleigh News & Observer* (February 8, 2018), https://www.newsobserver.com/news/politics-government/article199209144.html.

104. Campbell, *supra* note 103; Editorial, "NC Now Ranks Last among States in Unemployment Benefits," *Raleigh News & Observer* (February 8, 2018), https://www.newsobserver.com/opinion/editorials/article199162439.html.

105. Campbell, *supra* note 103.

106. Tazra Mitchell, "First in Flight from the EITC," North Carolina Budget and Tax Center (March 24, 2014), http://www.ncjustice.org/?q=budget-and-tax/btc-brief-first-flight-eitc-low-income-working-families-bid-farewell-ncs-earned.

107. Tazra Mitchell, "North Carolina's Earned Income Tax Credit," North Carolina Budget and Tax Center (February 2013).

108. John Frank, "Legislation Would Repeal NC Credit for Low Income Taxpayers," *Raleigh News & Observer* (February 14, 2013), http://www.newsobserver.com/news/weather/article10344959.html.

109. Michael Leachman, "Unhappy New Year, North Carolina Eliminates Its EITC," Center on Budget and Priority Policies (January 13, 2014), http://www cbpp.org/blog/unhappy-new-year-north-carolina-eliminates-its-eitc.

110. Colin Campbell, "NC Budget: More Sales Taxes in 2016, Income Tax Cuts in 2017," *Raleigh News & Observer* (September 19, 2015), https://www.newsobserver.com/news/politics-government/state-politics/article35825601.html.

111. "Altered State," *supra* note 5 at 5; Chris Fitzsimon, "The Ways Regressive Tax Hikes Will Harm the Poor," *Raleigh News & Observer* (September 18, 2015), http://www.newsobserver.com/opinion/op-ed/article35727654.html; Editorial, "Behind NC Tax Surge Is a Tax Shift," *Raleigh News & Observer* (January 16, 2016), http://www.newsobserver.com/opinion/editorials/article55101605.html; Gene Nichol, "North Carolina Tax Plan an Exercise in Villainy," *Raleigh News & Observer* (September 24, 2015), http://www.newsobserver.com/opinion/op-ed/article36473067.html.

112. Fitzsimon, *supra* note 111; Editorial, *supra* note 111.

113. Fitzsimon, *supra* note 111; Nichol, *supra* note 111. See also Alexandra Sirota, "State Budget Doubles Down Once More on Regressive Tax Policies," North Carolina Budget and Tax Center (June 26, 2016), http://www.ncpolicywatch.com/2016/06/29/state-budget-agreement-doubles-down-once-more-on-regressive-tax-policies; Colin Campbell, "NC Legislators Consider Expanding Sales Taxes, Cutting Income Taxes," *Raleigh News & Observer* (January 12, 2016), https://www.newsobserver.com/news/politics-government/state-politics/article54351470.html.

114. See Gene Nichol, "The Cold Cruelty of NC Leaders Is to Tax Poor to Render to Rich," *Raleigh News & Observer* (July 23, 2016), https://www.newsobserver.com/opinion/op-ed/article91364952.html. See also Sirota, *supra* note 113; Campbell, *supra* note 113.

115. Gene Nichol, "NC Tax Cuts Widen Inequality," *Raleigh News & Observer* (April 26, 2019), https://www.newsobserver.com/opinion/article229730559.html.

116. See Nichol, *supra* note 114; Sirota, *supra* note 113; Campbell, *supra* note 110.

117. See "Altered State," *supra* note 5 at 9–10.

118. Editorial, "North Carolina Would Save by Expanding Pre-K," *Raleigh News & Observer* (February 4, 2015), http://www.newsobserver.com/opinion/editorials/article10253654.html. See also "Childcare & Early Education," Washington Center for Equitable Growth, https://equitablegrowth.org/issue/childcare-early-education.

119. "Altered State," *supra* note 5 at 8.

120. Rob Schofield, "Cutting Food Assistance to the Poor? Really??," N.C. Policy Watch (October 6, 2015), http://www.ncpolicywatch.com/2015/10/06/cutting-off-food-assistance-to-the-poor-really. See also Jessica Murrell, "SNAP Truly a Lifesaver for Many North Carolinians," *Raleigh News & Observer* (February 24, 2016), http://www.newsobserver.com/opinion/op-ed/article62267887.html; Colin Campbell, "133,00 Would Lose Food Stamps under NC Senate Budget," *Raleigh News & Observer* (May 17, 2017), http://www.newsobserver.com/news/politics-government/state-politics/article151063487.html.

121. Laura Leslie, "North Carolina Shutting Down Work First," WRAL (October 14, 2013), http://www.wral.com/nc-shutting-down-work-first/12994151.

122. Gene Nichol, "Cuts to Legal Aid an Injustice to NC Poor," *Raleigh News & Observer* (October 24, 2015), http://www.newsobserver.com/opinion/op-ed/article41226495.html; Kirk Warner, "Cuts to Legal Aid a Disservice to the Economy," *Raleigh News & Observer* (October 1, 2015), http://www.newsobserver.com/opinion/op-ed/article37238517.html. See Ali Rizvi et al., "H.B. 2: A Timeline for North Carolina's Controversial Law," *Raleigh News & Observer* (February 9, 2018), http://www.newsobserver.com/news/politics-government/state-politics/article76726392.html; Colin Campbell, "Four Things to Remember about H.B. 2," *Raleigh News & Observer* (September 13, 2016), http://www.newsobserver.com/news/politics-government/state-politics/article101602642.html.

123. Campbell, *supra* note 120; Rizvi, *supra* note 122.

124. The poverty rate in the United States fell to 11.8 percent in 2018. See U.S. Census Bureau, "Income and Poverty in the United States," https://www.census.gov/library/publications/2019/demo/p60-266.html. The poverty rate in North Carolina in 2018 was 14 percent. See also N.C. Policy Watch, "North Carolina Poverty Rate Remains 15th Highest in the Nation," https://www.ncjustice.org/publications/north-carolinas-poverty-rate-remains-15th-highest-in-the-nation/.

125. Nichol, *supra* note 32 at ch. 10.

126. nchealthaccess, "NC House Speaker Tillis—Divide and Conquer!," YouTube (October 11, 2011), https://www.youtube.com/watch?v=O8ewESI51s4. See also Beutler, *supra* note 83; Rachel Maddow, "Tillis Eyes Divide and Conquer Strategy," MSNBC (May 7, 2014), http://www.msnbc.com/rachel-maddow-show/tillis-eyes-divide-and-conquer-agenda.

127. Kardish, *supra* note 6.

128. Adam Searing, "Senator Burr on Kids: Hogs at the Trough," Progressive Pulse (February 16, 2009), http://pulse.ncpolicywatch.org/2009/02/16/senator-burr-on-kids-hogs-at-the-trough. See also Saki Knafo, "George Cleveland, Republican Rep, Claims No Extreme Poverty in North Carolina as Preschool Cuts Weighed," *Huffington Post* (March 2, 2012), https://www.huffpost.com/entry/george-cleveland-poverty-north-carolina_n_1317554.

129. Congressman Robert Pittenger, Republican from Charlotte, also famously explained that the tense demonstrations following the shooting of an African-American Charlotte resident by local police arose because demonstrators "hate white people. . . . The grievance in their mind is—the animus, the anger. They hate white people because white people are successful and they're not." He also complained that the government has spent too much on welfare programs that ultimately hold people back. "Congressman Says Demonstrators 'Hate White People' Because "They Are Successful," *Washington Post*, September 22, 2016, https://www.washingtonpost.com/news/post-nation/wp/2016/09/22/charlotte-protesters-hate-white-people-because-white-people-are-successful-congressman-claims/?utm_term=.bcbfe6c7970a.

130. Alexander H. Jones, "Kicking the Unemployed While They're Down," Politics N.C. (September 2, 2015), https://www.politicsnc.com/kicking-the-unemployed-while-theyre-down (quoting Representative Speciale).

131. Schofield, *supra* note 120. See also Murrell, *supra* note 120; Campbell, *supra* note 120.

132. Knafo, *supra* note 128.

133. Gene Nichol, "Digging Deep into Districts Reveals Hardship," *Raleigh News & Observer* (March 26, 2013), 21A.

134. Lynn Bonner, "North Carolina Begins Drug Tests for Welfare Applicants," *Raleigh News & Observer* (February 9, 2016), https://www.newsobserver.com/news/politics-government/state-politics/article59389341.html.

135. Ned Barnett, "Drug Tests Dispel a Myth about North Carolina's Poor," *Raleigh News & Observer* (February 13 2016), http://www.newsobserver.com/opinion/opn-columns-blogs/ned-barnett/article60097156.html (quoting Representative Horn).

136. "Nationwide Trends," National Institute on Drug Abuse (June 2015), https://www.drugabuse.gov/publications/drugfacts/nationwide-trends.

137. Barnett, *supra* note 135.

138. "Stop the Madness," interview with Rupert Cornwell, *Toronto Globe & Mail*, July 6, 2006.

139. Eddie Huffman, *John Prine: In Spite of Himself* (University of Texas Press, 2015) (quoting *Taking the Star Out of the Window*).

140. Abigail Simon, "Why Ruth Bader Ginsburg's Confirmation Fight Still Matters, 25 Years Later," *Time* (August 3, 2018), https://time.com/5357068/ruth-bader-ginsburg-anniversary-confirmation-fight-standard (quoting Justice Ginsburg during her 1993 Senate confirmation hearings).

141. Roe v. Wade, 410 U.S. 113 (1973).

142. Planned Parenthood v. Casey, 505 U.S. 833 (1992).

143. Richard Fausset, "Law on Ultrasounds Reignites Abortion Battle in North Carolina," *New York Times* (January 10, 2016), https://www.nytimes.com/2016/01/11/us/law-on-ultrasounds-reignites-abortion-battle-in-north-carolina.html.

144. See "An Act to Require a Twenty-Four-Hour Waiting Period and the Informed Consent of a Pregnant Woman Before an Abortion May Be Performed," 2011 N.C. Sess. Laws 405, House Bill 854. See also Stuart v. Camnitz, 774 F.3d 238 (4th Cir. 2014).

145. N.C. Gen. Stat. § 90-21.85 (a)(3).

146. N.C. Gen. Stat. § 90-21.85(a)(2).

147. N.C. Gen. Stat. § 90-21.85(b). See also Stuart v. Camnitz, 774 F.3d 238 (4th Cir. 2014).

148. Stuart v. Camnitz, 774 F.3d at 254.

149. N.C. Gen. Stat. § 90-21.82.

150. N.C. Gen. Stat. § 90-21.82 (2)(e).

151. Stuart v. Camnitz, 774 F.3d at 243.

152. Stuart v. Camnitz, 774 F.3d at 244.

153. Ibid.

154. "Undue Burdens: A History of North Carolina Abortion Restrictions," ACLU of North Carolina (2016), https://www.acluofnorthcarolina.org/sites/default/files/field_documents/aclu-nc_undue_burdens_nc_abortion_restrictions_report_forprint.pdf.

155. N.C. Gen. Stat. § 90-21; ACLU of North Carolina, *supra* note 154 at 5.

156. Women and Children's Protection Act. See also ACLU of North Carolina, *supra* note 154; Fausset, *supra* note 143.

157. Fausset, *supra* note 143.

158. Ibid. (quoting Gerrick Brenner).

159. Abby Olheiser, "North Carolina Won't Stop Adding Abortion Measures to Unrelated Bills," *The Atlantic* (July 10, 2013), https://www.theatlantic.com/national/archive/2013/07/north-carolina-wont-stop-adding-abortion-measures-unrelated-bills/313459.

160. "Altered State," *supra* note 5.

161. See Gene Nichol, "Heaps of Hyperbole Drowning Honest Political Discourse," *Raleigh News & Observer*, July 21, 2013.

162. Fausset, *supra* note 143. See also Juliet Eilperin, "N.C. Gov. McCrory Vows to Sign Restrictive Abortion Bill," *Washington Post* (July 26, 2013), https://www.washingtonpost.com/news/post-politics/wp/2013/07/26/n-c-gov-mccrory-vows-to-sign-restrictive-abortion-bill.

163. ACLU of North Carolina, *supra* note 154.

164. Ibid.; "Altered State," *supra* note 5.

165. "Altered State," *supra* note 5.

166. Ibid.; Eilperin, *supra* note 162.

167. Bryant v. Woodall, 363 F.Supp.3d 611 (M.D.N.C. 2019).

168. See N.C. Gen. Stat. § 14-451(b); § 90-21-81(5). See also Bryant, 363 F.Supp.3d. at 611; Bryant v. Woodall, 1:16cv1368 (M.D.N.C. August 24, 2018).

169. Bryant v. Woodall, 363 F.Supp.3d. at 611; Will Duran, "North Carolina Abortion Law Is Unconstitutional, Federal Court Says," *Raleigh News & Observer* (March 26, 2019), https://www.newsobserver.com/news/politics-government/article228421354.html.

170. See Planned Parenthood v. Casey, 505 U.S. 833 (1992).

171. Simon, *supra* note 140.

172. Nichol, *supra* note 80.

173. Alexandria Bordias, "An Inside Look at the WNC Crisis Pregnancy Center," *Asheville Citizen-Times* (June 28, 2018), https://www.citizen-times.com/story/news/2018/06/28/north-carolina-budget-asheville-crisis-pregnancy-counseling-agency/715743002.

174. Aditi Kahrod, "Proposed State Budget Would Deal New Blows to First Amendment's Establishment Clause," N.C. Policy Watch (June 5, 2019), http://www.ncpolicywatch.com/2019/06/05/proposed-state-budget-would-deal-new-blows-to-the-first-amendments-establishment-clause.

175. Beth Holtzman, "Have Crisis Pregnancy Centers Finally Met Their Match? California's Reproductive Fact Act," 12 *Northwest Journal of Law & Social Policy* 78 (2017).

176. Amy Bryant and Jones Swartz, "Why Crisis Pregnancy Centers Are Legal but a Violation of Ethics," 20 *American Medical Association Journal of Ethics* 269 (2017).

177. Bordias, *supra* note 173.

178. Ibid.

179. Ibid.

180. Ibid. See also Dawn Baumgartner Vaughan, "Democrats' Attempts to Change Budget Were Cut Off—Along with a Microphone," *Raleigh News & Observer* (May 30, 2019), https://www.newsobserver.com/news/politics-government/article231003598.html.

181. Vaughan *supra* note 180.

182. Michael E. Miller, "Transgender Bathroom Law Is a National Embarrassment Says AG Roy Cooper," *Washington Post* (March 30, 2016), https://www.washingtonpost.com/news/morning-mix/wp/2016/03/30/nc-transgender-bathroom-ban-is-a-national-embarrassment-says-ag-as-pilloried-law-becomes-key-election-issue/?utm_term=.de77b842ab1e.

183. Editorial, "McCrory Joins a Dark List of Southern Governors," *Charlotte Observer* (March 24, 2016), https://www.charlotteobserver.com/opinion/editorials/article68005432.html.

184. Editorial, "Transgender Law Makes North Carolina Pioneers in Bigotry," *New York Times* (March 24, 2016), https://www.nytimes.com/2016/03/25/opinion/transgender-law-makes-north-carolina-pioneer-in-bigotry.html.

185. Lawrence v. Texas, 39 U.S. 558 (2003).

186. See N.C. Gen. Stat. §51-1.2 (1995).

187. "An Act to Amend the Constitution to Provide That Marriage between One Man and One Woman Is the Only Domestic Legal Union That Shall Be Valid or Recognized in This State," 2011 N.C. S.B. 514.

188. Samantha Oltman, "N.C.'s Amendment 1 Doesn't Just Screw Over Gay People," *Mother Jones* (May 8, 2012), https://www.motherjones.com/politics/2012/05/amendment-1-north-carolina-gay-people.

189. See "North Carolina's Ban on Gay Marriage Appears Likely to Pass," *New York Times, FiveThirtyEight* blog (May 4, 2012), https://fivethirtyeight.blogs.nytimes.com/2012/05/04/north-carolinas-ban-on-gay-marriage-appears-likely-to-pass.

190. See David Kaufman, "Tensions between Black and Gay Groups Rise Anew in Advance of Anti-Gay Marriage Vote in N.C.," *The Atlantic* (May 4, 2012), https://www.theatlantic.com/politics/archive/2012/05/tensions-between-black-and-gay-groups-rise-anew-in-advance-of-anti-gay-marriage-vote-in-nc/256695.

191. Adam Bink, "A Look at What Happened on Amendment 1 in North Carolina," *Huffington Post* (May 13, 2012), https://www.huffpost.com/entry/amendment-1-north-carolina_b_1510052.

192. "North Carolina Voters Pass Same Sex Marriage Ban," *New York Times* (May 8, 2012), https://www.nytimes.com/2012/05/09/us/north-carolina-voters-pass-same-sex-marriage-ban.html?mtrref=www.google.com&gwh=22FBF02EB00320F6EF9A3F1C187E4412&gwt=pay.

193. "Tillis: Marriage Amendment Likely to Be Reversed," WRAL (March 27, 2012), https://www.wral.com/tillis-marriage-amendment-likely-to-be-reversed/10911637.

194. See Bostic v. Schaefer, 760 F.3d 352 (4th Cir. 2014), *cert. denied*, 135 S.Ct. 314 (2014).

195. Ibid. (quoting W. Va. State Bd. of Educ. v. Barnette, 319 U.S. 624, 638 (1943)).

196. David Firestone, "In North Carolina, Thom Tillis is the Last Holdout Against Gay Marriage," *New York Times* (October 16, 2014), https://takingnote.blogs.nytimes.com/2014/10/16/in-north-carolina-thom-tillis-is-the-last-holdout-against-gay-marriage.

197. Ibid.

198. Colin Campbell, "Amendment One Gay-Marriage Ban Turns 5—Unenforceable, but Still in NC Constitution," *Raleigh News & Observer* (May 8, 2017), https://www.newsobserver.com/news/politics-government/state-politics/article149342339.html.

199. Obergefell v. Hodges, 135 S. Ct. 2071 (2015).

200. Colin Campbell, "Proposed Gay Marriage Ban Is Dead in N.C. House, Speaker Says," *Raleigh News & Observer* (April 12, 2017), https://www.newsobserver.com/news/politics-government/state-politics/article144169109.html.

201. Joe Killan, "Bill Filed to Defy Supreme Court Ruling, Oppose Same-Sex Marriage in N.C.," *Progressive Pulse* (February 14, 2019), http://pulse.ncpolicywatch.org/2019/02/14/bill-filed-to-defy-supreme-court-ruling-oppose-same-sex-marriage-in-n-c.

202. Mark Joseph Stern,"North Carolina Passes Law Allowing Magistrates to Refuse to Marry Same-Sex Couples," *Slate* (June 11, 2015), https://slate.com/human-interest/2015/06/north-carolina-passes-law-letting-magistrates-claim-religious-exemption.html.

203. Ibid.

204. Laura Leslie and Matthew Burns, "Few Magistrates Opt Out of Marriage Duties," WRAL (July 7, 2015), https://www.wral.com/few-magistrates-opt-out-of-marriage-duties/14760068.

205. Colin Campbell, "NC House Votes 65–45 to Exempt Magistrates from Marriage Duties," *Raleigh News & Observer* (May 27, 2015), https://www.newsobserver.com/news/politics-government/article22433973.html.

206. See Emma Green, "Why North Carolina Judges Can Still Refuse to Perform Same-Sex Marriages," *The Atlantic* (September 21, 2016), https://www.theatlantic.com/politics/archive/2016/09/north-carolina-magistrates-judges-same-sex-marriage-dismissals/500996.

207. Anne Blythe, "Should NC Magistrates Be Able to Opt Out of Performing Marriages on Religious Grounds? Case at 4th Circuit," *Raleigh News & Observer* (May 10, 2017), https://www.newsobserver.com/news/politics-government/state-politics/article149569774.html.

208. Gene Nichol, "Drawing the Line between Law and Religious Freedom," *Raleigh News & Observer* (June 10, 2017), https://www.newsobserver.com/opinion/op-ed/article155510484.html.

209. Amber Phillips, "The Tumultuous Recent History of North Carolina's Bathroom Bill Which Could Soon Be Repealed," *Washington Post* (March 30, 2017), https://www.washingtonpost.com/news/the-fix/wp/2016/12/19/the-tumultuous-recent-history-of-north-carolinas-bathroom-bill-which-could-be-repealed/?utm_term=.a7f7156ce337.

210. Amber Phillips, "How North Carolina's Bathroom Bill Could Backfire on Republicans," *Washington Post* (March 24, 2016), https://www.washingtonpost.com/news/the-fix/wp/2016/03/24/like-indiana-north-carolinas-controversial-lgbt-law-could-be-a-blessing-in-disguise-for-democrats/?utm_term=.e1fea7b3548c.

211. Dave Philipps, "North Carolina Bans Local Anti-Discrimination Policies," *New York Times* (March 23, 2016), https://www.nytimes.com/2016/03/24/us/north-carolina-to-limit-bathroom-use-by-birth-gender.html?module=inline.

212. David A. Graham, "North Carolina Overturns LGBT-Discrimination Bans," *The Atlantic* (March 24, 2016), https://www.theatlantic.com/politics/archive/2016/03/north-carolina-lgbt-discrimination-transgender-bathrooms/475125.

213. Michael Gordon, Mark S. Price, and Katie Peralta, "Understanding H.B. 2: North Carolina's New Law Solidifies State Role in Defining Discrimination," *Charlotte Observer* (May 2016), http://www.charlotteobserver.com/news/politics-government/article68401147.html#storylink=cpy (quoting Maxine Eichner). See also "Understanding HB2," *The State* (March 26, 2016), https://www.thestate.com/news/politics-government/article68401147.html.

214. Graham, *supra* note 212.

215. Miller, *supra* note 182.

216. Editorial, *supra* note 184.

217. Brady Dennis, "'Wrong Beyond Repair.' 'The Worst in U.S.' N.C. Papers

Blast Transgender Bathroom Law," *Washington Post* (March 25, 2016), https://www.washingtonpost.com/news/post-nation/wp/2016/03/25/wrong-beyond-repair-the-worst-in-us-n-c-papers-blast-transgender-bathroom-law/?utm_term=.13b34bd055ab.

218. AP, "'Bathroom Bill' to Cost North Carolina $3.76 Billion," CNBC (March 27, 2017), https://www.cnbc.com/2017/03/27/bathroom-bill-to-cost-north-carolina-376-billion.html.

219. Ibid.; "H.B. 2 Could Cost North Carolina Almost $5 Billion a Year," Williams Institute (May 11, 2016), https://williamsinstitute.law.ucla.edu/press/hb2-could-cost-north-carolina-almost-5-billion-a-year.

220. Maureen O'Hare, "U.K. Issues Travel Warnings About Anti-LGBT Laws in U.S.," CNN (April 22, 2016), https://www.cnn.com/travel/article/uk-lgbt-travel-advice-north-carolina-mississippi/index.html.

221. Chip Patterson, "Coach K Rips North Carolina Bathroom Bill: 'It's Embarrassing,'" CBS Sports, https://www.cbssports.com/college-basketball/news/dukes-mike-krzyzewski-rips-north-carolina-bathroom-bill-its-embarrassing.

222. Mark Berman, "Civil Rights Commission Says N.C. Bathroom Law Jeopardizes Physical Safety of Transgender People," *Washington Post* (April 19, 2016), https://www.washingtonpost.com/news/post-nation/wp/2016/04/19/u-s-civil-rights-commission-says-north-carolinas-bathroom-law-jeopardizes-the-physical-safety-of-transgender-people.

223. Jonathan M. Katz and Erick Eckholm, "Anti-Gay Laws Bring Backlash in Mississippi and North Carolina," *New York Times* (April 5, 2016), https://www.nytimes.com/2016/04/06/us/gay-rights-mississippi-north-carolina.html.

224. Michael Gordon, Mark S. Price, and Katie Peralta, "Understanding H.B. 2: North Carolina's Newest Law Solidifies State's Role in Defining Discrimination," *Raleigh News & Observer* (March 26, 2016), https://www.newsobserver.com/news/politics-government/article68401147.html.

225. Mark Joseph Stern, "It Looks Like NC's Anti-LGBT Governor, Pat McCrory, Is Out of a Job," Slate (November 9, 2016), https://slate.com/human-interest/2016/11/north-carolina-gov-pat-mccrory-lost-thanks-to-hb2.html.

226. Amber Phillips, "How Loretta Lynch's Speech Brought Some Transgender Activists to Tears," *Washington Post* (May 26, 2016), https://www.washingtonpost.com/news/the-fix/wp/2016/05/11/loretta-lynchs-speech-just-made-her-a-hero-to-transgender-activists/?utm_term=.94007d1b2e0e. See also Mark Berman, Sara Larimer, and Sari Horwitz, "North Carolina, Department of Justice, File Dueling Suits over Transgender Rights," *Washington Post* (May 9, 2016), https://www.washingtonpost.com/news/post-nation/wp/2016/05/09/north-carolina-justice-dept-face-monday-deadline-for-bathroom-bill/?utm_term=.a3b64aa71c33.

227. Berman, *supra* note 222.

228. Ibid.; Amber Phillips, "Why North Carolina Abruptly Flip-Flopped on Its 'Bathroom Bill,'" *Washington Post* (March 31, 2017), https://www.washingtonpost.com/news/the-fix/wp/2017/03/31/why-north-carolina-abruptly-flip-flopped-on-its-bathroom-bill/?utm_term=.659625ff8038.

229. Phillips, *supra* note 226.

230. David A. Graham, "North Carolina Is Finally Repealing Its Bathroom Bill," *The Atlantic* (March 30, 2017), https://www.theatlantic.com/politics/archive/2017/03/north-carolina-hb2-repeal/521301.

231. Ibid.

232. David A. Graham, "'I Don't Think You Can Compromise on Civil Rights,'" *The Atlantic* (March 31, 2017), https://www.theatlantic.com/politics/archive/2017/03/hb-2-what-happens-now/521394.

233. Mark Stern, "H.B. 2 Repeal Bill Is a Disaster for LGBTQ Rights and North Carolina," Slate (March 30, 2017), https://slate.com/human-interest/2017/03/hb2-repeal-bill-is-a-disaster-for-north-carolina-and-lgbtq-rights.html.

234. Amanda Holpuch, "North Carolina's New Discrimination Law 'Cruel and Insulting' Says LGBT Group," *The Guardian* (March 24, 2016), https://www.theguardian.com/us-news/2016/mar/24/north-carolina-discrimination-law-lgbt-groups-pat-mccrory.

235. Daniel Trotta and Frances Kerry, "NCAA Returns to North Carolina after Transgender Bathroom Law Repeal," Reuters (April 18, 2017), https://www.reuters.com/article/us-north-carolina-lgbt/ncaa-returns-to-north-carolina-after-transgender-bathroom-law-repeal-idUSKBN17K2AB.

236. See Melissa Boughton, "Federal Courts Hear Challenge to H.B. 2 Successor Law. Plaintiff: 'We Deserve Safety,'" N.C. Policy Watch (June 26, 2018), http://www.ncpolicywatch.com/2018/06/26/federal-court-hears-challenge-to-hb2-successor-law-plaintiff-tells-judge-we-deserve-safety. See also Rob Schofield, "Bathroom Law Victory: Federal Court Allows Challenge to H.B. 2 Replacement to Proceed," Progressive Pulse (October 1, 2018), http://pulse.ncpolicywatch.org/2018/10/01/bathroom-law-victory-federal-court-allows-challenge-to-hb2-replacement-to-proceed.

237. See Richard Craver, "Even after Partial Repeal, House Bill 2 Backlash Continues to Haunt N.C. Tourism," *Winston-Salem Journal* (October 30, 2018), https://www.journalnow.com/business/business_news/local/even-after-partial-repeal-house-bill-backlash-continues-to-haunt/article_2bcd8d50-e995-5768-a5b0-4f225b148bc6.html.

238. Joe Killian, "'Hate Crimes Prevention Act' Would Expand N.C. Protections," N.C. Policy Watch (March 7, 2019), http://pulse.ncpolicywatch.org/2019/03/07/hate-crimes-prevention-act-would-expand-n-c-protections.

239. "An Act to Protect All North Carolinians against Discrimination in All Walks of Life," 2019 N.C. Sess. Laws H.B. 514.

240. Martha Quillin, "House Dems Push for Trio of Bills to Promote Gay Rights, Ban Conversion Therapy," *Raleigh News & Observer* (March 28, 2019), https://www.newsobserver.com/news/politics-government/article228543209.html.

241. See Quillen *supra* 240; Ely Portillo, "After H.B. 2, NC Leaders Remain Divided About LGBTQ Protections in the State," *Charlotte Observer* (October 29, 2018), https://www.charlotteobserver.com/news/politics-government/influencers

/article220512460.html; Joel Burgess, "Asheville Lawmakers Propose Conversion Therapy Ban," *Asheville Citizen Times* (March 2019), https://www.citizen-times.com/story/news/local/2019/03/28/asheville-lawmakers-propose-ban-conversion-therapy-north-carolina-lgbtq-bill/3297320002; Elizabeth Friend, "NC Democrats Seek to Expand LGBT Rights," WUNC (May 11, 2016), https://www.wunc.org/post/nc-house-democrats-seek-expand-state-lgbt-protections.

242. Tom Donnelly, "John Bingham: One of America's Forgotten Second Founders," *Constitution Daily* (July 9, 2018), https://constitutioncenter.org/blog/happy-birthday-john-bingham-one-of-americas-forgotten-second-founders.

243. Plessy v. Ferguson, 163 U.S. 537 (1896).

244. See Erwin Chemerinsky, *Constitutional Law: Principles and Policies* (Wolters Kluwer, 2019).

245. Editorial, *supra* note 184.

246. Nichol, *supra* note 23.

247. William Faulkner, *Requiem for a Nun* (Random House, 1951), 73.

248. Hart v. State, 774 S.E.2d 281 (2015) (Hudson, J., dissenting).

249. Valerie Strauss, "North Carolina's Step-By-Step War on Public Education," *Washington Post* (August 7, 2015), https://www.washingtonpost.com/news/answer-sheet/wp/2015/08/07/north-carolinas-step-by-step-war-on-public-education.

250. See also Kris Nordstrom, *The Unraveling: Poorly-Crafted Education Policies Are Failing North Carolina's Children* (N.C. Justice Center, 2017).

251. See Jerry McBeath, Maria Elena Reyes, and Mary Ehrlander, *Education Reform in the American States* (Information Age, 2008), 115–30. See also Nordstrom, *supra* note 250.

252. Nordstrom, *supra* note 250.

253. T. Keung Hui, "How NC-GOP Lawmakers Have Changed K–12 Education," *Raleigh News & Observer* (February 2018), https://www.newsobserver.com/news/local/education/article200250829.html.

254. Reema Khrais, "NC Bill Keeps Groups from Collecting Dues by Paycheck," WUNC (January 29, 2015), https://www.wunc.org/post/nc-bill-keeps-teachers-group-collecting-dues-paychecks.

255. Laura Leslie, "Veto Overridden in Unprecedented Midnight Session," WRAL (January 5, 2012), https://www.wral.com/news/state/nccapitol/blogpost/10563086.

256. Matthew Burns, "NCAE Wins Challenge to Payroll Dues Ban," WRAL (January 3, 2013), https://www.wral.com/ncae-wins-challenge-to-payroll-dues-ban/11938870.

257. See Chris Fitzsimon, "The Outrage of Ending North Carolina's Teaching Fellows Program," *Raleigh News & Observer* (March 19, 2015), https://www.newsobserver.com/opinion/op-ed/article15384026.html#storylink=cpy.

258. Ibid.

259. Lindsay Wagner, "Ending Teaching Fellows Program One of the Biggest Mistakes Made in Public Education," N.C. Policy Watch (April 9, 2015),

http://pulse.ncpolicywatch.org/2015/04/09/new-nc-teacher-of-the-year-says-dismantling-the-teaching-fellows-program-one-of-biggest-mistakes-made-in-public-education.

260. T. Keung Hui, "New Report Praises NC Charter Schools," *Raleigh News & Observer* (February 2, 2018), https://www.newsobserver.com/news/local/education/article198017579.html#storylink=cpy.

262. Strauss, *supra* note 249.

263. T. Keung Hui, "Will Teachers Again Be Paid for Graduate Degrees?," *Raleigh News & Observer* (February 7, 2019), https://www.newsobserver.com/news/politics-government/article225632570.html.

264. John Wilson, "The Most Backward Legislature in the Country," *Education Week* (July 29, 2013), https://blogs.edweek.org/edweek/john_wilson_unleashed/2013/07/the_most_backward_legislature_in_america.html.

265. See WestEd Report to Judge David Lee in State v. Leandro, "Sound Basic Education for All: An Action Plan for North Carolina," reported at http://www.ncpolicywatch.com/wp-content/uploads/2019/12/Sound-Basic-Education-for-All-An-Action-Plan-for-North-Carolina.pdf. See also N.C. Policy Watch, "Leandro Report Is Out," December 12, 2019, http://www.ncpolicywatch.com/2019/12/12/the-leandro-report-is-out-the-future-of-public-education-in-north-carolina-starts-this-week/.

266. Lynn Bonner and T. Keung Hui, "North Carolina Public School Grades Reflect Wealth of Students' Families," *Raleigh News & Observer* (February 5, 2015), http://www.newsobserver.com/news/local/article10255961.html. See also Strauss, *supra* note 249; "Notable Numbers: School Grades, Zika Infections and Confidence in Trump," *Raleigh News & Observer* (September 9, 2016), https://www.newsobserver.com/opinion/editorials/article100898867.html.

267. Lindsay Wagner, "Virginia Governor Signs into Law Repeal of A–F School Grades," *Progressive Pulse* (March 23, 2015). See also Chris Fitzsimon, "Monday Numbers," N.C. Policy Watch (February 9, 2015), http://www.ncpolicywatch.com/2015/02/09/monday-numbers-237.

268. Nichol, *supra* note 32 at ch. 2.

269. Ned Barnett, "This Raleigh School Unfairly Got an F: It Merits an A For Effort," *Raleigh News & Observer* (September 7, 2018), https://www.newsobserver.com/opinion/opn-columns-blogs/ned-barnett/article218004435.html#storylink=cpy.

270. Nichol, *supra* note 32 at ch. 2.

271. Ibid.

272. Joe Ableidinger, "A Is for Affluent," EducationNC (April 15, 2015), https://www.ednc.org/2015/04/15/a-is-for-affluent. See also "Top Ten Educational Issues," Public School Forum of North Carolina (2019), https://www.ncforum.org/wp-content/uploads/2019/01/Top-10-Education-Issues-2019-PDF.pdf.

273. Hui, *supra* note 263.

274. North Carolina Ass'n of Educators, Inc., v. State, 786 S.E.2d 255 (N.C. 2016).

275. Ibid. at 782.

276. Craig Jarvis, "N.C. Supreme Court Rejects State's Appeal of Tenure Deci-

sion," *Raleigh News & Observer* (April 15, 2016), https://www.newsobserver.com/news/politics-government/state-politics/article72033607.html.

277. T. Keung Hui, "It's Not Tenure, But N.C. Teachers Will Get More Job Security," *Raleigh News & Observer* (December 20, 2017), https://www.newsobserver.com/news/local/education/article190767074.html.

278. Hui, *supra* note 263.

279. Hui, *supra* note 277.

280. Ibid.

281. Ibid.

282. "Altered State," *supra* note 5.

283. North Carolina Ass'n of Educators, Inc., v. State, 786 S.E.2d 255 (N.C. 2016).

284. Ibid. at 264.

285. Ibid. at 266.

286. Hui, *supra* note 263.

287. "Altered State," *supra* note 5.

288. *N.C. Const.* art. IX, § 2(1).

289. See Leandro v. State, 346 NC 336, 488 S.E.2d 249 (1997).

290. Hart v. State, 774 S.E.2d 281, 291 (2015) (Hudson, J., dissenting).

291. Ibid. at 297. (Hudson, J., dissenting).

292. Greg Childress, "Republicans, Education Advocates Square Off over Vouchers," N.C. Policy Watch (May 15, 2019), http://www.ncpolicywatch.com/2019/05/15/republicans-education-advocates-square-off-again-over-expanding-private-school-voucher-program.

293. Hart, 774 S.E.2d at 300.

294. Lindsay Wagner, "Last Minute Education Proposals That Didn't Survive the 2015 Legislative Session," N.C. Policy Watch (September 30, 2015), http://pulse.ncpolicywatch.org/2015/09/30/last-minute-education-proposals-that-didnt-survive-the-2015-legislative-session.

295. Kris Nordstrom, "Nine Ways in Which School Choice and Its Overzealous Backers Are Harmful to NC Public Schools," N.C. Policy Watch (June 12, 2019), http://www.ncpolicywatch.com/2019/06/12/nine-ways-in-which-school-choice-and-its-overzealous-backers-are-harmful-to-nc-public-schools.

296. Ned Barnett, "Three out of Four Voucher Schools Fail on Curriculum," *Raleigh News & Observer* (June 2, 2018), https://www.newsobserver.com/opinion/opn-columns-blogs/ned-barnett/article212352824.html.

297. Bonnie Bechard, "NC Private Schools Receiving Vouchers: A Curriculum Study," League of Women Voters of the Lower Cape Fear (2018), https://lwvnc.org/wp-content/uploads/2018/04/Voucher-Report-7.2-1.pdf.

298. Barnett, *supra* note 296. See also Bechard, *supra* note 297.

299. Barnett, *supra* note 296, and Bechard, *supra* note 297.

300. Lindsay Wagner, "Discriminatory Practices abound in NC Voucher Schools," N.C. Policy Watch (February, 26, 2014), http://www.ncpolicywatch.com/2014/02/26/discriminatory-practices-abound-in-north-carolinas-prospective-voucher-schools.

301. Hart v. State of North Carolina, Wake County Superior Court, 13 CVS 16771,

August 21, 2014, at https://s3.amazonaws.com/s3.documentcloud.org/documents/1279134/nc-ruling.pdf. See also Linsday Wagner, "Discriminatory Practices in North Carolina's Prospective Voucher Schools," N.C. Policy Watch (February 26, 2014), http://www.ncpolicywatch.com/2014/02/26/discriminatory-practices-abound-in-north-carolinas-prospective-voucher-schools/, and Capitol Broadcasting Company, "Editorial: Taxpayer Funded Vouchers Shouldn't Go to Schools That Discriminate" (April 23, 2019), https://www.wral.com/editorial-taxpayer-funded-vouchers-shouldn-t-go-to-schools-that-discriminate/18301351/.

302. Nordstrom, *supra* note 295.

303. Anne Blythe, "N.C. Supreme Court Upholds Voucher Program," *Raleigh News & Observer* (July 23, 2015), https://www.newsobserver.com/news/local/education/article28437271.html#storylink=cpy.

304. 406 U.S. 275 (1972).

305. N.C. State Department of Public Instruction, *The History of Education in N.C.* (1993), https://files.eric.ed.gov/fulltext/ED369713.pdf.

306. Jim Morrill, "N.C. Bills Would Ease Environmental Policies," *Charlotte Observer* (May 8, 2015), https://www.charlotteobserver.com/news/politics-government/article20549628.html.

307. Derb S. Carter, "This Is Not My State," Southern Environmental Law Center (April 15, 2015), https://www.southernenvironment.org/uploads/words_docs/Derb_Speech_NotMyState_digital.pdf. See also Derb Carter, "An Assault on the Environment," *Charlotte Observer* (April 18, 2015), https://www.charlotteobserver.com/opinion/op-ed/article18790962.html.

308. Dave Dewitt, "The State That Outlawed Climate Change," WUNC (May 4, 2015), https://www.wunc.org/post/state-outlawed-climate-change-accepts-latest-sea-level-rise-report.

309. Ibid. See also "The Word from Colbert to North Carolina: Sink or Swim," *Climate Central* (June 6, 2012), https://www.climatecentral.org/blogs/colbert-sink-or-swim; Alon Harish, "N.C. Bans Latest Science on Rising Sea Levels," ABC News (August 2, 2012), https://abcnews.go.com/US/north-carolina-bans-latest-science-rising-sea-level/story?id=16913782.

310. Erin Durkin, "North Carolina Didn't Like the Science on Sea Levels . . . So It Passed a Law against It," *The Guardian* (September 12, 2012), https://www.theguardian.com/us-news/2018/sep/12/north-carolina-didnt-like-science-on-sea-levels-so-passed-a-law-against-it.

311. Lori Montgomery, "On N.C.'s Outer Banks, Scary Climate-Change Predictions Prompt a Change of Forecast," *Washington Post* (June 24, 2014), https://www.washingtonpost.com/business/economy/ncs-outer-banks-got-a-scary-forecast-about-climate-change-so/2014/06/24/0042cf96-f6f3-11e3-a3a5-42be35962a52_story.html?utm_term=.e47d756b7a6f.

312. Abbie Bennett, "N.C. Banned a Study on Sea-Level Rise: Could It Mean More Hurricane Destruction?" *Raleigh News & Observer* (September 12, 2018), https://www.newsobserver.com/news/local/article218287205.html. See also Harish, *supra* note 309.

313. Harish, *supra* note 309.

314. Durkin, *supra* note 310.

315. Harish, *supra* note 309.

316. Durkin, *supra* note 310.

317. Dewitt, *supra* note 308.

318. Adam Wagner, "NC among Leaders in New Homes Where Sea Level Rise Could Increase Flood Risk," *Raleigh News & Observer* (August 7 , 2019), https://www.newsobserver.com/news/business/article233625927.html.

319. John Schwartz and Richard Fausset, "Warned of Rising Seas, North Carolina Chose to Favor Development," *New York Times* (September 12, 2018), https://www.nytimes.com/2018/09/12/us/north-carolina-coast-hurricane.html; Emily Atkin, "The Hurricane Damage That Didn't Have to Happen," *New Republic* (September 26, 2018), https://newrepublic.com/article/151362/republicans-responsible-hurricane-florence-damage-north-carolina.

320. Schwartz, *supra* note 319.

321. Colin Campbell, "New Abortion, 'Ag-Gag' Laws Take Effect Friday in North Carolina," *Raleigh News & Observer* (December 31, 2015), https://www.newsobserver.com/news/politics-government/state-politics/article52341745.html#storylink=cpy.

322. "Get the Facts," NC Farm Families, https://ncfarmfamilies.com/get-the-facts/; 2012 Census of Agriculture, USDA (June 2014), https://www.nass.usda.gov/Publications/Highlights/2014/Hog_and_Pig_Farming/index.php. See also Rob Verger, "North Carolina Ag-Gag Law Might Be the Worst in the Nation," *VICE News* (June 9, 2015), https://news.vice.com/en_us/article/7xap54/north-carolinas-ag-gag-law-might-be-the-worst-in-the-nation; Craig Jarvis, "McCrory Vetoes Workplace Bill," *Raleigh News & Observer* (May 29, 2015), https://www.newsobserver.com/news/politics-government/article22605054.html#storylink=cpy.

323. 2012 Census of Agriculture, USDA (June 2014), https://www.nass.usda.gov/Publications/Highlights/2014/Hog_and_Pig_Farming/index.php.

324. Editorial, "No More Exposés in N.C.," *New York Times* (February 1, 2016), https://www.nytimes.com/2016/02/01/opinion/no-more-exposes-in-north-carolina.html.

325. Jarvis, *supra* note 322. "No More Exposés in North Carolina," *New York Times* (February 1, 2016), https://www.nytimes.com/2016/02/01/opinion/no-more-exposes-in-north-carolina.html; Colin Campbell, "North Carolina Legislature Overrides Governor's Veto of 'Ag-Gag' Bill," *Governing* (June 4, 2015), https://www.governing.com/topics/mgmt/north-carolina-legislature-overrides-governors-veto-of-ag-gag-bill.html; Mark Binker and Laura Leslie, "Lawmakers Override McCrory Veto on Controversial 'Ag-Gag' Bill" (June 3, 2015), https://www.wral.com/lawmakers-override-mccrory-veto-on-controversial-private-property-bill/14687952/; Sarah Hanneken, "Principles Limiting Recovery Against Undercover Investigators in Ag-Gag States: Law, Policy and Logic, 50 J. Marshall L. Rev. 649 (2017)," https://repository.jmls.edu/cgi/viewcontent.cgi?article=2733&context=lawreview.

326. People for the Ethical Treatment of Animals v. Stein, No. 17-1669 (4th Cir. June 5, 2018), citing N.C. Gen. Stat. § 99A-2 (2016).

327. Ibid. See also N.C. Gen. Stat. § 99A-2(d)(1)-(4).

328. See Verger, *supra* note 322.

329. Opinion, "North Carolina's Boneheaded Ag-Gag Law Protects Corporate Wrongdoing," *Charlotte Observer*, https://www.charlotteobserver.com/opinion/opn-columns-blogs/o-pinion/article53141640.html.

330. People for the Ethical Treatment of Animals v. Stein, No. 17-1669 (4th Cir. June 5, 2018); William Vogeler, "Court Revives 'Ag Gag' Lawsuit in N.C.," *FindLaw* (June 14, 2018), https://blogs.findlaw.com/fourth_circuit/2018/06/court-revives-ag-gag-lawsuit-in-north-carolina.html.

331. Idaho's Ag-Gag law was invalidated by the federal courts. See Campbell, *supra* note 321; Editorial, "Time Is Running Out for NC's Atrocious Ag-Gag Law," *Wilson Times* (January 11, 2019), http://wilsontimes.com/stories/our-opinion-time-running-out-for-nc-ag-gag,156820.

332. Editorial, "No More Exposés," *supra* note 324.

333. Upton Sinclair, *The Jungle* (Dover, 2001; orig. 1906).

334. See Editorial, *supra* note 324.

335. See Verger, *supra* note 322.

336. Jarvis, *supra* note 322.

337. Lisa Sorg, "The War on the Environment in 2018—Five Stories That Mattered," N.C. Policy Watch (December 27, 2018), http://www.ncpolicywatch.com/2018/12/27/the-war-on-the-environment-in-2018-five-stories-that-mattered.

338. Anne Blythe, "Jury Awards 50 Million in Hog Farm Case," *Raleigh News & Observer* (April 26, 2018), https://www.newsobserver.com/news/business/article209927914.html#storylink=cpy.

339. Lisa Sorg, *Lawsuit Challenges Constitutionality of NC Laws Protecting Hog Industry From Nuisance Suits*, N.C. Policy Watch (June 26, 2019), http://www.ncpolicywatch.com/2019/06/21/lawsuit-challenges-constitutionality-of-nc-laws-protecting-hog-industry-from-nuisance-actions.

340. Greg Blount, William Droze, and Kathryn Warihay, "Punitive Damages in N.C. Hog Farm Cases Reduced," *Environmental Law & Policy Monitor* (August 7, 2018), https://www.environmentallawandpolicy.com/2018/08/punitive-damages-north-carolina-hog-farm-cases-reduced.

341. Sorg, *supra* note 339.

342. Complaint, Rural Empowerment Ass'n for Cmty. Help v. North Carolina, 19CV008198 (Wake Ct. Superior Ct. June 19, 2019). See also Sorg, *supra* note 339.

343. Sorg, *supra* note 339.

344. State v. Kelly, 119 S.E. 755 (1923).

345. Sorg, *supra* note 339.

346. Ibid.

347. Nichol, *supra* note 122.

348. Derb S. Carter, "This Is Not My State," *Southern Environmental Law Cen-*

ter (April 15, 2015), https://www.southernenvironment.org/uploads/words_docs/Derb_Speech_NotMyState_digital.pdf.

349. Derb Carter, "An Assault on the Environment," *Charlotte Observer* (April 18, 2015), https://www.charlotteobserver.com/opinion/op-ed/article18790962.html. See also Lisa Sorg, "Q&A: Environmental Attorney Derb Carter on DEQ's Power to Regulate GenX (or Not)," N.C. Policy Watch (August 21, 2017), http://pulse.ncpolicywatch.org/2017/08/21/q-lawmakers-hold-hearing-wednesday.

350. Southern Environmental Law Center, "Dismantled: N.C. Government's Attack on Environmental Protections" (2016), https://www.southernenvironment.org/uploads/words_docs/Dismantled_NCreport_0716.pdf.

351. Ibid. at ch. 2.

352. Sharon McCloskey, "Paradise for Polluters," in "Altered State," *supra* note 5; Southern Environmental Law Center, *supra* note 350; Carter, *supra* note 348.

353. Southern Environmental Law Center, *supra* note 350.

354. Ibid. See also Kirk Ross, *The N.C. Fracking Boom That Didn't Happen* (Carolina Public Press, 2018), https://carolinapublicpress.org/27699; S.B. 786 (2014); https://www.ncleg.net/Sessions/2015/Bills/Senate/PDF/S119v6.pdf.

355. Marti Maguire, "N.C. Governor Signs Law Paving Way for Fracking," Reuters (June 4, 2014), https://www.reuters.com/article/us-usa-northcarolina-fracking/north-carolina-governor-signs-law-paving-way-for-fracking-idUSKBN0EF1VC20140604.

356. Ibid. Southern Environmental Law Center, *supra* note 350.

357. Maguire, *supra* note 355; Southern Environmental Law Center, *supra* note 350; Ross, *supra* note 354.

358. See State v. Berger 781 S.E.2d 248 (N.C. 2016).

359. Kirk Ross, "The North Carolina Fracking Boom That Didn't Happen," *Carolina Public Press* (March 14, 2018), https://carolinapublicpress.org/27699/27699/.

360. Ibid.

361. McCloskey, *supra* note 352 at 30–32.

362. Laura Leslie, "Impeachment Justices Over Amendments Possible, GOP Chief Says," WRAL (August, 2018), https://www.wral.com/impeachment-of-justices-possible-gop-chief-says/17776194.

363. See Ned Barnett, Editorial, "An Independent Judiciary Is Under Siege in Washington and NC," *Raleigh News & Observer* (November 25, 2017), https://www.newsobserver.com/opinion/editorials/article186355103.html.

364. Gene Nichol, "Berger Misstates State of State," *Raleigh News & Observer* (March 5, 2019), https://www.newsobserver.com/opinion/article227136804.html.

365. Ibid.

366. Ibid.

367. Rick Hasen, "Chuzpah Dep't: N.C. Republican Legislative Leader Phil Berger Criticizes Democratic Governor Cooper for Not Appointing Republican to State Supreme Court," *Election Law Blog* (March 12, 2019), https://electionlawblog.org/?p=104125.

368. Melissa Price Kromm, "NC Should Restore Public Funding for Judicial Elections," *Raleigh News & Observer* (October 19, 2016), http://www.newsobserver.com/opinion/op-ed/article109283122.html.

369. Ibid. See also Billy Corriher, Michelr Jawando, and Lukasz Grabpowski, "N.C.'s Attacks on the Courts Lead to Fewer Judges of Color," Center for American Progress (November 16, 2017), https://www.americanprogress.org/issues/courts/reports/2017/11/16/442876/north-carolinas-attacks-courts-lead-fewer-judges-color.

370. Kromm, *supra* note 368. See also David Donovan, "Assembly Rushes New Appellate Changes," *N.C. Lawyers Weekly* (December 22, 2016), https://nclawyersweekly.com/2016/12/22/assembly-rushes-new-appellate-changes.

371. Kromm, *supra* note 368.

372. Billy Corriher, "The North Carolina Legislature Is Attacking Judges Who Rule against It," *American Bar Association Journal* (March 22, 2018), http://www.abajournal.com/news/article/the_north_carolina_legislature_is_attacking_judges_who_rule_against_it.

373. Anne Blythe, "N.C. Lawmakers Create Partisan Election Process for Courts That Review Their Laws," *Raleigh News & Observer* (December 17, 2016), http://www.newsobserver.com/news/politics-government/state-politics/article121449157.html.

374. Corriher, *supra* note 372.

375. Ibid.; Donovan, *supra* note 370.

376. Anne Blythe, "N.C. Democrats and Republicans Reveal Who They Want on Supreme Court and Appeals Court," *Raleigh News & Observer* (June 12, 2018), http://www.newsobserver.com/news/politics-government/article213010564.html; Jim Morrill and Michael Gordon, "How Fast-Moving Changes to the NC Justice System Could Reshape the State's Courts," McClatchy DC Bureau (January 12, 2018), http://www.mcclatchydc.com/news/crime/article194384414.html. See Craig Jarvis, "Shrinking of NC Appeals Court Becomes Law as House, Senate Override Cooper's Veto," *Raleigh News & Observer* (April 26, 2017), https://www.newsobserver.com/news/politics-government/state-politics/article146916714.html.

377. Blythe, *supra* note 373; Trip Gabriel, "In N.C., Republicans Stung by Court Rulings Aim to Change the Judges," *New York Times* (October 18, 2017), https://www.nytimes.com/2017/10/18/us/north-carolina-republicans-gerrymander-judges.html.

378. Gabriel, *supra* note 377.

379. Morrill, *supra* note 376.

380. Marcia Morey, "Justice in N.C. Under Attack," *Durham Herald Sun* (September 11, 2017), https://www.heraldsun.com/opinion/article172241102.html.

381. Mark Barrett, "Plan Could Push Buncombe Dems Off the Bench," *Asheville Citizen-Times* (January 27, 2018), https://www.citizen-times.com/story/news/local/2018/01/27/republicans-proposal-could-push-buncombe-democrats-out-judges-jobs/1069449001/; Melissa Boughton, "Surprise! Justin Burr Announces Maps on Twitter That Would Overhaul Judicial, Prosecutorial Districts," N.C. Policy Watch,

http://pulse.ncpolicywatch.org/2017/06/26/surprise-justin-burr-announces-maps-twitter-overhaul-judicial-prosecutorial-districts/.

382. Matthew Burns, "Vetoes on Judicial, Elections Bills Fall," WRAL (June 20, 2018), https://www.wral.com/vetoes-on-judicial-elections-bills-fall/17641615.

383. Corriher, *supra* note 372.

384. See David Donovan, "Assembly Rushes New Appellate Changes," *N.C. Lawyers Weekly*, December 22, 2016.

385. Gene Nichol, "When Dancing to the GOP Tune, NC Supreme Court Is Not a Court," *Raleigh News & Observer* (January 2, 2016), https://www.newsobserver.com/opinion/op-ed/article52544295.html.

386. Corriher, *supra* note 372.

387. See Donovan, *supra* note 370.

388. Phil Berger, "Legislative Leaders to Activist Judges: If You Want to Make Laws, Run for the Legislature" (February 7, 2017), https://www.philberger.org/legislative_leaders_to_activist_judges_if_you_want_to_make_laws_run_for_the_legislature.

389. Corriher, *supra* note 372.

390. Lynn Bonner, "Woodhouse Threatens Judges with Impeachment," *Raleigh News & Observer* (August 17, 2018), https://www.newsobserver.com/news/politics-government/article216886935.html; Mattias Miller, "Republican Party Executive Threatens to Impeach NC Supreme Court: Here's What to Know," *Daily Tar Heel* (August 23, 2018), https://www.dailytarheel.com/article/2018/08/republican-party-supreme-court; Jennifer Fernandez, "N.C. GOP Leader Threatens Judges with Impeachment," *Greensboro News & Record* (August 17, 2018), https://www.greensboro.com/ap/north_carolina/n-c-gop-leader-raises-possibility-of-impeaching-justices-over/article_13157db2-4e82-57cb-ba5d-9a15478d6e08.html.

391. Gene Nichol, "Phil Berger Rules by Whim to Gain Partisan Omnipotence," WRAL (October 29, 2017), http://www.wral.com/gene-nichol-phil-berger-rules-by-whim-to-gain-partisan-omnipotence/17065670.

392. Ibid. See also Anne Blythe, "Is Lawmakers' Proposal a Threat to Judges Who Won't Go Along with Their Agenda?," *Raleigh News & Observer* (October 30, 2017), http//www.newsobserver.com/news/local;/article181684616.html; Morrill, *supra* note 376.

393. Caryn McNeill, president of N.C. Bar Association, speaking in opposition to H.B. 717 on September, 19, 2017.

394. Corriher, *supra* note 372.

395. Blythe, *supra* note 392.

396. Editorial, "Relentless Partisan Manipulations of State Courts Threatens Justice for All," WRAL (April 11, 2018), https://www.wral.com/editorial-relentless-partisan-manipulations-of-state-courts-threatens-justice-for-all/17478252.

397. Morrill, *supra* note 376. See Anne Blythe, "Who Will Choose NC's Judges—Voters? Lawmakers? The Governor? New Plans Released," *Raleigh News & Observer* (January 3, 2018), http://www.newsobserver.com/news/politics-government/politics-columns-blogs/under-the-dome/article192867294.html.

398. Anne Blythe, "NC Lawmakers Push for Prominent Role in Selecting Judges Who Rule on Their Laws," *Raleigh News & Observer* (June 21, 2018), http://www.neesobserver.com/news/politics-government/article213577759.html.

399. Barnett, *supra* note 363.

400. Jim Morrill, "Former NC Chief Justices Join Former Governors in Opposing Proposed Amendment," *Charlotte Observer* (August 22, 2018), https://www.charlotteobserver.com/news/politics-government/article217210770.html.

401. Matthew Burns, "Voter ID and Three Other Proposals Pass, Power Shift Defeated," WRAL (November 7, 2018), https://www.wral.com/voter-id-three-other-amendments-pass-power-shift-proposals-defeated/17974397.

402. See Heather Hunt and Gene Nichol, "Court Fines and Fees: Criminalizing Poverty in North Carolina, N.C. Poverty Research Fund" (2017), https://scholarship.law.unc.edu/cgi/viewcontent.cgi?article=1443&context=faculty_publications.

403. See Gene Nichol, "What Happens When the NC Courts Criminalize Poverty," *Raleigh News & Observer* (September 18, 2018), https://www.newsobserver.com/opinion/article218411255.html.

404. Ibid.

405. Hunt, *supra* note 402.

406. Marbury v. Madison, 5 U.S. 137 (1803).

407. Melissa Boughton, "What Retired Judge Don Stephens Would Have Told Senators about Judicial Reform," N.C. Policy Watch (December 15, 2017), http://pulse.ncpolicywatch.org/2017/12/15 transcript-retired judge-don-stephens-judicial-reform; Will Doran and Anne Blythe, "Democrats Walk Out in Protest after Republicans Snub Roy Cooper," *Raleigh News & Observer* (December 13, 2017), https://www.newsobserver.com/news/politics-government/state-politics/article189621594.html.

408. Gene Nichol, "N.C. Legislators Are Pioneers in Constitutional Transgression," *Raleigh News & Observer* (August 31, 2018), https://www.newsobserver.com/opinion/op-ed/article217508760.html.

409. See Zack Beauchamp, "The Wisconsin Power Grab Is Part of a Bigger Republican Attack on Democracy," VOX (December 6, 2018), https://www.vox.com/policy-and-politics/2018/12/6/18127332/wisconsin-state-republican-power-grab-democracy.

410. Harper v. Virginia Bd. of Elections, 383 U.S. 663 (1966).

411. Reynolds v. Sims, 377 U.S. 533 (1964).

412. Voting Rights Act of 1965, Pub. L. 89-110, 79 Stat. 437.

413. U.S. Department of Justice, History of the Voting Rights Act (2017), https://www.justice.gov/crt/history-federal-voting-rights-laws.

414. See Robert Barnes and Ann E. Marimow, "Appeals Court Strikes Down North Carolina's Voter-ID Law," *Washington Post* (July 29, 2016), https://www.washingtonpost.com/local/public-safety/appeals-court-strikes-down-north-carolinas-voter-id-law/2016/07/29/810b5844-4f72-11e6-aa14-e0c1087f7583_story.html.

415. *N.C. State Conference of NAACP v. McCrory*, 831 F.3d 204 (4th Cir. 2016).

416. Ibid.; Barnes, *supra* note 414.

417. *N.C. State Conference of NAACP*, 831 F.3d 204; Barnes, *supra* note 414.

418. Adam Liptak and Michael Wines, "Strict North Carolina Voter ID Law Thwarted after Supreme Court Rejects Case," *New York Times* (May 15, 2017), https://www.nytimes.com/2017/05/15/us/politics/voter-id-laws-supreme-court-north-carolina.html.

419. Barnes, *supra* note 414.

420. Jack Healy, "Arrested, Jailed and Charged with a Felony. For Voting," *New York Times* (August 2, 2018), https://www.nytimes.com/2018/08/02/us/arrested-voting-north-carolina.htm.

421. Covington v. North Carolina, 316 F.R.D. 117, 124 (M.D.N.C. 2016), *aff'd* 137 S. Ct. 2211 (2017).

422. Rick Hasen, "Divided Three Judge Court Holds North Carolina Congressional Redistricting an Unconstitutional Partisan Gerrymander, Considers New Districts for 2018 Elections," *Election Law Blog* (August 27, 2018), https://electionlawblog.org/?p=100857.

423. Gene Nichol, "N.C. Has the Worst Gerrymander in US History: What Else Is New?" *Raleigh News & Observer* (February 1, 2018), http://www.newsobserver.com/opinion/op-ed/article197852639.html.

424. Rucho v. Common Cause, 279 F. Supp. 3d 587 (M.D.N.C. 2018).

425. Ibid.

426. Ibid.

427. Melissa Boughton, "NC Republicans Double Down on Partisan Gerrymandering Ahead of Tomorrow's Supreme Court Arguments," N.C. Policy Watch (March 25, 2019), http://www.ncpolicywatch.com/2019/03/25/nc-republicans-double-down-on-partisan-gerrymandering-ahead-of-tomorrows-supreme-court-arguments. See also Nichol, *supra* note 408.

428. Rucho v. Common Cause, 138 S. Ct. 2679 (2019).

429. Ibid.

430. Common Cause v. Lewis, Sept. 3, 2019, Judge Ridgeway, pp. 1–357, https://www.nccourts.gov/assets/inline-files/18-CVS-14001_Final-Judgment.pdf?Bwsege01VV20zhJsp9hoClvmoRp3A6AR.

431. Ibid.

432. Ibid.

433. See, Will Doran, "New Maps Ordered for NC 2020 Congressional Races, in Win for Democrats," *Raleigh News & Observer* (October 28, 2019), https://www.newsobserver.com/news/politics-government/article236752543.html.

434. Covington, 316 F.R.D. 176.

435. Ibid.

436. Covington, 270 F. Supp. 3d at 881.

437. Ibid.

438. Matthew Burns, Julia Sims, and Mark Binker, "Appeals Court Tosses District Maps for Wake County Commissions," WRAL (July 1, 2016), https://www

.wral.com/appeals-court-tosses-district-maps-for-wake-commissioners-school-board/15821358.

439. Editorial, "GOP Gets Wake County Districts It Wants," *Raleigh News & Observer* (March, 2015), https://www.newsobserver.com/opinion/editorials/article17155607.html.

440. Raleigh Wake Citizens Assoc. v. Wake Cty. Bd. of Elections, 827 F.3d 333 (4th Cir. 2016).

441. Ibid.

442. Ibid.

443. Golshan, *supra* note 29.

444. Ibid.

445. Ibid. (quoting Rick Hasen).

446. "Roy Cooper Wins N.C. Governor Race," *New York Times* (November 8, 2016), https://www.nytimes.com/elections/2016/results/north-carolina-governor-mccrory-cooper.

447. Dan Merica, "N.C. Gov. Pat McCrory Concedes Race," CNN (December 5, 2016), https://www.cnn.com/2016/12/05/politics/north-carolina-governor-concedes-race/index.html.

448. Golshan, *supra* note 29.

449. Matthew Burns and Mark Binker, "Cooper: GOP Proposals 'More Ominous' Than Power Grab," WRAL (July 13, 2018), https://www.wral.com/cooper-gop-proposals-more-ominous-than-power-grab/16342840. See also Amber Phillips, "Serious Political Drama in North Carolina," *Washington Post* (December 15, 2016), https://www.washingtonpost.com/news/the-fix/wp/2016/12/15/a-coup-a-power-grab-theres-some-serious-political-drama-in-north-carolina-right-now/?utm_term=.1270bdfad6f1.

450. Mark Stern, "North Carolina Republican Legislative Coup Is an Attack on Democracy," Slate (December 15, 2016), https://slate.com/human-interest/2016/12/north-carolina-legislative-coup-an-attack-on-democracy.html. See also Steven Bennen, "N.C. Republicans Launch a Legislative 'Coup,'" MSNBC (December 16, 2016), http://www.msnbc.com/rachel-maddow-show/north-carolina-republicans-launch-legislative-coup; John Nichols, "State Republicans Are Refusing to Honor the Peaceful Transition of Power," *The Nation* (December 4, 2018), https://www.thenation.com/article/wisconsin-michigan-republican-lame-duck-power-grab.

451. Golshan, *supra* note 29.

452. Isaac Becker, "Wisconsin Lawmakers Vote to Strip Power from the Incoming Democratic Governor Attorney General," *Washington Post* (December 5, 2018).

453. See Beauchamp, *supra* note 409; Mitch Smith and Monica Davey, "Stung by Election Losses, Republicans in the States Seek a Way to Neutralize Democrats," *New York Times* (December 3, 2018), https://www.nytimes.com/2018/12/03/us/wisconsin-lawmakers-republicans-power.html; Nichols, supra note 450 (arguing it is a "radical assault" on democracy).

454. "Totalitarianism," *The Free Dictionary*, https://www.thefreedictionary.com/Totalitarian+temptation (quoting Arthur Schlesinger).

455. Lewis Carroll, *Through the Looking Glass* (1872).

456. U.S. Dep't of Commerce v. New York, 588 U.S. (2019).

457. Harper Lee, *To Kill a Mockingbird* (1960).

458. Galatians 5:14.

459. Perjury typically requires: "the willful giving of false testimony under oath or affirmation, before a competent tribunal, upon a point material to a legal inquiry." I'm not talking, here, about declarations under oath "before a competent tribunal." I do refer, however, to the willful, knowing proffer of false testimony or justification to explain governing choices. "Perjury," *Dictionary.com*, https://www.dictionary.com/browse/perjury.

460. Andrew Young and Kabir Sehgal, *Walk in My Shoes* (St. Martin's, 2010). See Devin Dwyer, "Post-Racial America? Not Yet, Civil Rights Legend Andrew Young Says," ABC News (May 25, 2010), https://abcnews.go.com/Politics/andrew-young-civil-rights-legend-book-race-politics/story?id=10731590.

461. Isaac Chotaner, "Does Democracy Need Truth?," *New Yorker* (January 31, 2019), https://www.newyorker.com/news/q-and-a/does-democracy-need-truth-a-conversation-with-the-historian-sophia-rosenfeld.

462. Gene Nichol, "Lawmakers Back 'In God We Trust'—Say Its Not Supporting Religion," *Raleigh News & Observer* (June 22, 2018), https://www.newsobserver.com/opinion/article213613949.html.

463. See Lynch v. Donnelly, 465 U.S. 668 (1983).

464. Fausset, *supra* note 143; Eilperin, *supra* note 162.

465. "Between H.B. 2 Supporters and Colleges: A Cultural Divide," *Charlotte Observer* (April 16, 2016), https://www.charlotteobserver.com/news/local/education/article72096322.html.

466. Leonard Goenaga, "2016 Champions of the Family," N.C. Family Values (2016), https://www.ncvalues.org/2016_champions_of_the_family.

467. "N.C. Reverses Transgender Bathroom Ordinance," MSNBC (March 25, 2016), http://www.msnbc.com/mtp-daily/watch/north-carolina-reverses-transgender-bathroom-ordinance-652461123838 (quoting Dan Bishop).

468. Elizabeth Baier and Jeff Tiberii, "How Did We Get Here?," WUNC (March 23, 2017), https://www.wunc.org/post/hb2-how-did-we-get-here.

469. Editorial, *supra* note 9.

470. Katy Steinmetz, "Why LGBT Advocates Say Bathroom 'Predators' Argument Is a Red Herring," *Time* (May 2, 2016), https://time.com/4314896/transgender-bathroom-bill-male-predators-argument.

471. *N.C. State Conference of NAACP v. McCrory*, 831 F.3d 204 (4th Cir. 2016), and discussion, more broadly, in chapter 9.

472. *N.C. State Conference of NAACP v. McCrory*, 831 F.3d 204 (4th Cir. 2016).

473. Nichol, *supra* note 161.

474. See Planned Parenthood v. Casey, 505 U.S. 833 (1992).

475. Ibid.; Carey v. Population Servs. Int'l, 431 U.S. 678 (1977).

476. Lynn Bonner, "Court Gives Roy Cooper a Win on Constitutional Amendments at Least Temporarily," *Raleigh News & Observer* (August 21, 2018), https://www.newsobserver.com/news/politics-government/article216880225.html.

477. Lynn Bonner, "Courts Have No Role in Constitutional Amendments, Argues Lawyer for NC Legislators," *Raleigh News & Observer* (August 15, 2018), https://www.newsobserver.com/news/politics-government/article216689835.html.

478. Lynn Bonner, "Court Blocks Two North Carolina Amendments," *Governing Magazine* (August 22, 2018), https://www.governing.com/topics/politics/tns-north-carolina-ballot-constitutional-amendments-blocked-roy-cooper.html.

479. Nichol, *supra* note 98.

480. "Plaintiff Lawyers Speak after Gerrymandering Trial Ends," WRAL (July 26, 2019), https://www.wral.com/nc-gerrymandering-trial-concluding-friday-in-raleigh-plaintiff-attorneys-hold-press-conference-attorneys-hold-press-conference/18534519; Will Doran, "Lawyers Want Files Kept Secret," *Raleigh News & Observer* (June, 19, 2019), https://www.newsobserver.com/news/politics-government/article229997404.html.

481. Will Doran, "North Carolina Gerrymandering Trial Begins," *Raleigh News & Observer* (July 15, 2019), https://www.newsobserver.com/news/politics-government/article232677422.html.

482. Will Doran, "Hofeller Files Can Be Used in NC Gerrymandering Trial, Judges Rule in Win for Democrats," *Raleigh News & Observer* (July 12, 2019), https://www.newsobserver.com/news/politics-government/article232612182.html.

483. "Plaintiff Lawyers Speak after Gerrymandering Trial Ends," WRAL (July 26, 2019), https://www.wral.com/nc-gerrymandering-trial-concluding-friday-in-raleigh-plaintiff-attorneys-hold-press-conference-attorneys-hold-press-conference/18534519; Igor Derysh, "N.C. Republicans Lied to Federal Court About Racial Gerrymander Report," *Salon* (June 7, 2019), https://www.salon.com/2019/06/07/n-c-republicans-lied-to-federal-court-about-racial-gerrymander-report.

484. Steve Harrison, "State Gerrymandering Trial: GOP Says Democrats Creating Bogeyman," WFAE (July 15, 2019), https://www.wfae.org/post/state-gerrymandering-trial-gop-says-democrats-are-creating-bogeyman#stream/0; See also Melissa Boughton, "NC Lawmakers Deny Misconduct in Latest Court Filing," N.C. Policy Watch (June 19, 2019), http://pulse.ncpolicywatch.org/2019/06/19/hofeller-files-lawmakers-deny-mapmaking-misconduct-in-latest-court-filing.

485. "Plaintiff Lawyers Speak after Gerrymandering Trial Ends," WRAL (July 26, 2019), https://www.wral.com/nc-gerrymandering-trial-concluding-friday-in-raleigh-plaintiff-attorneys-hold-press-conference-attorneys-hold-press-conference/18534519. See also Michael Wines, "Deceased Strategists Files Detail Republican Gerrymandering in North Carolina, Advocates Say," *New York Times* (June 6, 2019), https://www.nytimes.com/2019/06/06/us/north-carolina-gerrymander-republican.html.

486. Editorial, "Three North Carolina Judges Step In Where the Supreme Court Refuses," *New York Times* (September 4, 2019), https://www.nytimes.com/2019/09/04/opinion/north-carolina-gerrymandering.html.

487. Common Cause v. Lewis, 18 CVS 014001 (N.C. Dist. Ct. Wake Cnty. 2019); Will Doran, "NC Gerrymandering: Legislative Districts Declared Unconstitu-

tional," *Raleigh News & Observer* (September 3, 2019), https://www.newsobserver.com/news/politics-government/article234668747.html.

488. Common Cause v. Lewis, 18 CVS 014001 (N.C. Dist. Ct. Wake Cnty. 2019).

489. "North Carolina House GOP Overrides Budget Veto with Few Democrats Present," *Wall Street Journal* (September 11, 2019), https://www.wsj.com/articles/north-carolina-house-gop-overrides-budget-veto-with-few-democrats-present-11568233883.

490. Dawn Baumgartner, "NC House Overrides Budget Veto in Surprise Vote with Almost Half of Lawmakers Absent," *Raleigh News & Observer* (September 11, 2019), https://www.newsobserver.com/news/politics-government/article234962017.html. See also Gene Nichol, "NC-GOP: Grand Old Prevaricators," *Raleigh News & Observer* (September 22, 2019), https://www.newsobserver.com/opinion/article235313602.html; Paul Spect, "Democrats Want Lie Detector Test," *Raleigh News & Observer* (September 23, 2019), https://www.newsobserver.com/news/politics-government/article235312417.html.

491. Bruce Springsteen, "The Ghost of Tom Joad (Introduction)," YouTube (December 13, 2018), https://www.youtube.com/watch?v=y2IeNmbhHjs.

492. *N.C. Const.* art. IX, § 2(1).

493. Stern, *supra* note 450; Bennen, *supra* note 450; Nichols, *supra* note 450.

494. Richard Rorty, *Achieving Our Country: Leftist Thought in Twentieth-Century America* (Harvard University Press, 1999).

495. Fletcher, *supra* note 1; Vanden Heuvel, *supra* note 1.

496. Golshan, *supra* note 29.

497. Graham, *supra* note 28.

498. Cox, *supra* note 3.

499. Rucho v. Common Cause, 138 S. Ct. 2679 (2019).

500. Cox, *supra* note 3.

501. Ibid. (quoting Mac McCorkle).

502. Robert Kennedy, "A Speech on Race," Berkeley, CA (October 22, 1966), https://www.mfa.org/exhibitions/amalia-pica/transcript-a-speech-on-race.